Tail Fins and Two-Tones

The Guide to America's Classic Fiberglass and Aluminum Runabouts

Tail Fins *and* Two-Tones

The Guide to America's Classic Fiberglass and Aluminum Runabouts

PETER HUNN

DEVEREUX BOOKS
MARBLEHEAD, MA

Published by Devereux Books
PO Box 503
Marblehead, MA 01945

Internet address: www.devereuxbooks.com

Library of Congress Cataloging in Publication Data

Hunn, Peter, 1953 –
Tail fins and two two tones: the guide to America's classic fiberglass and aluminum runabouts / Peter Hunn.
p. cm.
ISBN 1-928862-10-1 (alk. paper)
1. Motorboats—United States—History. 2. Fiberglass boats—United States—History.
3. Aluminum boats—United States—History. I. Title: Tailfins and Two-Tones. II. Title.
VM341.H858 2006
623.82'31' 0973—dc22

2005051941

Design by Paige Davis, Fish Tank Media.

Printed in Singapore

On the cover: Created by famed industrial designer Brooks Stevens, the mid-'50s Evinrude Lark combined automotive and nautical themes to become among the most dramatic American runabouts ever built.

On the Back Cover: Restored runabouts and cruisers gather at meets throughout the country. These boats showed up for an event in California. (Neda Atash photo). Rare boating literature like the Feather Craft brochure is eagerly sought out today by collectors and restorers.

Table of Contents

Acknowledgments

This book isn't so much about old boats as it is about people who love boats and enjoy sharing their classic marine interest with others. The Antique Boat Museum's Barton Haxall comes to mind. Throughout the fall and early winter of 2002, he set this work's cornerstone by graciously photocopying period *Motor Boating* and *The Boating Industry* outboard boat manufacturers' lists until the stack of resulting paper was almost too tall to stand unaided. Richard T. Curvin's positive influence is also present herein, as his impressive collection of original brochures was offered to me without any stipulations other than, "Have fun!" When, as primarily an outboard motor person, I really needed some direction about the unique fiberglass craft, Kevin Mueller quickly answered the call. Thanks to Gene E. Wagner for the loan of pictures from Mercury's *Boat House Bulletin*. Other good boating friends like Bill Loveland, Doug Penn, and Art DeKalb provided vintage brochures and insight instrumental in piecing together historical puzzles. I am also grateful for the antique boating chronicle groundwork installed over the past several decades by Bob Speltz, Lee Wangstad, Larry Carpenter, Daniel Spurr, *fiberglassics.com*'s Kelly Wood, and a host of other tireless contributors to the labor of love known as preserving pleasure boating's rich past. In California, Denise Goodwin, president of Golden State Classics (the local FiberGlassics chapter) helped arrange a photo shoot and identify the boats. Thanks, too, to editor Stan Grayson for sticking with this project throughout its behind-the-scenes series of fits and starts — no doubt experienced in those proverbial mid-20th-century manufacturing shops where a few determined boat lovers contributed to an American pastime by building new kinds of boats.

Introduction

This book chronicles the uniquely American boats responsible for a boating boom that has never really stopped booming. Our story harks back to the years immediately following World War II when Americans in ever greater numbers found the time and money to buy themselves not just a new family car but a new boat and motor as well. Then, thanks to the use of aluminum and fiberglass that reduced enormously the time and expense traditionally associated with wooden boats, people flocked to marine dealerships and trailered home an incredible variety of the sorts of craft we consider here — the outboard-powered runabout.

It was a vibrant time. Colors and stylish touches created a new market appeal and gave a whole new face to the boating world. Famous designers like Raymond Loewy and Brooks Stevens were called upon by major boat manufacturers to create dramatic models that, if comparatively expensive and made only in low numbers, attracted attention to the bread and butter family runabouts that most folks bought. More and more, the boat-building companies aligned themselves with the Big Three carmakers in terms of how they named and marketed their products. When Ford unveiled its famous Mustang, several boat companies — even Chrysler Marine — were ready to associate themselves with the exciting new model and launched their own Mustang sporty runabouts.

Many boat makers worked hard to introduce a new vocabulary to the waterborne world, one whose terminology had more in common with a car catalog than traditional marine usage. Copywriters produced brochures full of terms that had distinctly automotive echoes such as "gull wing design," "groovy center console," "feather-soft ride," "mono-flite hulls" "o'matic" this or that and evocative color names intended to inspire dreams of ownership on the reader. Even the name "runabout" had its origins in the automotive world as it was used to label the early car makers' more sprightly, usually two-seater models.

Within a decade of the first production line molding of fiberglass hulls around 1946, hundreds of companies throughout the country were producing runabouts for regional markets or, in the case of the major manufacturers, all of the United States and Canada. By 1957, the whole business had become so big that even the general press took notice. That April, one of *Newsweek*'s cover stories was "The Outboard Comes of Age." The mainstream magazine was amazed to report that a small dealer in rural Clovis, New Mexico, had rather effortlessly sold 112 outboard motors in 1956, even though "the nearest boating water to Clovis is 85 miles away."

Time followed with its own article that pictured the then head of Chris-Craft, a company whose wooden boats had taken such a big hit from the newcomers that the company reluctantly began offering some fiberglass boats of its own. Soon, the entire world of boat building would be stood on its stern and fine old wooden boat-building companies that didn't make the transition were doomed.

This book was created to tell the story of the classic American runabout and the companies that built them.

While the appeal of the varnished mahogany wooden boat is undeniable and such boats and their builders have been widely chronicled, it is only rather recently that the aluminum and fiberglass models have begun to generate ever-growing interest as boats worthy of collection and restoration. Once sometimes scorned as quickly outdated, factory-produced products for the masses, these boats now reflect no less an important phase in America's cultural, technological, and recreational history than their wooden sisters, or automobiles of the period.

We define "runabouts" here as any aluminum or fiberglass powerboat of up to twenty feet long with a deck and steering wheel, and intended for general family use. An exception is the outboard utility craft, typically more open and basic than the runabout, and sometimes sans steering wheel. Semantics and nuances that we need not worry about can be at play here. What one maker declares to be a utility, another might brand an "economy/specialty runabout."

Whatever the label, however, many skippers are now discovering the boats' classic qualities. There's lots to appreciate, too, ranging from flamboyant winged designs to tenacious durability. Because many runabouts are now a quarter-century old or older, this book also aims to answer historical questions about pedigree. Our goal, too, is to serve as a guide to those seeking information on how to decide whether that interesting "tin" or "plastic" craft wearing a hand-lettered *For Sale* sign represents a good buy, be it a freebie or rare hull auctioned on eBay for $10,000. One thing is for sure, these aluminum and fiberglass runabouts represent great fun at what are still affordable prices. Welcome aboard!

PETER HUNN
Fulton, New York
January 2006

Chapter 1

From Fighter Planes to Runabouts

AN ALUMINUM BOAT OVERVIEW

"Rust-proof, lightweight aluminum displays its versatility in application to a wide variety of hull types. Tough and seam-free, they withstand both wear and weather."

— *Motor Boating*, January 1955

In the midst of what many term "boating's golden age," the June 1959 issue of *Boats* magazine reported that a third of all of pleasure craft in America were aluminum. When, during the Kennedy era, boat buyers compared hours spent doing hull maintenance with time that could be better enjoyed on the water in aluminum (or fiberglass) craft, much of the remaining market for wooden boats dried up.

Aluminum is among the five most common elements contained in the earth's crust. Even so, it wasn't identified until 1808 when an English scientist, Sir Humphrey Davy, gave aluminum its name. The 1855 Paris Exhibition featured an aluminum ingot, then touted as a bar of precious metal. Eleven years later, a pair of researchers — one American and the other from France — independently patented a process to electrically harvest molten aluminum from its ore, paving the way for the establishment of several aluminum companies in 1888.

Arguably, the Mullins Manufacturing Corporation gets the nod as having offered the first few "production" aluminum hulls. During the late 1920s, the Salem, Ohio-based firm — most widely known for making automotive fenders and steel boats — introduced a series of aluminum outboard boats that included a

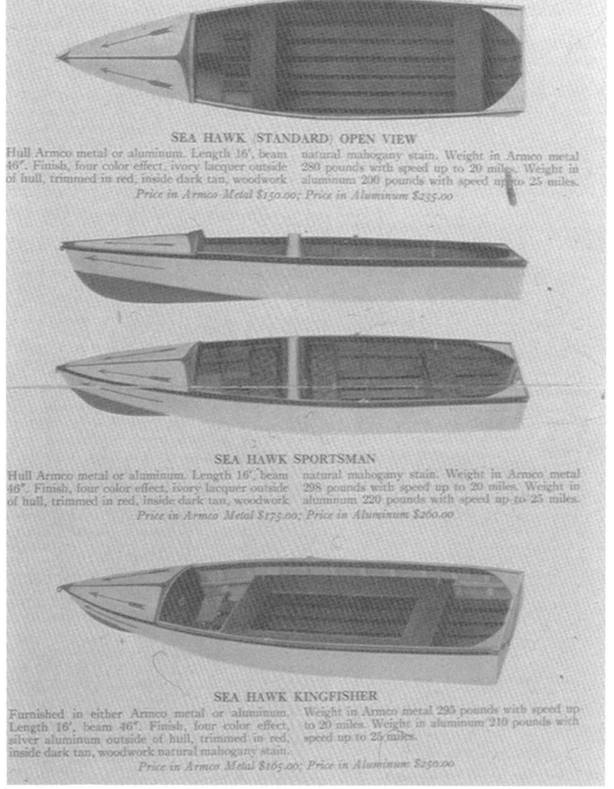

The 1928 Mullins catalog included the 16-foot Sea Hawk, which was offered in either "Armco metal" (steel) or aluminum. The latter offered a weight savings of about 80 pounds but cost a whopping $235 vs. $150 for the base model. The Sea Hawk was finished in ivory lacquer with red trim and was lavishly fitted out with mahogany stained wood.

16-foot family runabout and a 12' 9" racer. Even for Mullins, however, its aluminum offerings were more like footnotes to its otherwise all-steel line of boats. Like others in the pioneering group of pre-World War II alloy boat makers, Mullins didn't appear to believe that the lightweight metal was ready for prime time. This contrasts with outboard motor manufacturers gaining remarkable successes with the adoption of aluminum parts, starting in 1921.

Shortly before and in the years following World War II, other builders of metal boats like Gil-Boat Distributors (rolled steel), Pioneer Manufacturing Company (galvanized iron), and Star Metal Boat Company (sheets of Copper-Steel) began to actively spread the "alloy hull" gospel. In colorful brochures, small magazine ads, and displays at sportsmens' shows, such publicity always focused not upon the comparatively light weight and low maintenance inherent in an aluminum boat, but instead upon the fact that a metal boat couldn't sink.

"*Safety* is the most important factor," Pioneer's 1940 catalog shouted. "The large built-in air chambers make every Pioneer boat not only unsinkable, but a life raft as well. When full of water, a Pioneer boat will support two people sitting inside . . . and ten people could cling to the sides."

Deciding to forego head-on competition with a wooden boat's aesthetics and smooth ride, copywriters

Like Star, Pioneer was a major name in pre-World War II metal boating, but even longer than Star, the Middlebury, Indiana manufacturer resisted moving into aluminum.

of the 1940 Star sales pamphlet noted, "The paramount factor in boating is not beauty or performance. It is *safety!* Large airtight compartments make a life raft of every Star — even when it's full of water!" One tiny Spokane, Washington, maker of steel rowboats attempted to convey the safety message in his product's trade name — the Kant-Sink-Em!

After the "straight-to-the-bottom" aspect of metal boats was sufficiently debunked (though millions of middle-aged Americans who clearly remembered the unsinkable *Titanic* would never be completely convinced), manufacturers played their products' best

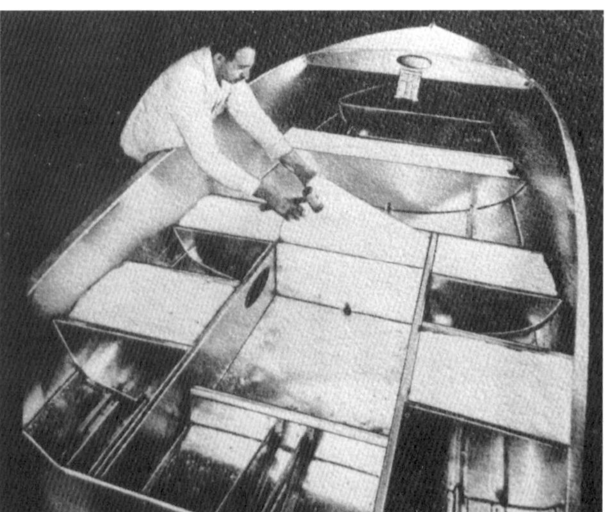

Because everyone knew that metal wouldn't float, few early aluminum boats catalogs were without at least one serious picture of an employee installing generous blocks of buoyant Styrofoam under the seats.

card — simple upkeep. "A yearly painting and the boat looks like new," claimed Star. What's more, most makers suggested that accidental damage could be rectified by any auto body shop possessing a rubber mallet, and soldering or welding equipment. Of course, buyers were promised they could instantly "forget the backaching upkeep work of the wood boat."

Research indicates that commercial or governmental entities, rather than private individuals, generated the lion's share of the pre-World War II metal boat business. Easy maintenance despite rough usage seems to be the key to these fleet buys by the likes of Yellowstone National Park; Westchester County, New York; Denver City Parks; and Camp Pontoosuc/Camp Wahconah in Pittsfield, Massachusetts. The latter's director wrote to the Pioneer factory not only to praise the safety aspect of his camp's newly purchased metal boats, but "add[ed] to this fact that they are considerably cheaper and easier to handle than wooden boats." He confessed being "at a loss to understand" why anyone who knows about metal craft would buy any other type. Despite this glowing testimonial, however, through the onset of the war, alloy hull sales never made much of a dent in the pleasure boating picture. It took a military-inspired, patriotic paradigm shift to move metal boat makers from steel to aluminum, and to get consumers to recognize marine aluminum as a legitimate heir to wooden boats.

Perhaps the most romanticized of all the weaponry sent to topple Axis powers were the fighter aircraft. In a remarkably short span, America's military air arsenal became transformed from an obsolete fleet to legions of sleek aircraft fabricated largely of aluminum. Only the coldest-hearted citizen wasn't moved by the emotion of a shiny new P-47, P-51, or P-38 as it flew by — whether overhead or in a movie newsreel. What's more, thousands of men and women came to appreciate the beauty and technical virtues of aluminum as they worked with the alloy in aircraft plants. At war's end,

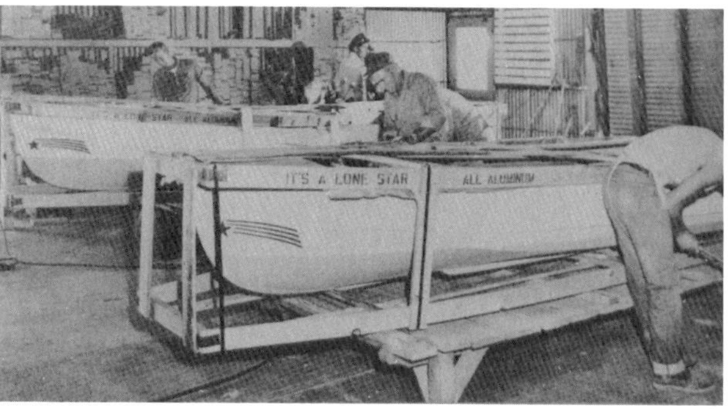

Even the fellows who hammered together the open crates that kept completed Lone Star boats protected during shipping helped publicize their ware's most notable feature. "All Aluminum," boasted stenciling on framing the crew used for the crate's top pieces.

the stage was set for those savvy in aviation aluminum to transfer their knowledge to boat building, and for a public thoroughly appreciative of aluminum's properties to take a serious look at aluminum boats. In fact, some of the plane makers themselves would enter boat production as a sideline. Both Douglas Aircraft and Grumman were offering aluminum hulls — a skiff and canoes, respectively — by 1946.

Who built the first postwar aluminum boat? In fact, it is now difficult to provide a pinpoint answer. A parenthetical phrase on page 124 of the January 1949 *Motor Boating* appears to indicate that Feather Craft of Atlanta, Georgia, can be credited for debuting the earliest aluminum hulls. But this is probably erroneous. Instead, the first modern aluminum boats were likely fabricated by a St. Charles, Michigan, firm, Harwill, Inc. Its Aero-Craft were so named to confer the company's products with an aircraft provenance. According to early catalogs, Harwill, Inc., was "founded in early 1946

Some of the world's first aluminum boats were built in Aero Craft's modest St. Charles, Michigan, plant.

for the manufacture of lightweight aluminum boats according to the sound principles of aircraft construction developed during and since World War II." The local *St. Charles Union* newspaper ran a mid-May 1946 story noting that the first Aero-Craft boats were then under construction and would be ready for summer sales.

Aluma Craft, the now-famous Minneapolis alloy boat builder, was also early on the scene. The brand appeared in *Motor Boating* magazine's "outboard boat" specs for January 1947, a year before the appearance of either Aero-Craft or Feather Craft. But we make a distinction here between when boats were actually produced and sold and when a company name first appeared in print. Not far behind any of the companies already named was Little Falls, Minnesota-based Larson Watercraft, later dubbed Crestliner. Larson began delivering its aluminum boats to dealers around Thanksgiving 1946.

Like Aero-Craft advertising, initial Larson Watercraft brochures touted "aeronautical inspired aluminum watercraft," and "the family boat with an aircraft heritage." By 1947, with the aeronautical connection established, these early aluminum boat companies used precious catalog space previously devoted to aircraft industry parallels to exclusively sing the praises of their sturdy boats. In any flyer worth its ink, however, at least a page was dedicated to explaining, in sometimes hyperbolic terms, the intricacies of hull construction. While welding was mentioned as the method of choice for out-of-sight, under-seat components like flotation chambers, rivets were touted as the most preferred method. This associated the boats with the wartime grit of Rosie the Riveter. Customers were assured that the same kind of rivets used in a P-51 Mustang plane secured their aluminum boat's components.

Admittedly, some makers welded together their smaller craft, but riveting hit a positive engineering (as well as a publicity) chord. It also had economic benefits. Long-time boat enthusiast Paul Hansson still remembers a visit in 1957 to the Lowell Aluminum Boat Works near his boyhood home in Spokane, Washington. There, a workman told Hansson, "We can rivet together a boat lots faster than we could weld her. Plus, rivets make for a lighter boat and are cheaper and cleaner to install than welding. Some shops do make welded boats, but welding aluminum is pretty tricky compared to welding steel." It would not be until the 1980s that new technology made aluminum welding easier to practice and teach.

Rather than rivets-versus-welds debates, brand-to-brand comparisons instead involved such details as the number and manufacturing method of ribs and struts (press-formed or die-formed), the presence and quantity transom knees, aluminum thickness, and whether spray rails were separately applied or embossed, as key areas of distinction between brands.

A check of *The Boating Industry* magazine's annual "stock boatbuilders selling through dealers" listing from 1945 through 1956 indicates over 50 companies

A triple 1947 shipment of Larson Watercraft aluminum craft is caught by the photographer. The brand was later renamed Crestliner, but long continued to be built on Larson's riparian Minnesota manufacturing campus.

jumped onto the aluminum boat bandwagon during that period. Many were fledgling outfits eyeing the big time and hoping that their trade name would be one of the lucky few to become a household word in pleasure boating circles. Among those achieving such success were Aero-Craft, Crestliner (née Larson Watercraft), Lone Star, Aluma Craft, and Star. Star's decision to adopt the *craft* suffix used by many of its peers clicked and small-boat buyers quickly snapping up the renamed Starcraft models from coast to coast. Some suggest that the modified nomenclature was in part an effort to differentiate Star from Lone Star.

In addition to the best-known brands, there were the minor labels content to serve their particular region or niche market. New England's do-it-yourself *Aluma Kit* is but one example. Such companies often had a yearly output of just several hundred hulls. Understandably, most were swept away as the bigger names got bigger, the cost of doing business ballooned, and the boating boom calmed down in the 1960s. By then, the promotional swing from heralding an aluminum boat's safety to touting its style, was complete.

From early postwar days to the 1960s, marketers also redirected the image associated with aluminum boating. Initially depicting happy anglers gently motoring to some favorite fishing spot, many aluminum boat company catalog covers soon featured young couples or families seated in the firm's fastest, most colorful, and curvaceous runabout. Style became a more topical subject. Arguably one of the most fondly remembered practitioners of this publicity was Feather Craft. Starting with designs it had put in the water in the late 1940s, the Atlanta-based company netted an enviable reputation for forming aluminum into sports car–like designs. When Feather Craft offered some models, including the sexy, two-place Rocket Runabout, in space-age anodized hues of green, gold, and blue, any last aesthetic arguments against alloy boats really sprouted leaks.

Though few other aluminum boat makers got into anodizing, most operated automotive-type painting facilities offering style-conscious boaters color choices. For example, Arkansas Traveler offered a now evocative palette of "horizon blue," "beacon red," "spray white," and "marine bronze." Upholstery also became part of the amenity package for aluminum boat shoppers, as did removable plywood flooring for those who didn't want to chill their toes as cold water rushed under the metal hull. On some models, wooden seats could be had to keep one's derriere from experiencing the cold or heat transmission natural to metal.

Some industry observers suggest that early postwar

As a boat trailer maker, Lone Star had the material and engineering wherewithal to fabricate proprietary trucking trailers nicknamed "mule trains." They were used to transport the growing company's craft throughout the US.

boaters who casually purchased an aluminum rowboat used it as an initial steppingstone to a nice wooden hull — something an adult in the late 1940s and early 1950s would still have considered optimum boat material — and then on to a colorful, curvaceous fiberglass runabout. Because of its forgiving nature, aluminum was often viewed as entry-level and something simply to use and outgrow. While functional virtues sold many run-of-the-mill aluminum fishing boats, it took sleeker, faster craft with a steering wheel to lend the alloy some romance.

Usually developed at first from a small marine manufacturer's bread and butter line — 12- to 14-foot rowboats — it is the aluminum outboard runabouts that are central to this book. However, just as many of the brands discussed here were getting started, material shortages precipitated by the Korean War promptly squelched anticipated output. But whenever the miracle alloy could be commandeered from early 1950s bureaucrats, some of it was set aside for "developing" runabouts.

In 1954, by adding a deck and dashboard to its popular Sportsman "12" rowboat, Crestliner created the Commander "12" runabout, which the maker predicted was "destined to be more popular than the companion [rowboat] open model." With an eye on the baby boom generation and parents looking for ways to provide wholesome family fun, Crestliner knew it had a winner.

To give their aluminum boats a bit of a traditional feel, early players like Larson Watercraft accented the alloy hulls with varnished wooden seats, gunnels, and spray rails. (Richard Holm photo)

"Add a [steering] wheel and a big [25-hp] motor," Crestliner copywriters urged boat shoppers, "and you have the ideal combination for pulling [kids on] water skis or [for] general sports use."

Such boats provided a way to be a part of the family boating culture without spending big money or free time on wooden hull maintenance. As a bonus, the average lightweight aluminum runabout wasn't a chore to launch, beach, or trailer. What's more, there was a far greater variety in looks than one might think. In the early postwar years, and especially during the 1950s, *Trailer Boats*'s Larry Carpenter liked to say, "Aluminum boat makers had vastly different ideas as to how to design and build their products. The results gave buyers a glorious variety [of] choices, [as] every make took on a distinct character all its own."

As we'll see in the following sections that highlight each manufacturer, when the marketplace gained greater sophistication, the basic, economy runabouts were soon joined by fancier and larger aluminum hulls. Contributing mightily to this urgent need to upgrade was the increasing level of outboard motor horsepower. It leaped from the industry's top end 25-horsepower model in 1953, to 60 hp just four years later, and then moored briefly at a milestone 100 horses by 1962. After that, horsepower continued to skyrocket, forcing boat makers to offer craft that could best take advantage of this burgeoning muscle.

Today, the sheer variety of outboard runabouts and their longevity have made the boats desirable to a new breed of boat enthusiast. Suffice it to say that vintage examples make up a diversely beautiful and hardy fleet, a genre of craft that led the way to today's more sophisticated and exponentially more expensive aluminum craft.

Chapter 2

Paint and Polish

THE MAJOR ALUMINUM BUILDERS

"Indeed, every make took on a distinct character all its own..."

— Larry Carpenter, *Trailer Boats*, January 1988

One day, while researching at the Clayton, New York, Antique Boat Museum library, I was approached by an enthusiastic newcomer to the vintage boating hobby waving a Firestone aluminum runabout brochure. He'd just acquired the literature at a nautical flea market. The fellow immediately asked for leads in finding such a craft. "Must be a lot of them still around," he figured, "After all, there are Firestone service centers from coast to coast." Quite frankly, before examining that 1957 flyer, I had no idea that the famous tire company ever marketed boats — outboard motors, yes, but not boats. He invited me to copy the paperwork and, upon noticing my rough outline segregating major and minor brands, announced that I now had another marque for the majors. "Why wouldn't it go there?" he reasoned. "Everybody has heard of Firestone!"

This parable is offered as a good-natured disclaimer to anyone whose feelings might be hurt if his or her classic aluminum runabout's pedigree isn't herein classified as being major league metal. Though this roster was compiled with the help of several knowledgeable small craft cronies, it is admittedly subjective, as there were no computer categorized caches of just how many aluminum boats each maker sold from 1946 to 1970. So, like this book's sections on fiberglass boats, the selection process was largely based upon estimates of U.S. and Canadian sales, plus how "nationally" a company advertised. There were some regional manufacturers (like Hewescraft, and Lowell in Spokane, Washington) that cranked out remarkable numbers of aluminum craft in their particular geographic venue, but were promotionally nonexistent elsewhere. Additionally, a company's overall 1946–70 distribution performance was estimated as a benchmark. Consequently, firms (like the contemporary aluminum "major," Lowe) on the short end of that time line can be found among the "minors" in Chapter 3. The category to which a boat is moored in no way reflects upon its quality or collectibility.

Typically, the information presented here is catalog or periodical based. Unless otherwise indicated, quotation marks denote material gleaned directly from that firm's magazine advertising or flyer. Space limitations did not allow for details on each model produced, nor were even the most extensive period brochure collections complete as to the entire tenure of each manufacturer. Still, it is my belief that the following material should provide classic aluminum runabout buffs useful benchmark details about their favorite brand. *Note that additional photos of various models appear in Chapter 7.*

Aero-Craft (Aero-Line)

Though a 1958 Feather Craft flyer headlines that company as "America's oldest manufacturer of aluminum boats," arguably the honor would later be owned by Aero-Craft because it lasted a bit longer. In fact, an Aero-Craft ad claimed the "oldest" title in the June 1959 edition of *Boats*. Aero-Craft was based in St. Charles, Michigan, and accounts in the local newspaper in June 1946 report that Aero-Craft production had commenced.

Tracking Aero-Craft's lineage requires being on the lookout for the brand's parent company, Harwill, Inc. — a mnemonic amalgamation of the names of its founders, L. B. Harkins, his brother Leon Harkins, and Douglas Wilste. According to Harwill historian, Andreas Jordahl Rhude, the trio formed their company in Bay City, Michigan, during February of 1946, but conducted manufacturing startup in St. Charles when that community made its erstwhile waterworks building available to Harwill for a nominal charge. Reportedly, the founders figured on producing plastic items, but quickly settled on the manufacture of aluminum boats when president L. B. Harkins reminded his partners that, several years earlier, he had successfully completed a "How to Work with Aircraft Sheet Metal" class. He'd marketed his new skills at an aircraft plant and the Bay City, Michigan, Dow Chemical facility where magnesium goods, including some 12- and 16-foot Dowcraft boats, were being fabricated.

Once the fledgling St. Charles firm got rolling, initial production figures indicate that about a dozen boats were built weekly. Rhude reports Harwill was

This late 1940s Aero-Craft model "AD" is deluxe version of the firm's cornerstone 12-foot rowboat. Add a period 10-hp Mercury Lightning and you've got the makings of an official American Power Boat Association Class "BU" stock outboard utility racer. Fit her with the classic 5.4-hp, four-cylinder Evinrude Zephyr fishing motor she's wearing here, and this Aero-Craft can't be beat for trolling.

Aero-Craft offered several bargain/second-string models under the Aero-Line name, including this "snappy [1958] 14-foot model RSD runabout featuring styling, performance and safety at a rock bottom price."

sufficiently swamped with orders for more boats so that, by March 1947, 60 employees were helping to crank out 50 boats each week. This encouraged the founders to buy acreage in an undeveloped part of town for the construction of a bigger factory. The building project necessitated a public stock sale, which lead to a major investor, A. S. Brennan, assuming the Harwill presidency. Painted on the new plant were the company logo, the words "aluminum boats," and "light metal products." Among the latter was an interesting assortment of military-related items — aluminum card tables, laundry tables, and parachute-packing tables — as well as a few 27-foot boats that the Army wanted to try.

By the time its 1954 catalog was printed, Harwill, Inc., had a relative army of 100 workers "equipped with the latest precision machinery [to produce] quality aluminum boats at the rate of several hundred every month." The brochure noted that Harwill "had become one of [the] leaders in the aluminum boat field by late 1947," had tripled factory space, and "once more [was, during late 1953] in the process of enlarging plant facilities to step up production capacity still further." Aero-Craft's success was credited in large part to one "Rene Beauvais, noted aircraft engineer [who] adapted the special aluminum alloys and production techniques of the aircraft industry to the manufacture of lightweight aluminum boats." Brochure copy also cited leading but unnamed marine designers and metallurgical engineers.

While Aero-Craft brochures through about 1955

For 1958, the 16-foot Blue Sabre Deluxe represented Aero-Craft's upper-end runabout. Polished tailfin/tail light covers provided stylish borders for the pair of Oliver 16-hp motors used in this catalog picture.

typically chronicle nearly 20 boats, those germane to our study include the 12-foot Model AD and 14-foot Model DD. Both are center "wheel-deck" runabout versions of rowboats central to the Aero-Craft line. Both of these semi-vee bottom runabouts and an 18½-foot Model JOR front deck runabout had a late 1930s "mechanical" look with boxy lines. Enigmatically, though, their sterns exhibited a curvy tumblehome reminiscent of Feather Craft. It was almost as if the Aero-Craft designer had spied a Feather Craft only minutes before his blueprints were due. The 18½-foot version was also available in sedan cruiser form as the Model JCC with either standard or deluxe options and enough portholes and cabin glass to make it look like it was wearing a gas mask.

Vintage marine columnist Larry Carpenter says boats such as these are like "a crotchety old aunt" — sometimes disagreeable, but lovable anyway and never boring. He mused about his DD in the June 1988 issue of *Trailer Boats.* Thirty years earlier, he'd picked up a nice, secondhand example, but "soon found a defect peculiar to [his] particular boat. Many of the rivets were unexplainably corroded and a sharp wave tap while underway could send a half-dozen streams of water

Blue Sabre, the 1958 Aero-Craft flagship measured 16-feet could handle a 70-horse Merc and came standard with that convertible top and big windshield. Interestingly, though, the tailfins were "optional at extra cost. [And] cut aluminum sheets, rivets, and other basic materials [were] available for those who wish to further customize their Aero-Craft boats."

into [his] lap." Carpenter's father "bought some oversize rivets, and frequently [dad and lad] would haul the boat up on the dock and roll it over on one side. After drilling out several holes, [they'd] take turns peening the new rivet heads while the other held a two-pound hammer firmly on the other side." This boat must have been made on some gloomy St. Charles Monday or with economy rivets, as I've never encountered any other Aero-Craft owner who recalls his hull being equipped with an *optional shower nozzle bottom.* "Another characteristic of this hull," Carpenter notes, "could catch you unaware if you weren't paying attention. The shallow vee forward and minimal bow flare up from the hard chine could cause trouble in a following sea (or crossing the heavy wake of a large cruiser) taken any way but straight on, because the boat could go shooting off at a crazy angle. On the other hand, with a little attention to the wheel and throttle, the boat could, under the same conditions, send a solid sheet of water a considerable distance."

Though there were instances when the AD and DD competed in the speed and spray of stock utility outboard races (in Class AU and BU, as well as Class CU and Class DU, respectively) circa 1950 listings showed Aero-Craft deliberately chased the checkered flag with Model K-Racing (12 feet) and L-Racing (13½ feet) runabouts. Also footnoted is mention of a standard service Model H runabout at 15' 11".

An interesting Aero-Craft accessory seldom seen on surviving boats are bottom-mounted "Sta-Foils." These long, hollow (and open on the aft end) aluminum feet would "fill up with water and become ballast tanks that increase [the boat's] dead weight for safety and stability when anchored or moving slowly. As the boat picks up speed, the water drains out of the Sta-Foils, and they become fast planing foils that help increase speed and maneuverability and give a soft, knee-action ride."

From its earliest years, Harwill rode on a solid reputation that its boats' quality equaled that of aircraft. A 10-year warranty against hull punctures (while in the water) was upped to a lifetime guarantee by 1958. By then, boxy characteristics (as seen in the AD, DD, et al.) had faded, and the runabout lineup (now with foredeck steering) consisted of the tail fin-equipped 16-foot Blue Sabre; the 16-foot HD16, delivered as a utility; the 14' 2" Lancer and Sea Mist; and the 14-footers Sea Dart and Special. Offered in the same catalog, although considered a separate marque with a distinct logo, were "the economy line of quality boats," Aero-Line. These carried only a one-year hull puncture guarantee. The 14-foot Model RSD was that bargain brand's sole runabout offering for 1958.

Central to the early boats' identity were non-skid paint jobs on the inside bottoms, a model/serial number nameplate riveted to the deck, and "a wide blue stripe around the boat [as] a mark of distinction." From the latter 1950s, however, the stripe was replaced (on most models) with a colorful array of enamel finishes above the spray rails. Such accenting as well as tasteful tail fins are evidenced on the 1958 Blue Sabre, a 16-foot runabout with a convertible top option and a 70-hp rating. Aero-Craft often pictured this one in a dark blue/silver two-tone with a tall, 60-horse Mercury Mark 75 engine.

Having added a fleet of fiberglass craft to complement Aero-Craft aluminum boats and canoes, the operation was speeding along in 1968 when acquisition-minded officials of the Browning gun organization took notice. Harwill accepted an early 1969 offer on speaking terms with $2,000,000 from Browning, with additional compensation to the Harkins brothers and Brennan, who stayed on in a management capacity. (Some boats from the Browning years are labeled "Browning-AeroCraft.") As did most recreational vehicle makers, Browning's Aero-Craft marine division took a direct shot in 1973 from the first of several gasoline shortages and price hikes. By the end of that year, it began major staff downsizing in St. Charles and sold off the then idled boatworks in the summer of 1974 to Atlanta-based Fuqua Industries/Signa Corporation.

Manufacturing was restarted by September and, as Rhude notes, ramped up to "250 aluminum boats and 30–35 fiberglass boats per week." Production was seriously affected by a fire in the winter of 1976. Three years later, the last Aero-Craft were fabricated in St. Charles, before Signa shifted Aero-Craft operations to a Decatur, Indiana, factory, and then took the line dark shortly thereafter. It was an unceremonious end for the world's first production aluminum boat company.

Aluma-Craft

"Rounding the turn — SWISH! You see the sleek shiny train as it streaks over the rails. You marvel at its aluminum beauty! Its durability! ZOOM! — A high-powered plane skyrockets through the air. It's aluminum, of course to withstand the strain of the elements. And on the water — it's the same aluminum sturdiness, this lifetime metal that gives you the last name in boats today… Aluma Craft!" So touted the fledgling pleasure craft company's 1949 brochure, as it also promised aluminum boat buyers that Aluma Craft could keep them from "wasting precious weekends with blow torches, caulking irons, paintbrushes, and tar pots" — scary eternal provinces of wooden boat ownership.

The brand's advertising and quickly acquired reputation for tank-like rugged quality precipitated a line of small craft about which an entire book could be written. The story began with the 1893 founding of Flour City Ornamental Iron, a Minneapolis firm that, after World War II, found itself with a stockpile of military-grade aluminum and employees who had learned how to work with the alloy. The result was entry into the boatbuilding business in late 1946 with the production of some aluminum rowboats.

Along with Douglas Aircraft, which marketed its 10-foot "Dural" (for durable aluminum) dinghy; plane maker Grumman, championing aluminum canoes; and

Aluma Craft's Kodiak 14.

a Long Island–based refrigerator company offering an aluminum skiff, Aluma Craft was one of the first firms to receive notice in *Motor Boating*'s "outboard boats" postwar specification chart. The first Aluma Craft of interest to our study was the late 1940s 14-foot Model F decked utility. It was one of four models of from 12 to 16 feet that were listed in *Motor Boating*'s January 1947 issue. That gives Aluma Craft the press distinction of being viewed as a pioneer marine aluminum manufacturer. Competitors Aero-Craft and Feather Craft hadn't yet activated the venerable magazine's radar.

By the fall of 1947, the *Aluma Craft News* publicity paper sought to sign dealers with a promise to cut out the middleman and sell directly to them at a one-third discount. "Continuous heavy consumer demand plus improved production methods," Aluma Craft announced, "have made possible [a] price reduction on [the] world's number one small boat." Although such a positioning claim could be disputed, it was clear to the manufacturer, dealerships, and early customers alike that Aluma Craft was a serious contender.

Marine designer Erich Swenson got catalog credit for creating the line's products (including canoes). Double-row welding — which the maker dubbed "stronger than welding without defining the difference — "served to join hull panels. Extruded aluminum gunwales, ribs, stiffeners, and splash rails also received note (as did the cast fittings). To test each hull for leaks, the company subjected every one to 3,000 pounds of water pressure in a factory immersion tank.

The firm's 1953, 1954, and 1955 catalogs all had the same front and back cover motifs with only the year being changed. The back cover presented a healthy lineup that defines quality in mid-century carefree small boating. It's home to the now coveted, notably basic 11' 7" Model R wheel deck runabout; the 16-foot wheel deck Model K, also spartan but with Aluma Craft's useful "Aqueduct" transom that, as a sort of backsplash compartment, added strength to the stern while keeping dripped outboard fuel off the floor; a deluxe upholstered, center-decked (with steering mounted on the deck as opposed to the dash) Merry "M" available in 14- and 16-foot lengths, and the 14-foot wheel-decked Model FD. All of these boats have since found favor with vintage outboarders seeking sturdy, virtually maintenance-free craft on which a large variety of motors can be tried without fear of swamping.

At the high end of this book's 20-foot length cutoff is another Aluma Craft introduced in 1953 as the Big Boy (also offered in cabin guise as the Day Cruiser and Luxury Liner) and revamped a few years later as the Cruiseabout. At 19' 2" with a 78-inch beam, it provided 68 square feet of cockpit space, had plywood flooring, weighed about 700 pounds, and begged for 120 hp, nearly quadruple that of any then-contemporary Evinrude or Johnson.

Swenson's runabout designs became more colorful with Aluma Craft's 1957 series. This included the center-decked, richly upholstered 15-foot Super C, Super CS (with a walk-through center deck), and the more modest, bench-seat, front-steered Deep C. Color options on the former pair were so plentiful that dealers were simply instructed to give boat shoppers a color sample card. In 1959, runabout buyers saw the 14-foot Flying D, the 15-foot Flying C, the Queen Sixteen (16 feet), and the 18-footer Queen Merrie. The trend toward outboards being equipped with electric starting caused Aluma Craft to position the steering and other controls forward.

In 1960, the Minnesota manufacturer unveiled a 14-foot Model FDR, a front-steered runabout with modest upholstery. In an apparent effort to target different markets, this was dubbed part of the "family cottage fleet," as opposed to the higher "yacht club fleet" in which only the Queen Merrie and Queen Sixteen shared catalog space with the new glass offerings. A nine-year (Why didn't they make it 10?) warranty accompanied the aluminum boats.

In 1958, the company introduced fiberglass models. By 1961, Aluma Craft had become a division of the Hupp Corporation, which initially gave glass and aluminum models equal billing before highlighting the plastic soon thereafter. To keep up with the increasingly sophisticated (and some say by then highly female-influenced) family boating marketplace, most Aluma Craft runabout models received color and upholstery upgrades. New for 1962 were the 14-foot Maracaibo 14, the center-side control-decked Kodiak, the entry-level front-steered Model F-6, and a reintroduced Model FD, dubbed FD-6. For some reason, it later morphed back to the FD.

Having finally given the fiberglass boats their own brand name (Alpex) and promotion, Aluma Craft had palpably thinner catalogs by 1964. Among the new runabout products were the Bel Mara (at 17' 1"), the 15' 3" Tampico II, and the larger (15' 3") Maracaibo. That latter was fitted with rear-facing back seats to accommodate water skier observation.

By 1971, even the casual observer would notice a huge change in Aluma Craft runabout offerings. Only one made the catalog that year, a welded 18-foot tri-hull primarily designed for inboard/outboard installation, but also available in an outboard format. The brochure's cover was rather oblique, too, featuring a series of washed-out watercolor sketches that seemed to affix an old fisherman's head on a bikini-clad body. A stray bikini top and bottom added dissonance to the literature — a far cry from the evocative, richly colored family boating scene of Aluma Craft's 1953–55 flyers. Something seemed to be amiss.

An early 1970s move to manufacturing facilities in St. Peter, Minnesota, yielded an even smaller flyer, but one that appeared logically focused on the canoe and fishing boat marketplace. The only vestige of the classic Aluma Craft runabouts was a 14' 7" Model F-7 with side steering deck. Pinpointing anglers has since caused Aluma Craft's line to grow and prosper in the 21st century, with no need to convince small-craft shoppers that aluminum — the material it helped bring to pleasure boating — makes sense.

Arkansas Traveler

Officially known as the Southwest Manufacturing Company, which was located in Little Rock, Arkansas, the firm joined the small but growing ranks of aluminum boatbuilders in the late 1940s. It began by offering 12- and 14-foot versions of the Sportsman series in standard and, on the 14-footer, center deck–forward windshield versions. All had wood slat floors and dual-toned paint jobs. Sexiest of the early boats was the limited production 1950 Playboy. This 14-foot stock utility racing runabout was initially designed for

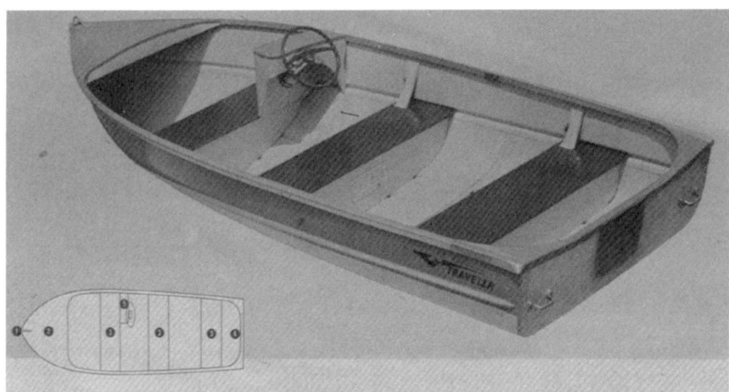

A side-center steering pod (either factory installed or as a dealer accessory) instantly upgrades an erstwhile Arkansas Traveler rowboat into a fun utility begging for her maximum 35-horse mate.

a single kneeling driver, even though the craft had a modest bench seat ahead of its wheel deck to meet American Power Boating Association competition rules. A 40-cubic-inch Mercury KG-9 would provide a fast mate for this craft. The 1955 models included the more pedestrian DUT-14 and Sportsman SP-14 with "a much longer [than previous incarnations] fore-deck, twin cockpits, and a fantail deck under which [was] space for battery and gasoline tanks."

Speaking of lengthy foredecks, the 1955 fleet featured a sexy, two-place 12-foot runabout with decking that extended to the sole seat. It had been designed with the 16-horse, conservatively rated Mercury Mark 20 or family-friendly Evinrude 15 in mind. Given a choice, the boat would have chosen the Merc. In any event, this admittedly special interest speedster must have been a low-production item because few show up today. Southwest Manufacturing also made a toy version.

Behind the scenes, Arkansas Traveler engineers were working to make obsolete the old standbys by perfecting "a revolutionary new die-formed hull, in one piece from spray rail to spray rail." Unveiled in the 1957 line, the resulting Royal Series runabouts were the CSP-15 Marquise Custom Sportsman and the DUT-15 Dutchess Deluxe Utility (both 14' 9" long). One had been torture tested in a Mississippi River run from New Orleans to St. Louis being pushed for two days straight at up to 40 mph, thanks to a couple of 40-hp motors. Besides capturing the multi-toned, finned, space-age essence of the era, the Royal Series models were especially interesting because of their "gleaming fiberglass superstructure" decking and coaming.

Surprisingly, Southwest Manufacturing was one of only a few aluminum boatbuilders that used fiberglass components as part of its boats' construction. Eventually, Arkansas Travelers entered the fiberglass boat arena for the 1959 model year. A fiberglass foredeck was used during that period to modernize the old 14-foot utility into the Deluxe Utility (DUT-14) and at the top, a nice little entry-level bench-seated 12' 10" runabout dubbed Ski-Tor, just right for a bargain-priced 25-hp outboard from some catalog store and a pair of brand-X water skis. By 1960, steering had long since moved up front on all Arkansas Traveler wheel-steered models (except a 15-foot UT-15F utility with side foredeck partly attached to the front seat). The DUT-14 got treated to front seat backs, as did the basic DUT-15 Deluxe Utility, which had no rear seating at all. Fiberglass models appeared on most post–1950s Arkansas Traveler brochure covers, the inside of which sometimes mentioned the company's boats as having been designed by Reinbeck and Associates of Los Angeles.

To come up with this sporty model, Arkansas Traveler generously decked over one of its 12-foot rowboats. The results made the pages of many 1955 boating magazines, but few of the neat two-seaters are accounted for today.

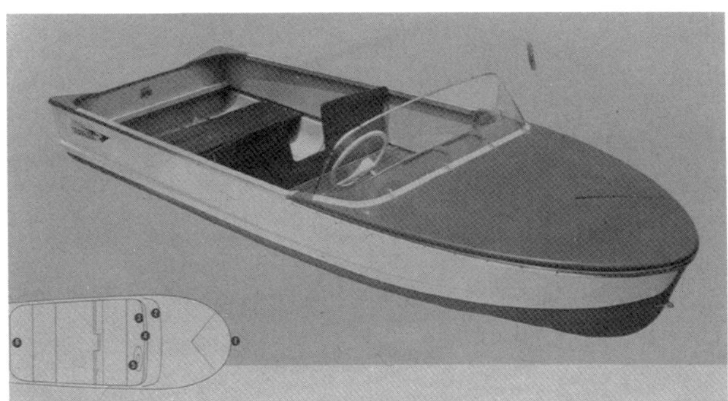

Enigmatically, only a very few makers of aluminum and fiberglass boats copied Arkansas Traveler's sensible technique of decking some of its aluminum hulls in attractively contrasting glass, as in this 14-foot model DUT-14 Deluxe Utlity.

To meet the anticipated mushrooming marine marketplace, production facilities in Amsterdam, New York; Adams, Wisconsin; and Peterborough, Ontario, Canada (home of Evinrude/Johnson's Canadian subsidiary) had joined the original Little Rock plant. By 1963, the company had become Traveler Manufacturing and offered what it termed the aluminum Corsair series with the Lark sport runabout and utilities in 12- and 14-foot versions. The following year saw Traveler listed as a division of the Chicago-based Stan Ray Corporation. Its locale switched to Danville, Illinois, in 1965 and the company mentioned marketing 12- and 14-foot aluminum "utility runabouts." As per subsequent *Motor Boating* rosters, the marque faded from sight shortly thereafter.

Cadillac

Understandably, this boat line was sometimes thought to be a General Motors product, as it shared a trade name and logo script with GM's top-of-the- line cars. In fact, Cadillac Marine & Boat Company's (originally, just called the Cadillac Boat Company) aluminum runabouts did represent quality products, even though the name had disappeared from the boating scene in the early 1960s after merging with Wagemaker. Some sources indicate that Wagemaker, of Grand Rapids, Michigan, best known for Wolverine molded plywood craft, closed out the Cadillac line in 1959.

The Cadillac, Michigan-based firm's first boats were built in 1953, an assortment of molded ply-lap, cedar strip, and molded plywood hulls. The 1956 Cadillac catalog, however, shows the aluminum boats for which the manufacturer is best recalled. Aluminum runabouts for 1956 defined the marquee's sturdy, silvery quintessence — the "sweetest boats afloat." Although a short-lived brand, Cadillac's hulls hit during the middle of the big boating boom and were pictured in most of the day's pleasure boating periodicals, thus earning Cadillac mention as a major player.

Center wheel-deck fans had a choice of three versions of Avalon, in 12-, 14-, and 16-foot options. The embossed aluminum seats on these and sister aluminum Cadillac's were advertised as "specially treated, glare-proof" so that they "will not discolor clothing." The Daytona series offered front-deck steering in 12-, 14-, 16-, and 18-foot varieties. Permanent front- and rear-seating upholstery was standard on the more deluxe Coronado 14-foot runabout, which was also fitted with a detailed topside that included an aft-deck and combing. Finally, the Isle Royal could handle 75 hp, and featured a full topside like Coronado's, as well as a hardtop, making this 18-foot craft Cadillac's "Cadillac."

By 1962, Ash-Craft Company, a Madison Avenue, New York City firm, was marketing aluminum boats under the Cadillac name.

The basic aluminum finish Cadillac Daytona could be ordered in sizes ranging (in two-foot increments) from 12- to 18-feet. The smallest incarnation is shown here.

Crestliner (Larson Watercraft/Crestliner)

Lineage research on this brand can confuse vintage small-boating buffs who wonder why the hulls bear *a pair* of famous boat manufacturer's names —Crestliner and Larson. The simple explanation is that prolific small-craft builder Paul Larson lent his name to two companies based in Little Falls, Minnesota. The first was Larson Boat works, begun a year or so before the United States entered World War I, and housed in a modest facility just a stone's throw from the Mississippi River.

Visiting Larson during the first days of the 1946 boating season, veteran Robert Wold gave an enthusiastic presentation on why small boats should be built with war-proved aircraft aluminum. Larson was quickly convinced, and by mid-August, he, Wold, and several local investors had established Larson Watercraft to fabricate aluminum boats. Initially, production occurred in some spare Larson Boat Works space, and then at a separate factory close by. It's a testament to simpler times, less government regulation, and probably fewer lawyers, that Larson Watercraft had sped from idea to a shipment of aluminum 12-footers by Thanksgiving 1946. According to historian Andreas Jordahl Rhude, the first of these boats had been designed by Larson and a trusted staffer, Jack Oestrich, "using sheets of plywood as a model." The 1949 listings note a 12' 1" Commander, a 14' 2" Commodore, and a 16' 2" Admiral. A 12-foot Commander, Commodore Speedster 14, Seaman 14, and 16-foot Admiral Speedster are noted in 1950's *Motor Boating* lineup.

Brochures from 1952 show a newly introduced mix of plywood and aluminum in Larson Watercraft boats dubbed "PLY-A-LUM." These 12- and 14-foot rowboats are tangential to our study because they "combined the advantages of waterproof mahogany marine plywood, and tempered aluminum." The wood-to-metal joints were secured by an aluminum keel and seams using rivets so there were "no nailed or screwed joints to work loose and require time-consuming caulking." This quasi-aluminum boat was an answer to alloy shortages brought about by the Korean War, but apparently gained enough of a following (according to Rhude, about 15 percent of Larson Watercraft production) to be continued in catalogs after a ceasefire was declared.

Metal shortages caused by the Korean War motivated Larson Watercraft/ Crestliner to offer the Ply-A-Lume plywood boats braced with strips of aluminum.

In 1954 brochures, the now familiar name and logo "Crestliner" appeared, although mated to a small script "Larson," and by the fall of 1957, all mentions of Larson Watercraft, Inc. and/or Larson were dropped, this to avoid the brand confusion that boat buyers would understandably otherwise experience. This change was decreed from Crestliner executive offices at a new plant opened in 1954 several miles away from the original Larson-based locale.

Crestliner's 1954 Commander "12" served nicely as the line's debut runabout. With red bottom and deck trim, the interior bottom finished in green non-skid paint, and optional oak (as opposed to aluminum spray rails as standard) spray rails, this decked craft might have looked like an upgraded rowboat. Despite appearances, thicker aluminum (.064-inch vs. .051-inch for the sister Sportsman rowboat) and substantial supports allowed it to be teamed with an outboard up to 25 hp. The flyer shows it being pushed by an Evinrude Big Twin 25. Surely some lucky young speedsters fitted a late model Mercury KG-9 25+ horse mill to their Commander "12's" transom. What a ride that could produce! It's a good thing that the steering and other controls were front-dash mounted. From a classic outboarding perspective, this 130-pound Crestliner (also friendly to low-power motors) makes for a useful vintage craft.

In 1955, the company established a factory in Strasburg, Virginia, to help with ever-expanding orders. This added manufacturing capacity assisted in the introduction of both updated and completely new models. The former category included four versions of the Commander 12, from an open craft and a bench-seat decked model to a center-decked hull and a deluxe incarnation with individual front seats, generous combing, and aft-decking. These 12-footers were upgraded to take 30 hp. For those wanting to try a recently introduced Mercury Mark 75 (six cylinder in-line, 60-horse giant), a 14-foot Viking 14, available in options similar to Commander 12, was just the ticket. Fifteen- and 18-foot editions of the Buccaneer — offered in Crestliner's four runabout styles — were rated for 70 hp, as were the three variations of the Voyager 15- and 18-foot Convertible, so named for its canvas top. The Commodore 14 fit the moderate-size, entry-level family runabout sector with four versions (from open to 40-inch deck and 60-inch deck with a center deck and various seating options), though only suggested to be used with up to 35-hp outboards.

A debut fiberglass fleet took Crestliner's center stage publicity in 1958, though *Motor Boating* editors saw fit to picture the company's new aluminum Jetstreak 12 in the January show issue. Any classic outboarder would love to find one of these generously finned, two-place, fore- and aft-decked speedsters today. They also came in 14- and 15-foot versions. Each offered several color schemes.

By 1960, most of the marque's aluminum runabout hulls were painted white (although other colors were available) and treated to the firm's "invisible rivet construction" (above the spray rails) in order to mimic their smooth glass sisters. The 1960 brochures touted a recently christened Morrilton, Arkansas, plant, plus a division in Waterloo, Ontario, Canada. New to the aluminum runabout roster were a richly appointed

Entry-level aluminum runabouts like this Crestliner with its Spartan interior and plain (rowboat-style) bench offered a way for lots of young moms and dads to get their fledgling clan into boating fun economically. Besides, who cared about upholstered seats, padded dashboards, and carpeted flooring when simply experiencing the joys of teaching the baby-boomers to ski?

The Commander Deluxe 12 and a rowboat from which the model sprang provide contrast to Crestliner's "family boat shopping" theme. Boat and motor manufacturers understood that a good local dealer could move product better than low price and national advertising, so often depicted a happy hometown marine dealership experience in its catalogs.

14-foot Falcon, an entry-level Commodore 16, and the Imperial Flying Crest 17 (-footer) sporting lots of seating, instrument panel, side panel upholstery, and a "folding snack tabl-ette [between stern seats] and simulated teakwood floor." Wildwind and (with a "completely customized interior) Imperial Wildwind topped Crestliner's alloy line. Both of these 19-footers were recommended for twin outboards totaling 105 horsepower.

As the 1960s got under way, Bigelow-Sanford bought the company, and briefly added a northeastern manufacturing branch in Thompsonville, Connecticut. It also licensed an Italian outfit to build boats — Crestliner S.P.A. in Como, Italy. Then, in 1964, Crestliner sold out to the Molded Fiberglass boat company. MFG's influence was evident in the 1964 models, which, amidst a sea of fiberglass, featured only a pair of 14-foot aluminum runabouts. These included the rather basic Shipmate, the better appointed Sea Scout, and the 16-foot Crest Rider. The Shipmate and Crest Rider were fabricated in "Fairlap," Crestliner's term for the embossed lapstrake design, while Sea Scout was constructed with "Crest-Weld, the first all-welded boat in its class. . . through interlocking heavy gauge aluminum plates and automatically Crest-Welded [its] full length."

For 1966, "Crest-Weld" was central to the line's aluminum runabouts: the Norseman 19, Dane 15, Flying, and Sea Scout 14. Entry-level runabouts the Flying Crest 16 and bench-seat-basic Commodore Speedster 14 were advertised as being formed with standard "lapstrake aluminum" construction. It was around this time that the crown appeared above the "C" in Crestliner's now well-known logo.

North American Rockwell Corporation's marine division acquired the Little Falls–based boat company around 1970 and sold it to American Machine & Foundry (AMF) in 1972. AMF was battered in the 1980 economic storm and sold the now-idled Crestliner aluminum boat operation to a locally financed group of erstwhile Crestliner staff. Under the banner of Nordic Boat Company, production resumed with a small crew in the late spring of 1981. A final twist in the story of this long-respected boat maker came seven years later when the owner of Larson Boats, Genmar, Inc., made a deal to acquire Nordic and renamed the resulting craft Crestliners.

Chrysler

It's clear from perusing the 1967 Chrysler boats catalog that executives there hadn't acquired Lone Star two years earlier in order to increase aluminum runabout sales. By then, fiberglass models constituted the lineup, the sole exception being the 14' 11" lapstrake pattern Del Ray 15, an "all-aluminum, all-value runabout." Comfortable with a Chrysler 45-hp long shaft outboard, the Del Ray was likely cataloged as a nod to entry-level, fair-weather family boaters or maybe as an ode to those looking to replace their vintage Lone Star with something newer but familiar. Neither was reason enough, however, to cause Chrysler Marine management to continue the boat into the 1970s.

Duratech

For western readers who might suggest that an eastern bias is showing for my having included Duratech in the majors, the company long claimed to enjoy national distribution. A sales rep at the 1964 New York Boat Show told my dad that the company had satisfied customers all over the United States and Canada. In fact, the 1958 brochure bragged that there were "over five hundred Duratech dealers throughout the country."

Though a New York state–based firm, Duratech was notably transient. *Motor Boating*'s January 1951 roster first notes it as Duratech Manufacturing Corporation of Tarrytown. The debut line had only a couple of versions of a basic nine-foot flat-bottom jon boat from which a rudimentary wheel deck, Class JU racer was subsequently developed. By 1953, the firm had moved to 12 Paulding Street, Pleasantville, New York, added a sail option to its pram and introduced rowboats and canoes up to 16 feet. Though for 1954, the company's Pramline series was expanded, inexplicably that racing pram was deleted from the fleet, which then included a Veeline series with basic 12- and 14-foot runabouts. After testing prototypes at "high-speed" in often rough Long Island sound, Duratech reported the Veeline's features such as "elimination of the outside chine joint, addition of a non-skid floor paint, full length spray rails, increased gunwale beam, 20 percent thicker side skins, and one-piece bottom skins" showed improvement over previous models.

Duratech had again relocated by 1958, this time to a Route 202 address in Peekskill, where literature touted a supply relationship with Alcoa. "Duratech rivets, sheets, and extrusions are supplied by the Aluminum Company of America, and are inspected for thickness, hardness and alloying elements." To be sure, the other aluminum boat "majors" also obtained their enviable market shares based upon similar quality control. Internal structure details, on most Duratech craft, though, show

For outboard speed buffs, the model 92RA, Class "JU" stock utility racer is Duratech's most interesting offering. It's likely that some of the few surviving 1953 output have long since been converted to fishing prams or duck boats by owners who never realized what an uncommon craft they own.

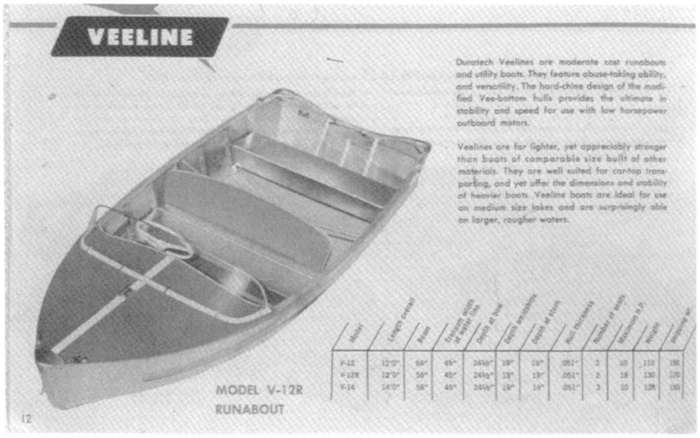

VEELINE

Duratech Veelines are moderate cost runabouts and utility boats. They feature abuse-taking ability, and versatility. The hard-chine design of the modified Vee-bottom hulls provides the ultimate in stability and speed for use with low horsepower outboard motors.

Veelines are far lighter, yet appreciably stronger than boats of comparable size built of other materials. They are well suited for car-top transporting, and yet offer the dimensions and stability of heavier boats. Veeline boats are ideal for use on medium size lakes and are surprisingly able on larger, rougher waters.

Model	Length overall	Beam	Transom width at water line	Depth at bow	Depth amidships	Depth at stern	Hull thickness	Number of seats	Maximum H.P.	Weight	Shipping wt.
V-12	12'0"	58"	45"	24½"	19"	19"	.051"	3	10	110	150
V-12R	12'0"	56"	45"	24½"	19"	19"	.051"	2	18	130	170
V-14	14'0"	56"	45"	24½"	19"	19"	.051"	3	10	125	[illegible]

MODEL V-12R
RUNABOUT

12

Duratech's economy 12-foot Veeline runabout weighed only 130-pounds and even with its maximum 18-hp, made for a very trailerable, versatile craft.

aggressive ribbing, which contributed to the line's good reputation, backed by "a lifetime puncture guarantee, five-year watertight guarantee, and a five-year salt water guarantee." The latter pledge was meant to reassure coastal buyers who had long been taught that salt and aluminum don't make for a pleasant mix.

A runabout survey done around 1958 shows Duratech with a pair of heavy-duty 19' 1" boats, and a trio of 15' 9" models that included the nicely upholstered and aft-decked Deluxe (S-168RD), a Standard version (S-168R) with modest front upholstery and L-shaped rear bench seating, and the basic Fishing model (S-168RF), sans rear seats. The 13' 7" "Fourteens" came in Deluxe (S-148RD) and Standard (S-148R) runabout formats, and like the larger versions, were categorized as the Sealine Series. A 12-foot Veeline (V-12R) runabout was available for entry-level boaters. Its compactness and plain aluminum rear bench seat would make it a nice craft for vintage outboarders. Many of these models featured the company's colorful Duradeck, "an abrasive-resistant vinyl, bonded with heat and pressure to the aluminum decks. Even the twist of sandy shoes cannot mar its beauty," Duratech claimed.

Besides its well-known aluminum models, Duratech made a late-1950s foray into fiberglass when it manufactured some boats for Glass Magic. This output was distributed throughout the northeast. By the mid-1960s, the company had been acquired by Penn Yan Boats, Inc. and moved to the parent's Penn Yan, New York, facility. Aluminum runabouts of this era (typically appointed with a blue deck and white hull) included the 14-foot Skier, "the water-skier's dreamboat, family pleasure craft par excellence. Designed and priced for those choosing their first power runabout, or for folks who think young!" The 15½-foot Neptune was advertised (on the same catalog page) as "a step up from the Skier. Heftier craft included Duratech's Orion at 16' 10", and the 18' 2" Galaxy. A 1966 price sheet mentioned

Standard and Deluxe editions of Duratech's 16-foot Sealine runabouts. Note side rear bench seating in the Standard model, perfect for fishing or observing a skier.

the Marlin at the bottom end of the price scale ($649), but this 4-foot runabout earned no catalog space.

Duratech was conspicuously absent from the 1967 *Motor Boating* listing of active builders, although it continued receiving footnote mentions throughout the late-1960s boat name directories published by *The Boating Industry*. After that, someone there who hadn't heard anything from the marque in a while subjected it to an editorial housecleaning.

Feather Craft

"As manufacturers since late 1945," the January issue of *Motor Boating* said, Atlanta-based Feather Craft "designers entered the field with a flat-bottom utility fishing boat, and recruited skilled aluminum fabricators and riveters formerly employed in airplane plants." If interpreted to mean that the company began building boats sometime in the fall or early winter days of that year, the wording suggests that Feather Craft wins the "first modern aluminum boat" prize.

Questions about the 1945 date are raised by Frank Kibler, who was long associated with Feather Craft, first as staff and then as owner. Lee Wangstad's February 2003 *Boating World* article reports Kibler as recalling, "The company was founded in 1947 by my uncle, W. Douglas Knight. He was associated with J. T. Knight, a metal dealer involved in scrap metals and aluminum

Sixteen feet worth of nicely curved aluminum, a trusty 33-horse Scott-Atwater outboard, loyal pooch, picnic supplies, canvas top, and lovely companion give Feather Craft's Falcon and its captain reason to soar.

before he went out on his own. After the war years, the aircraft companies were all shifting their production to other goods. The aluminum companies were looking for new markets and gave us a lot of assistance in gearing up for boat production."

Finally, as if this "who's on first?" debate isn't sufficiently murky, I offer an innocent-looking 1964 Feather Craft sales pitch to dealers subscribing to November 1963's *The Boating Industry*. Published there, a hand-rendered outline of a boxy rowboat is depicted above the caption, "'45 — Simple then, but eighteen years later aluminum's high strength, low upkeep and dependability tell the tale. Now it's worth more." While it's unclear exactly what worthy tale the copywriter was attempting to convey, we can assume that part of the message identified 1945 with the first Feather Craft, which might have been a homebrew prototype. No matter the neck-and-neck nature of different start dates, Feather Craft easily wins most vintage marine buffs' "best-loved aluminum boats" honor.

To be sure, much of Feather Craft's output served the fishing boat (and later canoe) market, but it was about a decade's worth of streamlined runabouts that truly defined the brand and give it a cherished spot in pleasure boating history. Those circa 1945 designers *Motor Boating* referred to quickly proposed interpreting classic 1930s mahogany speedboat lines in an aluminum format. Feather Craft's creative follow-through gave boaters an option for carefree eye-pleasing streamlining and a rolled tumblehome reminiscent of expensive wooden hulls.

By 1950, those aesthetic and engineering distinctions were present in the 12' 1" Standard Runabout, the 13-foot Deluxe Runabout, the 12-foot Flyer, the 15-foot Vagabond, and the 10-foot Firefly racing hull. Each had seen at least a year of service by that time. For 1951, Vagabond's beam went from 55 inches to 62 inches, making it "far roomier with greater freeboard and heavier gauge metal than [the] last year." Also in 1951, the Flyer grew 12 inches and was doing some nice stock utility outboard racing work, especially when mated to a 25+ hp Mercury KG-9 motor. Replacing the Firefly that year was a 10½-foot Flash racer built to compete in both Class AU and BU outboard racing. Tests with a Mercury KF-7 rated at 10+ horses planed Flash almost immediately and took her up to 45 mph. Today, both Firefly and Flash are considered Feather Craft's most sought-after models in a vintage outboard boat milieu that often dubs Feather Craft as *the* brand to find. The fast, cute pair proved to be short-lived catalog offerings and were gone by 1954.

The sleek 12-foot Cartopper circa 1955 deserves mention because its lines mimic those of the classic early Feather Craft runabouts. Its bookend was the 16-foot Super Chief, rated for up to 40 hp and sometimes owner-converted to runabout status through the installation of steering at its front dash. On some dashes and decks, Feather Craft offered a no-glare, non-skid finish that was "embossed [into the aluminum] for extra strength." A 10-year warranty came with each boat.

A Canadian company had begun building Feather Craft products under license by 1956. Fleet Manufacturing, Ltd., of Fort Erie, Ontario, Canada, tagged its Feather Craft output accordingly. Anyone discovering a Feather Craft near or over the Canadian border might find it interesting to see where the boat originated. With the boating boom in full percussion mode, 1956 Feather Craft catalogs diversified the company's pitch with a combination of publicity stills and cartoons. Cleverly drawn by Mark Trail comic strip creator Ed Dodd, the strips cut to the chase about why one should select a Feather Craft.

The designer who drew up plans for the firm's new Rocket Runabout garnered attention for Feather Craft, too. That's because this single cockpit, 12½-foot nautical sports car was fabricated with anodized aluminum. "Attractive color contrasts," the brochure shouted, "are obtained by sensational 'fast color' processing of sides and deck. The process, like galvanizing, assures a long-lasting coating many times harder and tougher than paint." Generous aft decking, non-skid step pads aft of the seat, a glove compartment, and up to 30-hp motor capacity added to the Rocket Runabout's appeal. The boating public's reaction to the anodization was positive enough for the firm to give other models the color treatment. Gold, green, and aqua hues were typical.

To the untrained eye, most Feather Craft runabouts probably look alike, but variety was truly present in the rest of 1956's offerings. Witness the 15' 9" Falcon I and Falcon II. The latter had a walk-through center deck, high windshield, and convertible canopy. Because it possessed no center obstructions, bunk inserts were available for Falcon I. The 14' 7" Vagabond came in a I and II series with the II having the walk-through center deck option, as well as a windshield, bow light, wheel, pennant and pole, pulleys, tiller rope, deck cleats, and cushions. Several Vagabonds were bought by an amateur marine stunt group called The Flying Boatmen of Knoxville, Tennessee, "who have entertained thousands with closely coordinated barrel rolls, tight V and trail maneuvers, spin-outs and various other thrill-a-minute tactics." While there are no figures to prove it, I bet that the various versions of Vagabond provided Feather Craft with its best-selling runabout model.

Four versions of the 14' 1" Ranger runabout were introduced in 1956. One version offered a short 14-inch foredeck so that the front seating is possible together with a stern-facing rear seat. A second version had a 47" foredeck, and a third had a long foredeck with non-glare embossed pattern, four stern supports, and a walk-through center deck. The fourth version had seat backs. Also for 1956, the 15' 11" Super Chief had a walk-through rear wheel deck.

Choices diminished in the 1958 line as incarnations of the Rocket, Ranger, and Vagabond, though all attractively anodized, were the only surviving Feather Craft runabouts to keep some of their characteristic tumblehome. A pair of 14-foot Hawk family of runabouts and the 15' 11" Clipper showed up, with the deluxe Hawk II and Clipper treated to tail fins — admittedly more a sign of the space age than were rolled tumblehomes.

On several previous occasions, company catalogs had typos or juxtapositions noticeable enough for disclaimers (on small slips of paper) to be inserted or affixed to subsequent advertising. As an example, the

1958 sales sheet heralded a Feather Craft fiberglass boat fleet with boats supposedly all "anodized for family fun," while the aluminum boats were "molded by the scientific autoclave [resin curing] method." In fact, the section that proclaims "NEW MODELS... NEW MATERIALS...NEW SALES PROGRAM," is crossed out in deliberate red marker on my sample copy. That and the reduced lineup for 1958 suggest that times were tough and the boat business was really becoming a challenge for all but the best-financed.

No matter how one spelled it, by 1961, the classic tumblehome Feather Craft runabouts were history. Hefty fins were still integrated into the 1961 Clipper Deluxe, but not evident on the standard family service Hawk III. A trio of Clippers had starred in a Paramount Pictures' film short *Boats-A-Poppin'* shot at the old Cyprus Gardens. A frame of the action graced brochure covers. The flyer also pictured Ski Bo, a boat that looked like it could belong to almost any manufacturer of that period. A hint of aft side deck, though, gave the 15-footer nuances of Feather Craft's traditional style. "High glass color-weld and anodized finishes" could be had on the aforementioned boats and were promised for the Ski Bo spin-off dubbed Starflite.

There was a noticeable logo shift by 1962 with an "F" and "C" suddenly scripted over a feather. For many enthusiasts who agree that the original feather trademark design needed no improvement, the change seems to signal that the line had lost its luster. It was almost like a former millionaire was now living in a duplex. Feather Craft's last *Motor Boating* 'Outboard Boats' preview listing came in 1963 with the brief blurb reporting that the Atlanta company "builds a line of 27 boats in 17 models from 14-foot runabouts to 16-foot fishing boats with a modified catamaran hull. Construction is of aluminum with prices for unpainted boats ranging from $95 to $310, and from $105 to $530 for painted craft."

Although most of Feather Craft's mid-1960s catalog covers were printed in color, they began departing from wholesome, family-friendly themes. One example featured a bikini-topped brunette with her cleavage literally jammed around a rowboat's bow handle. Things went to black and white for the 1969 pamphlet, which noted that the operation had relocated to Lawrenceville, Georgia. On that year's brochure cover, only a bit of a boat's stern was visible, the focus being on a curvaceous, cheerleader-type model. Inside, in addition to canoes, and a proposed trihedral hull dubbed Triad ("to be announced at mid-season"), the catalog pictured the line's sole surviving runabout, the Ski Bo.

A further indication of hard times was the catalog's offering of "Topper Kits," unfinished, generic, car-top rowboats. Apparently, this was not an entirely new strategy, as *The Boating Industry* for November 1957 lists Feather Craft as offering "rowboats, outboard utilities & runabouts" in kit form. "For easy do-it-yourself assembly," that late '60s flyer euphemized. "Fun as your home project. [Put together] with screwdriver and hand drill. Kit includes finished hull, parts box complete, no riveting." As a way to move inventory, Feather Craft encouraged interested parties to save even more money on these boats by ordering "nested shipments" of several hulls, one inside another. It is plausible to suppose that, as the manufacturer sang this veiled swan song, those who picked up one of the bargain Feather Craft kits had no idea that the boat was linked to a true cornerstone of pleasure boating history.

Grumman

A 1944 Adirondack fishing trip, an unwieldy canvas-covered wooden canoe, and an aircraft company vice president provided the recipe for cooking up the Grumman marine line. That heavy canoe prompted vice president William Hoffman to have his Bethpage, New York, firm build an aluminum canoe using the same

Understandably Grumman recommended a long shaft motor for its 14' 6" Sea Wings hydrofoil-equipped runabout. "On turns," the maker noted, "the boat banks inward and skidding is virtually non-existent." The hydrofoils were retractable, equipped with shear pins, and would float if knocked away.

materials as Grumman's fighter planes. A 1946 brochure heralded, "just as it has replaced other materials (wood, dope and fabric) in aircraft — so now does aluminum alloy replace these materials in canoe construction."

Lightweight, stretch-formed Grumman aluminum canoes, which by 1953 were being produced in a former skate factory at Marathon, New York, quickly became the standard by which others were judged. But the Korean War caused materials shortages and manufacturing delays. An undated single-sheet flyer (believed to be for the 1953 season, though only mentioning the Bethpage venue) noted "production will not start until aluminum is again readily available. Keep in touch with your Grumman dealer and watch for national advertising."

When material permitted, Grumman planned to add fishing skiffs and runabouts to its lineup. These models were said to have been originally "built and tested in 1952, and have fulfilled hopes . . . of exceptional eye-appeal [as well as being] very dry, maneuverable, fast and seaworthy." Included in the lineup for 1953 fleet was the 14½-foot Deluxe Runabout. By 1956, Grumman output spanned the range from an eight-foot dinghy and 14' 3" wide-beam, square-stern canoe Sport Boat that could be rowed, paddled, motored, or sailed, to the enlarged 15½-foot edition of Deluxe Runabout. True to Grumman "military" specs, this Deluxe was a substantial craft that weighed 255 pounds versus Aero-Craft's comparably sized but 140-pound Model DD. The company was "frank to admit that [this one was] not a boat for everyone. It would be a shame," Grumman speculated, "to waste her talents in the old mill pond, even though the Deluxe Runabout is admired wherever she floats. [Rather, it was designed] for the person who wants the ultimate in outboard runabouts, she's fast (30 mph with a 25-hp Evinrude or Johnson), dry, and combines beauty with ruggedness and the ability to weather-out the roughest water."

Early Grumman hull colors included red, blue, green, white, and "dead-grass." By 1957, while the marine division's manufacturing facilities were expanded, gray and yellow got added, as were several runabouts that most Grumman fans define as *the* models to own. These included the 13' 4" Junior Runabout, a modestly appointed entry-level hull comfortable with ten horsepower motors; the '50s style 14½-foot Custom Runabout with "sports fins and stern deck"; (also available in a quasi-inboard version pushed by the Fageol 44 VIP Vertical-Inboard-Power 4-stroker.) the 18½-foot G-19 Sportster; and the remarkable 15½-foot Sea Wings runabout. The latter derived its name from hydrofoils that lifted a throttled-up Sea Wings right out of the water. Grumman noted that these fascinating appendages were "equipped with shear pins. The wings float and can be easily retrieved and refastened in case of accidental grounding." Among other neat Grumman accessories was the mid-ship "half deck" (for the steering wheel and other controls) that made a utility version of the line's open hulls.

By the late 1960s, Grumman brass noticed its boat sales diving, while canoe output was still moving well. This led to a quick discontinuance of rowboat and runabout models. Some 10 years later, this decision was reversed, though the new Grumman high quality boats were commensurately expensive and not good sellers. A course correction called for boats that could be priced more in keeping with the competition. By 1990, a slump in marine-related sales caused Grumman to sell the canoe and boat business to Outboard Marine Corporation, which soon moved OMC's subsidiary DuraNautic boat operation to the Marathon factory. But, OMC's troubles precipitated an idling of the plant several years later.

Lone Star

Not even the dustiest old Lone Star documents explain why founders Lamar and William Moody sold their tiny Grand Prairie-based company in 1946, only about a year after its debut on paper. During most of the ensuing decade, the buyer, R. W. McDonnel, would grow the operation into one of the world's most prolific builders of non-wooden boats. He and a couple of dozen workers began cranking out about 10 aluminum fishing hulls a week from a plant roughly the size of an auto repair shop. Rowboats were reportedly offered in 1946, making this brand one of the first postwar fabricators of marine aluminum. The Lone Star Boat Manufacturing Company appears in *The Boating Industry* magazine's 1950 national listing, indicating that the brand had outgrown its early regional boundaries. By 1951, when Lone Star entered the outboard runabout market and finally netted a *Motor Boating* listing, a new factory and warehousing had been added. To help pay for the expansion and obtain help in overseeing some 200 employees, McDonnel sold a 30 percent interest to E.

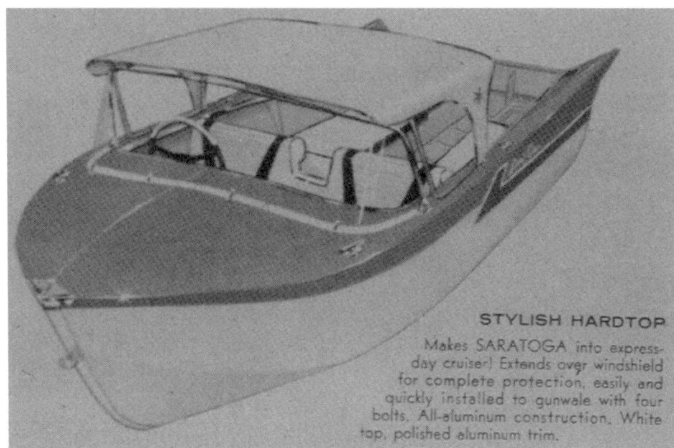

Accessory hardtop dresses up a 1960 Lone Star Saratoga.

This 1964 Lone Star Malibu featured the company's famous multi-tone finish. The 14-foot hull was white with red stripes while the decking and dash board area were blue.

M. Bishop.

The earliest of the runabouts was the 14-foot Admiral, "a handsome, colorful (exterior — aluminum and red; interior — green) boat [with] big air chambers, full spray rails, full width leatherette kapok cushions, windshield, steering wheel, and throttle." The dual-cockpit, center-decked craft could step lively with a 10-horse Mercury Lightning, or really plane under heavy loads with the 33.4-hp Evinrude SpeediFour for which it was capacity rated. A trio of less fancy models, the 12-foot Sportster Runabout, the 14-foot Commander Runabout, and the 16-foot Speed King, were offered in a bench-seating, decked format with "seagull white/Newport green" finish. It should be noted that Lone Star's option list included a center deck for modifying the line's semi-vee-bottom boats into runabouts. Sometimes such "uncataloged" examples confound boat show judges, but if equipped with this Model S-12 factory Lone Star accessory, they can be considered kosher. By the way, a side-steering bracket option was current then, too. Riviera came aboard the 1955 brochure as a combination 18-foot big runabout/cruisette.

In the meantime, Lone Star announced it was "the world's largest producer of boats," and had set up a sister plant in Bremen, Indiana (711 North Center St.). Mr. McDonnel sold his share of the expanding company to Continental Insurance of Alabama, which transferred it to Standard Steel Works, Inc. in 1956. Aluminum runabouts for 1956 started out with the 12-foot Sportster Deluxe, a basic two-bench-seated oarlock-equipped model with a 60-inch deck. The 14-foot Admiral came in standard and deluxe versions, the Clipper checked in at 16 feet, and the 18-foot Riviera could be had with a hardtop. Most stylish was the Holiday, a 16-footer with stepped topsides (aft of the front seats) and an open area in which Lone Star recommended deck chairs for water skier observation. A separate motor bracket was affixed to the transom.

Lone Star's parent organization had an eye for further growth, and so oversaw the addition of a Tallahassee, Florida (330 Mabry St.), facility in 1957 and a McAdoo, Pennsylvania (Tresckow Rd.), factory two years later. Business was booming as seemingly everybody in North America wanted a recreational boat! Fiberglass hulls accounted for a respectable portion of the nearly 44,000 Lone Star boats sold in 1958–59, but aluminum craft were the company's bread and butter.

By 1958, the old shooting star logo (near the bow) had been dropped in favor of an "asterisk" star shining between the "Lone" and "Star" script. For 1958, runabouts like 14-footers the Coronado and the upholstered Malibu version, and the 16-foot Nassau combined high freeboards with a tasteful hint of tail fins.

The 1960 aluminum runabouts included 15-footers Newport and Saratoga, and the 16-foot Holiday, which had a hinged bow hatch. Somebody at Lone Star must have been into family cruising, as the firm's outboard (and, prior to 1958, inboard) cruiser offerings were among the most robust in the business. Lone Star accessorized its runabouts with canopies and sliding aluminum hardtops for "cruisette" conversion. The 1960 catalog devoted nearly two pages to seating options, some of which flipped into bunks or served as galley tables suitable for several paper plates piled with a picnic lunch.

The public's new boat appetite had slowed somewhat by 1962. It's likely that the durability and relative timelessness of 1950s aluminum craft either kept existing pleasure boaters satisfied with their present rigs or introduced quality, late model aluminum inventory into a marketplace that (in the erstwhile used wooden boat milieu) would have otherwise bought new. Lone Star's 1962 sales were over 5,000 boats softer than those in 1958. It had inaugurated a new Plano, Texas

(1001 Industrial Ave.), "home office" plant in 1960, thus closing the old Grand Prairie facility.

To accommodate the big outboards emanating from midwestern factories, Lone Star built some of its runabouts like the 15' 9" Champlain and 15' 11" Holiday with "long shaft transoms." Short-shaft motor owners could buy the family budget friendly Malibu, a 14-foot job with the company's famous multi-toned finish that truly made the boats look festive.

During the early 1960s, Lone Star published a clever advertising piece disguised as a small boating magazine. Of course *Boats Illustrated* covered only one brand, but probably enjoyed a longer life than a catalog. Because few new aluminum Lone Star boats were introduced in this period, the publication devoted space to showing off its Plano plant's "automobile-industry-size, 1,000 ton Hydro-Press that makes possible the precision-formed, smoothly contoured hull and deck sections." The products of the huge machine were backed by "the large full-time staff in Lone Star's research and development section and enhanced by the creative services of Thomas L. Faul & Associates, internationally renowned marine architects."

A continuing slow leak in sales caused company officials to do some downsizing by selling off all but the main Plano facility throughout 1964. Before the next boating season ended, Lone Star's more than 1,600 dealers learned that the boat manufacturer itself had been sold. It was grabbed by Chrysler, which would also add West Bend outboards to its new marine division. Both the motors and boats were soon re-christened with the Chrysler name.

Mirro-Craft

No doubt Mirro Aluminum Company executives noticed rival West Bend aluminum's success in the marine field. Both were venerable Wisconsin aluminum fabricators best known for their respective cookware products ranging from cookie presses and Jell-O molds to pots, pans, and popcorn poppers. But where West Bend embraced outboard motor production (both with its own brand and the likes of Sears and Roebuck's Eglin), Mirro decided to build boats.

The inaugural Manitowoc, Wisconsin-built Mirro-Craft fleet cruised into the marketplace in 1956. The key distinction by which many boating buffs vividly remember the boats is their lapstrake hulls. "The use of lapstraking in boat building is almost as old as sailing itself," Mirro Craft catalogs noted. "Traditionally, it has been preferred where strength, handling, and stability are prime factors. It's only natural then, that modern boat engineering has seen the development of the lapstrake aluminum hull. [That's why] all Mirro-Craft boats utilize this practical construction feature, which greatly increases hull impact and yield strength and reduces drag.

During the 1960s, the line ranged from a 10-foot pram to an 18-sport fisherman, and included canoes, even though Mirro-Craft's 14-foot Sportsman, as well as the 14- and 16-foot Ski 'N' Troll runabouts were the marque's quintessential offerings. While notably rugged by contemporary standards, these were rather Spartan, though ranked among the best "starter" family runabouts. Consequently, there wasn't much potential for things to break or wear out. It's not uncommon for the purchaser of a used Mirro-Craft to be flabbergasted to learn that it hails from the late 1950s.

An optional steering console was offered for upgrading Mirro-Craft rowboats (often in a turquoise finish) to utility runabout status. Imbued with the line's plushest upholstery were runabouts like the Titan 15 (15' 3") and the 17' 3" Apollo 17. Like their sisters, Mirro-Craft advertised them as "virtually fireproof," a quality few other aluminum boat manufacturers stressed.

In 1982, Mirro sold the Mirro-Craft assets —including the trade name — to a group of erstwhile

Mirro employees who set up shop in Gillett, Wisconsin, under the corporate banner, Northport. In the fall of 2003, ClearWater Marine acquired Northport to add respected Mirro-Craft aluminum boats to its other lines of watercraft.

Starcraft

Arthur Schrock built some of the first metal boats around 1927 with materials he also used to fabricate water and feeder tanks for farms near his Goshen, Indiana, home. His Star Tank Company reportedly began in 1903. As these rugged metal boats found a niche, Schrock and his son Harold expanded the first generation of Star Metal Boats into a wide lineup of craft (from rowboats and sailboats to runabouts) typically constructed of "20-gauge galvanized Copper-Steel formed over a sturdy one inch channel frame and given new strength by heavy stamped metal keelsons."

After World War II, Star's sailboats and deluxe outboard hulls were de-emphasized in favor of craft like the 1949 stainless steel Sportsman rowboats (12- and 14-feet long) and the 12-, 14-, and 16-foot Super Deluxe Sportsman, one of which was shipped to President Truman's Camp Shangri-La. Understandably, Star realized that lugging the 280-pound rowboat would not provide any chief executive with inner peace, so the company formed a subsidiary, Starcraft Boat Division, to market a new boat of lightweight alloy known as…magnesium! Actually, Star bought its way into this business. In late 1948, Star acquired the Dowcraft magnesium boat business from Dow Chemical.

"The Dowcraft trade-name will be gradually supplanted by the new Starcraft name in the ultra-lightweight boat field," indicated a press release picked up by the January 1949 *Motor Boating*. "Tests by Starcraft with the new FSA alloy magnesium showed it to be tougher and more durable than any other light metal tried," the publicity promised. Starcraft tagged the

Only several years before introducing attractive aluminum boats like the 15-foot Jet Star, Starcraft was decrying the alloy in favor of steel and magnesium.

statement by pointing out that its new material of choice "weighs almost one-third *less* than aluminum."

Through 1950, the Star Tank & Boat Company and Starcraft were publicized as separate operations. Both criticized aluminum boats for either being heavier than magnesium craft or not being as impervious to wear as steel. By the time the *Sports Afield* 1951 Fishing Annual hit magazine racks, however, the two Goshen, Indiana, boat companies were identified as one. Wisely, Star brass recognized that any connection to the word "tank" was not conducive to marketing small boats. Period ads still bore the Star Metal Boats ID, but with the name "Star" crossed out and the new STARCRAFT above it.

It was not until the release of the 1953 Starcraft "metal boats" catalog, a product offering in aluminum appeared on the last page. It was dubbed the STARLITE rowboat, available in either 12- or 14-foot lengths. "The newest thing afloat!" read the Starlite copy. "Lightweight, easy to carry, no maintenance problems, low cost, long life." Star and Starcraft had forgiven its erstwhile enemy alloy, although the steel hulls remained in the catalog through 1957.

It's the 1957 line that Starcraft buffs will recognize as foundational to our study. Runabouts included the 12-foot Speedster and 14-foot Speed Queen (both with a split center deck option), as well as the Ski Champ in either 14- or 15-foot versions. Any of these colorful examples would look right at home with a "Holiday Bronze" or white and chrome Johnson Javelin 30-hp or a two-tone finished Mercury Mark 30.

With the steel boats having tanked for 1958, there was room in the line for a small introductory fiberglass fleet and the 15-foot aluminum Jet Star runabout with a flared clipper-style prow and unobtrusive tail fins. Its large foredeck was "supported underneath by plywood for double protection and strength." Also new was the hefty 16-foot Jupiter, designed for long-shaft outboards. Interestingly, both of these had plywood sub-decks "for double protection and strength." The Super Constellation, at 16 feet, could be had in a split center deck option. The Jet "15" was added to the aluminum runabout roster for 1959 as a nice entry-level family boat with a surprisingly generous equipment package ("beautifully upholstered seats, 16-inch high windshield, steering, running lights, step pads, bow cleat, chocks, tie ring, stern handles, drain, control mount, mahogany dashboard, and attractive aluminum corner castings.")

New for 1958 was the 12-foot Speedster rated for 35-hp mill for daredevils, but advertised to fair-weather folks on small, horsepower-restricted lakes as "a low priced runabout that will give exciting performance with even a five-hp motor." Also offered was the 14-foot Speed Queen. Like the Speedster, it was available with either a foredeck or foredeck and center deck.

With front steering, the sturdy, nicely painted, 12-foot Speedster had the look of a bigger late '50s runabout and helped set the stage for Starcraft's renown among boaters in subsequent decades.

The Speedster became the line's "most popular model" during the late 1950s. On this and sister Starcraft, the boat maker gave a 15-year written guarantee against skin punctures and popped rivets.

By 1961, the smooth-sided Bonanza and lapstrake 13' 7" Ski Champ served as the marque's low-priced runabouts, with the Jet '61 providing the next step. The big 18-foot Holiday looked best with its convertible top in place. Also a lapstrake aluminum hulled model, the 16-foot Viscount was rated for motors from 10 to 75 hp, even though it was photographed for the catalog with an 80-horse West Bend on its transom. From a similar hull, Starcraft offered the Viking as a nuanced offering somehow "engineered to make your motor act as if it had double the horsepower…fast, fast, fast!" However, it weighed 50 pounds more than Viscount, also touted as capable of "thrilling lapstrake speed and performance." Like most Starcraft runabouts, the Viking was nicely appointed in stock form. When the company's 1967 brochure pondered, "What makes Starcraft the largest selling boat in the U.S.A?" the answer suggested was that "one of the big differences [customers] found was that many of the 'extras' that they want most are included as 'standard equipment' on Starcraft boats."

O'Day sailboats and several other brands became Starcraft's sisters in 1969 when the Schrock family sold their boating and travel trailer business to conglomerate Bangor Punta. Catalogs during BP's first year of ownership pictured center console aluminum models known as Sportabouts such as the 15' 1" Star Trek-V. Rather than promote the model with a fishing focus, catalog copy noted that the lapstrake boat was "light enough for mom to handle easily at shopping time and one the kids will use, too." The 14-foot Falcon was the line's entry-level runabout during the late 1960s–early 1970s, and could be traced to the classic Eisenhower-era Starcraft.

Those center-console sport boats, meanwhile

appeared to be the contemporary way to get a family into boating, as lots of small boat buyers eyed them over traditional basic runabouts. Still, enough folks asked for entry-level Starcraft runabouts for the genre to be continued into the 1980s when the company moved to Topeka, Indiana. In the latter part of the decade Mercury Marine added the Starcraft's aluminum and fiberglass operation to its stable of boat brands. But Merc sold it in 1996. Without having to jeopardize happy endings, I note that Starcraft landed with an investment group headed by Doug Schrock, the grandson of the quality boat manufacturer's founder. He soon decided to focus exclusively on marine aluminum.

Chapter 3

In Shops Throughout the Country

SMALLER ALUMINUM BUILDERS

"You know Pop, we've got some good guys who are pretty handy with sheet metal. Why not have 'em build a few aluminum boats in the off-season?"

— Enthusiastic new partner in his family's plumbing and heating business, circa 1952

The bulk of the historic detail herein comes from the *Motor Boating* and *The Boating Industry (TBI)* annuals of the period. These magazines now harbor the sole surviving records of numerous long-expired small boat manufacturers. That said, even at the time of publication, the latter magazine's editors admitted "that possibly there are omissions." More than 2,000 questionnaires were sent to boatbuilders, trying to get their listings (without charge), but some did not reply. "Possibly," said *TBI,* "there are others we have missed. Nevertheless, we believe the list is as accurate as it is humanly possible to be."

In 1957, a decade after *The Boating Industry* began offering its January (and later, November or December issue) list of builders, the publication still prefaced it with the notice of possible incompleteness, but noted that any company included had to be a "stock" (as opposed to one-off custom) boatbuilder "and [must] have sold at least twenty-five boats through dealers during the past year." Consequently, a January 1956 entry wasn't technically current for the upcoming 1956 season (although it was the case with the January *Motor Boating* rosters); it looked back instead to 1955 production. This seemingly minor point is vital when trying to pinpoint an exact production year. What's more, it meant that some tiny firms were already out of business when their first listing made the small print. (This scenario applies to the minor aluminum makes considered here and the fiberglass companies covered later.)

While some of the following outfits come through the decades with just a company name, what its line was called, an approximate first year of having offered aluminum utilities or runabouts, and last known address (so that nearby marine history sleuths can have fun investigating), others are presented in more detail by a description of at least one of their products. As you peruse the information, please remember that the author wholeheartedly welcomes additions at *www.devereuxbooks.com* or by regular mail in care of the publisher.

Aero Mfg. Co. Not to be confused with Aero-Craft, this Syracuse, Indiana, firm entered the small boat industry around 1949 as Aero Welding & Mfg. Co. For 1950, Aero dropped the welding part of its name and introduced aluminum utilities to its line. The 1958 Sea Nymph model RR is representative of the company's prolific entry-level runabouts. The sturdy 14-footer could take a 40-horse motor and was essentially a beefed-up, decked-over rowboat. By 1967, the corporate identity as Aero Mfg. Co. changed to Sea Nymph Mfg. Corp. Today, the firm is considered a major producer of fishing boats.

By 1958, Aero Manufacturing had already begun emphasizing its Sea Nymph trade name, as the corporate identity was often confused with Aero-Craft by boat shoppers. Sea Nymph survived its then better known competitor to become a large producer of aluminum boats.

Alexandria Boat Works, Inc., Highway 52 East, Alexandria, Minnesota, first built its "Lady of the Lakes" line in 1960.

Alumakit Co., Inc. Beginning around 1960, this Salem, Massachusetts, firm (35 Congress Street, and later Shetland Industrial Park) was one of the few to offer aluminum boat kits, including runabouts and utilities. Typically, the brand name got embossed into a gusset connecting the gunwale to the transom. The short-lived line appears to have been long gone by 1965. (see Northline)

Aluminum Boats & Canoes, Inc. By 1956, "Prince Craft" hulls were emanating from this Princeville, Quebec, fabricator.

Aluminum Boat and Canvas, Inc. One of several 1950s mystery manufacturers that appeared in a small print aluminum boat listing, sans locale.

Appleby Mfg. Co. "Neat, trim, good-looking boats that are made strong, roomy and easy to handle," was the sales pitch for Lebanon, Missouri's Appleby Manufacturing Co. J. B. Appleby began offering Jon boats, utilities, and runabouts in 1961, but soon concentrated only on the fishing craft.

Aqua-Car. (see Roby-Hutton)

Aqualine Boat Corp., Mackall St., Elkton, Maryland, was first listed as having outboard utility craft for 1954. This brand is highly representative of "flash-in-the-pan" aluminum boat makers that made a debut splash but were apparently gone before the ripples hit the shore. Specifically, Aqualine sprang for an expensive, full-page advertisement in the key (January boat show number) *Motor Boating* issue for 1955, seemed to have disappeared the following year, resurfaces in Yorklyn, Delaware by 1957, and vanishes sometime before the '50s closed. "Aqualine outboard boats feature a rugged, modified vee hull…rivet-locked throughout [and] all seams lapped and sealed. High-speed [with] low horsepower" was promised in the January 1955 ad. Though 12- and 14-foot open fisherman and runabout versions were offered, pictured was the larger runabout, unique because it featured a small foredeck and two wheel decks! That formed two sets of seats with backs

Triple cockpits, instead of two, make this rare 1955 Aqualine utility runabout particularly unique.

— and a resulting sturdily braced hull — as well as a small cockpit for the skipper to tiller the motor, if wheel steering wasn't installed. This model would make for a great classic outboarder's boat, though it might be a very tough one to find.

Aqua-Queen Boat Div., B & N Mfg. Co. 1954 listings show B & N Aluminum Welding Corp., of Elkhart, Indiana, as offering rowboats. By late 1956, the maker's name had changed to reflect manufacturing, and the line expanded to include Aqua-Queen–branded utilities and runabouts.

Aqua Swan Div. of Milco Tank & Boat Co. Starting in 1957, this White Pigeon, Michigan, maker marketed small aluminum craft. For 1963 it offered six "outboard runabouts with simulated-lapstrake aluminum hulls, welded seams, extruded gunwales, vinyl-covered flooring and tinted windshield." An example included the 15-foot K-5 Kamper rated for 50 hp.

Arnolt Corp. "Unitized welded hull construction" served as the sales point for this Warsaw, Indiana, firm's early 1960s **So-Lite** boats, a few of which might have been utilities.

Barnes Boat Co., Inc., 40 Brooklyn St., Rockville, Connecticut. One of a very few New England aluminum boat makers, Barnes built the Dolphin line, starting around 1961.

Barracuda Marine Co., 33 South LaSalle St. (and later 311 Ashland Ave.) Aurora, Illinois. A full line of aluminum and glass Barracuda Boats starting in 1959, but de-listed by 1967.

Guy Barnette & Co., Inc. 239 South Dudley St., Memphis, Tennessee (1956)

Beeching Craft. 444 Transit Road, Victoria, British Columbia (1955)

Blue Mfg. Co., Inc. "Blue Star." It appears that one Max Blue set up an aluminum boatbuilding shop in Goodard, Kansas, during 1950. His firm's 1951 model year output included Blue Star-branded fishing craft and modest runabouts. By 1954, the small company had relocated to 2221 North Main St., Miami, Oklahoma, where brochures pinpointed it "at Grand Lake." For this period, distribution was advertised as occurring in "23 states where Blue Star boats are widely accepted." Michigan was Blue's star sales venue in 1956, with more product moved there than throughout the outfit's home territory. Distributor John T. Fulbright's Watercraft sales center at Bostwick Lake in Rockford, Michigan, had enough clout with Blue to net catalogs with his name and address printed (as opposed to locally stamped) on the cover.

Possessing Blue's "round chine, full bow hull," the 1957 line featured an entry-level runabout, Sky Rider, "the 12-foot version of carnival thrills on the water. She's a colorful two-tone honey of a boat — as thrilling in design as in action. If you demand thrilling action," catalog copy suggested, "then the lively spirit of this all-aluminum runabout belongs in your life. You'll go fast, [and] turn quickly without boat worry." On the surface, Sky Rider looked like a decked-over rowboat, but a

The two-seater, Sky Rider by Blue Star is ready to embarrass even the biggest inboard on the lake. That modest 1957 dozen-foot hull is wearing a 40-cubic inch, 4-cylinder Merc!

closer inspection revealed its beefed-up transom, which invited "bigger" motors like the 30-hp, four-cylinder in-line Mercury Mark 30. With a light driver and trim feminine passenger (as typically shown in the catalog), this Merc with a two-blade bronze speed prop would produce quite a ride!

Also in the fleet were the 14-foot Surf Rider, with lots of nicely polished aluminum trim, two-tone vinyl seats, and contrasting hull coloration; the 15-foot Islander with "Safety Dry Transom" motor well, tasteful aft fins, and one-piece molded fiberglass deck; and the 18-foot Flightliner, also with fins and glass decking, as well a hardtop option. "Harmonious two-tone hue possibilities on Blue Star runabouts ran the spectrum from "flame red, jade green, aqua blue, and jet black, to cloud white, autumn yellow, horizon blue, and emerald green." Any selected combo finish consisted of the "finest vinyl plastic, over an etched and primed hull."

A check of Blue Star flyers indicates that the line didn't change much into the early 1960s. Mention of the firm disappears from *The Boating Industry* listings by 1965. Seldom chronicled were the rarest and arguably most desirable Blue Star boats — its early-to-mid-1950s stock outboard racing craft. Among this fast fleet, were the 11½-foot Warrior, a Class AU/BU utility runabout,

Tasteful tailfins provide the 15-foot Blue Star Islander with a hint of its 1957 lineage while subsequently allowing her to appear moderately contemporary into the next decade.

as well as aluminum hydroplanes designed for the likes of a Mercury KG-4H or Mark 20H racing mill.

Bowman Manufacturers, Inc. 1823 Woodrow St. (and later, 713 Izard St.), Little Rock, Arkansas. First noted in1957, the company had moved Lake Providence, Louisiana by fall 1958 and focused on fiberglass.

Canadian Canoe Co., Ltd. Peterborough, Ontario. "Canadian Flight-Craft." (1961)

Cherokee Boats (see McKenzie)

Chestnut Canoe Co., Ltd. Fredericton, Newfoundland (1959)

Clipper Line (see Charles Eaton)

Consolidated General Products, Inc., Rexcraft Boat Div. 611 West 22nd St., Houston, Texas. "Boxy, pointy sponsons and fins," is the description levied on a 1957 debut Rexcraft runabout by one boat show observer.

Consolidated Metal Products. Elkhart, Indiana (1959)

Corsair Boats, Inc. 10400 Hines Blvd., Dallas, Texas (1955)

Cruiser Craft of Dallas, Inc. 3108 Sylvan Drive, Dallas, Texas. First noted in 1955, Cruiser Craft offered 11 models for 1956, including what looks to be a scow-bow cruiser reported to have "won the Mississippi Marathon. Exclusive hydro-keel increases speed without loss of maneuverability. Fast, yet so safe," touted their ads. "A Cruiser Craft has never been sunk."

Chicoutimi Aluminum Products, Ltd. Chicoutimi, Quebec (1951)

Currier's of Arkansas. 3525 Fair Park Blvd., Little Rock, Arkansas (1957)

Delhi Mfg. Corp. Delcraft Boats. Illinois Ave., Delhi, Louisiana (1961)

Phillip A. **Dill, Inc.** 1209 Castle, Dallas, Texas. Same address as General Manufacturing Co., which began offering aluminum outboard utility craft in 1954. The Dill name shows up around 1957.

Dorsett Plastics Co., Industrial Div. 2550 Scott Blvd., Santa Clara, California. The January 1966 *Motor Boating* publicized this firm's unusual "aluminum outboard 'icebreaker' as a special-purpose hull tested in Northern California to combat ice in the canals of the Pacific Gas & Electric Co." The Dorsett Ice Breaker was "a 140-pound 12-foot aluminum utility with 30 pounds of steel backbone from stem to stern." Interestingly, the accompanying photo shows the craft powered by a late 1940s Johnson Sea Horse 10, as opposed to a motor more contemporary with the boat's mid-1960s intro.

Douglas Aircraft Co., Inc. 3000 Ocean Park Blvd., Santa Monica, California. The 10- and 14-foot "Air Skiff" utilities were a side business of this airplane maker, starting in the 1947 model year. Arguably a glorified rowboat, these were lightweight open craft. The bigger version was rated for a hefty 16-horse motor but, if later fitted with something like a 1957 Mercury Mark 25, would probably have delivered quite a ride!

Dow Chemical Co., Dowcraft Boat Div. Bay City, Michigan. Dow's short-lived magnesium boat division offered (for 1947) standard and deluxe 12-foot utility craft (the later with an amazingly low weight of 45 pounds), as well as a 55-pound, 16-foot magnesium canoe. For the 1949 model year, the operation was acquired by Star Tank Co., and morphed into the Starcraft aluminum line.

Dunphy Boat Corp. Broad at Parkway, Oshkosh, Wisconsin. Best-known for molded plywood hulls, Dunphy offered some aluminum boats by 1956. It may be that these were another maker's product and simply badge-engineered. Whatever the source, Dunphy never got too excited about marine alloy. One of its 1961 ads in *The Boating Industry* proudly concluded, "Wood is naturally best for boats."

Duo Marine, Inc., Decatur, Indiana, shows up in the trade literature for 1961 with a pair of fiberglass boats, but had added aluminum runabouts by 1965. These included the 14-foot XL-4, the 15-foot XL-5, and the 16-foot XL-6.

DuraCraft Boats, Inc. Monticello, Arkansas. Having begun aluminum boatbuilding operations as Ward Brothers Mfg. Co. sometime in 1950, a newly named DuraCraft Boats, Inc., enjoyed four legal-sized small print pages of authorized dealers by the early spring of 1956. In fact, the growing organization even noted several South American dealerships. For 1956, the DuraCraft runabout line consisted of Custom and Deluxe versions of "the finest, most beautiful all-aluminum runabout ever built — DURAflite." This overarching model was available in either 14½- or 16½-foot lengths.

Custom and Deluxe versions of DuraCraft's DURAflite (with a lower case "flite" similar to Glastron's model nomenclature), were both worthy competitors in the colorfully robust late 1950s runabout market.

"Baked two-tone vinyl [paint] coating, custom fitted kapok cushions, and a [short] molded wrap-around windshield" created a nicely finished look for these well-built boats. The Deluxe edition, with arrow design deck and side paint accent, motor well/rear seat backs, and a hint of aft fins, made it mildly reminiscent of a wooden Aristo-Craft speedster. While the firm added a line of fiberglass boats and continued on into the next decade, the mid-to-late 1950s aluminum offerings represent DuraCraft's penchant for sturdily built, though nicely appointed runabouts.

DuraNautic Mfg. Corp. 1 East Main St., Beacon, New York, and later Scranton, Pennsylvania, and Marathon, New York. "Since the early 1960s," notes a 1996 catalog, "the DuraNautic nameplate has stood for outstanding [boating] value." Interestingly, the company doesn't show up in trade publications until the late '60s. For 1969, it offered "six aluminum fishing utilities" such as 12- and 14-footers. Along the way, some DuraNautic craft were fitted with console steering. Many of the hulls were finished in a greenish-blue. Reportedly, the venture was originally begun by some erstwhile personnel of Duratech, a boat maker headquartered near to Beacon. The Evinrude and Johnson outboard folks once owned DuraNautic. (see Grumman)

Charles E. Eaton, Corp. RFD 5, Portland, Maine, is listed as first offering utilities in 1955. By 1956, its trade name Clipper Line appears.

Eckenroth Motor & Boat Manufacturers. 3601 Detroit Ave., Cleveland, Ohio (1956)

Elgin. (see Sears & Roebuck)

Eradlab, Inc., 1600 Water St., Conneautville, Pennsylvania, is listed as starting out with utility craft in 1955. Though some mid-1950s sources indicate that Feather Craft offered its boats in kit form, the 1955 *Outboard Boating Handbook* identifies Eradlab's Hoppencraft as the "only make of aluminum kits." Eradlab, Inc., is a later incarnation of Hoppenstand Industries Co., original maker of the Hoppencraft line.

Cheston L. Eshelman Co., 109 Light St., Baltimore, Maryland. This delightfully wacky outfit's 1957 Rocket Boat was actually built with 16-gauge cold rolled steel (as opposed to all aluminum), but is included here because it's sometimes categorized in obscure aluminum craft listings. At 14 feet, 425 pounds, and with a conical pointed bow that would scare the pilings off any dock the freaky looking boat approached, this was a real attention-getter. Touted as "the ideal boat for open water fishing or racing with your friends in their old-fashioned boats," Eshelmans were dangerously fast with the likes of a 40-horse Mercury Mark 55, but were better suited visually for a science fiction "B" movie. So were the tiny, lawnmower engine–powered "commuter cars" the company offered at around the same time. Vintage runabout buffs dream of finding one of these little autos and an Eshelman Rocket Boat, as well as a special trailer to link the two.

Fabricated Steel Products (Windsor) Ltd. (see Thornes)

Firestone. (see Olympian)

Fisher Marine, Inc. West Point, Missouri (1968)

Flotel Boats, Div of Gennett & Sons, Inc. 1 Main St., Richmond, Indiana (1957)

Freeland Sons Co. Wenzel Ave, Sturgis, Michigan. Debuting for the 1951 season with a flotilla of 12- to 16-foot aluminum (as well as galvanized steel) open craft and an outboard runabout, Freeland soon became a recognized small boat name throughout the Midwest. For 1957, its flagship was Ski-Master, a novel 14-footer because of the hull's "one-piece fiberglass deck, available in four colors." Freeland, Duratech, and Blue Star were among a tiny cadre of aluminum boat manufacturers to utilize this sensible aluminum and glass construction technique, whereby a rowboat hull could be colorfully crowned with a shapely superstructure. Ski-Master's entire topside appears to be fiberglass-reinforced plastic and constitutes the deck, seats, gunwales, and a motor well. This "classy, but sturdy" model could handle 40 hp. The marque had disappeared from *The Boating Industry* directories by 1967.

General Boat Corp. (see Sports-Kraft)

General Marine Sales. 2615 East Krist Blvd., Dallas, Texas (1957)

General Mfg. Co. 1209 Castle St., Dallas, Texas. Also connected with Phillip A. Dill, Inc., this southwestern aluminum boat maker began building utilities around 1955.

Glasspar Co. This famed fiberglass boat maker is listed as offering aluminum hulls in 1965. It is believed they were private-branded for Glasspar by some other manufacturer.

Heating Assurance, Inc. Nelson Boats. 124 East Augusta, Spokane, Washington. This mystery listing appeared in *The Boating Industry* for December 1960 and December 1961. This is probably a classic case of an outfit savvy in sheet metal for heating duct fabrication that attempted to apply its skill to small boats under the Nelson (for company president, R. L. Nelson) trade name. It is believed that Nelsons were offered through the much of the 1960s in a wide range of styles from fishing boats to small cruisers.

Spied during late fall 2004 in the side yard of a northern Idaho muffler shop was this Nelson aluminum cruiser. Boat makers often fitted their largest runabout with a modest cabin in order to attract buyers who envisaged exciting family vacations highlighted by a peaceful night moored off the leeward side of some little island. The porthole served to give this craft a hearty nautical look. Nelson was one of a cadre of regional aluminum boat manufacturers to set up shop near a major aluminum plant in Spokane, Washington.

Hewes Marine Co. Municipal Airport, Colville, Washington. Ralph E. Hewes is noted as head of the Hewescraft line, which started around 1959. The 1967 Hewescraft fleet sported three vee-hull runabouts with a water ski theme, like the Ski Maid 14 (13' 9"), Ski Master 15 (14½ feet), and Ski King 16 (15' 5"). Its 1970 catalog shows an otherwise basic outboard runabout that was stylized by a bright paint job.

Hoppenstand Industries Co. Greenville, Pennsylvania (1950) (see Eradlab Inc.)

Hollywood Boat & Motor Co. Hollywood Boats. 4301 South Union Ave., Tacoma, Washington (1961)

Hydro Keel Draft Co. 605 Singleton, Dallas, Texas (1957)

Kaysea Kraft Boat Co. 1706 Euclid Ave., Cleveland, Ohio (1957)

F. E. Kilbourn. 510 East Columbus Drive, US-12, East Chicago, Indiana (1955)

Lowell Aluminum Boat Works. Market St., Hillyard, (Spokane) Washington. Along with the likes of Nelson Boats and Hewes Craft, Lowell was one of several small, regionally distributed Spokane area makers that began because of a convenient supply from the nearby Kaiser Aluminum smelter and rolling plant facilities. Lowell is believed to have been operational from the 1950s to mid-1960s.

Lund Metalcraft, Inc. New York Mills, Minnesota. Although this contemporary major brand doesn't appear in *The Boating Industry* rosters until 1961, a company history from the once regional manufacturer indicates "in 1948 G. Howard Lund built his first aluminum duck boat, which took about a week to build. The boat was on top of the family car along highway 10 [in New York Mills], and this unintentional advertising brought a boat salesman from Inland Marine Corporation to his doorstep. He inquired where he could get a boat like that. Howard explained that he had built it himself, and that he was willing to build more. The salesman put in an order for fifty boats, and with that Lund's [boating enterprise] was created.

"The business started with three employees in his garage, and a year later he had moved to a new building, and hired fifteen employees. Since then the company has expanded to take up twenty-nine acres, and employ over five hundred people." Though long known as a fishing craft maker, Lund buyers could almost always obtain a runabout. Perusing, for example, a 1967 catalog, one sees Lund's 16-foot Surfrider, "a deep and roomy hull rated for 90 hp that may be used for fishing as well as flashier pursuits such as water skiing. Standard equipment include[d] lights and hardware, ski racks, and folding back-to-back padded seats."

Maritime Products Corp. Alliance, Ohio. A 1967 ad for Maritime's "five-boat fleet of Indestructibles" showed the 18-foot vee-hulled Prince Edward, and the 17-foot tri-hulls Nova Scotia and Sandpiper. Reportedly, the novel craft were dubbed "indestructible" because their aluminum plate, welded seam hulls had a "tough vinyl acrylic hide." Anyone requesting a company catalog would also be sent a free sample of the aluminum used in fabricating these unique boats.

McKenzie Boat Mfg. Co., 121 North Highland Drive, McKenzie, Tennessee, first offered its Cherokee Boats in 1959.

MFG Boat Co. Union City, Pennsylvania. After MFG's acquisition of Crestliner, Molder Fiber Glass cataloged some MFG-branded/Crestliner-built aluminum boats starting in 1967.

Milco Tank and Boat (see Aqua Swan)

Minnetonka Boat Works, Inc. Wayzata, Minnesota (1955)

Mitchell Boat Co., Inc. Highland Blvd., Elkhart, Indiana. Starting around 1960 and trade-named Mitch-Craft, and sometimes just Mitchell, these aluminum runabouts should not be confused with output from Mitchell Boat Company of Costa Mesa, California. The latter was a fiberglass marque.

Mohawk Boat Co. Grand Rapids, Michigan (1959)

MonArk Boat Co. Monticello, Arkansas, began around 1960, and by the 1968 model year offered "aluminum runabouts, canoes, pontoon boats, and utility boats in sizes from ten to thirty-six feet." MonArk runabouts and utilities featured "hulls that have a deep vee-shaped entry and built-in spray rails in 12-foot, 14-foot, and 16-foot lengths." In addition to flat-bottomed center-steered models (essentially early versions of what we'd now call bass boats) MonArk cathedral hull runabouts were also available. So were custom workboats and "jumbo ice chests." As is the case with other makers that focused on anglers, MonArk offered optional steering consoles and side steering mounts that would essentially convert a Jon Boat (some with long decks/front seating) into an outboard utility.

Montgomery-Ward. Like its biggest competitor, Sears & Roebuck, "Monkey-Ward" shopped around each year for the best possible price on aluminum boats that could be badge-engineered with Ward's Sea King trade name. For some boating seasons, M-W would contract with several makers to satisfy anticipated demand in particular distribution regions of its chain store operation. Wards (and Sears & Roebuck, et al.) would reportedly pick up a manufacturer's excess stock or factory leftovers and offer them as "unadvertised specials," or offer the boats through a single page flyer at maybe one store or several area locales. A circa 1957 newsprint handbill pertinent to seven Chicago-land Wards serves as an example. It advertises five boat bargains, including a $475, 14-foot aluminum Sea King runabout on sale for $447. "Full 60-inch foredeck for plenty of storage space. Flooring finished in gray non-skid paint," read the flyer. Suffice it to say, the boat's modest description and generic appearance makes pinpointing parentage perplexing! Unless one discovers period documentation related to chain store suppliers, such mysteries are typically the case with all private brand craft.

Huge retailers such as Sears and Montgomery-Ward bought boats from the most reliable and reasonably priced suppliers. Consequently, Sea King-branded craft on this Chicago area single-sided flyer might have each originated in a different factory. The trailered 12-footer netted the biggest space because Wards marine market was typically entry-level oriented.

Multi-Plastics, Inc. 2411 Weaver St., Fort Worth, Texas. This firm marketed Fiber-Flite fiberglass boats before adding aluminum hulls to the catalog in 1964.

Meyers Aircraft Co., Boat Div. Tecumseh, Michigan. Begun by aviation pioneer Allen H. Meyers, Meyers Aircraft Co., was responsible for notably safe small planes like the two-seat MAC-145 and Meyers 200 series, the latter often rated by private aviation buffs as the best factory-built single-engine aircraft. By 1955, Meyers's organization spawned an aluminum boat division that produced rowboats, utilities, and some runabouts of basic design, but "reinforced with heavy aluminum extrusion." A bit heavier than most of its competitors, Meyers hulls were seemingly built with Federal Aeronautic Administration regulators — rather than an angler new to boating — in mind. The company's early boat catalogs refer to the products as "Sabre Craft," although brochures show hulls simply branded, "Meyers." No matter what the name, the boat's ruggedness is the reason why it's not surprising to encounter an older Meyers model today. One model to look for is the mid-to-late 1950s model 112 WR. Rated for 25 hp, this Meyers Custom 12 Runabout was fitted with both a forward and center wheel deck, plus a modest motor well that allowed for tiller steering. It was one of the few boats to offer such a feature. The interior layout included seat backs fore and aft, another convenience not normally found in a small aluminum runabout designed for either tiller or remote control. Because Meyers Aircraft built boats and boat trailers, the firm touted products for "Land, Water, and Air." Be advised that the firm's name is sometimes misspelled (without its first "e") in boat maker listings. And there was another small boat manufacturer operating under the name Myers.

Naden Industries. "Naden" boats. 505 Fair Ave., Webster City, Iowa (1956)

Nelson. (see Heating Assurance.)

North American Marine, Inc. "American" and "North American" branded boats. North Warsaw, Indiana (1959)

Northline Mfg. Co. 31 Congress St., Salem, Massachusetts. First listed in 1964, this could be the successor to Alumakit (as the addresses are similar), though Northline's boats were noted as factory-built, not kits.

Olympian by Valley Aluminum. A 1957 Firestone catalog shows badge-engineered craft built by Fresno, California-based, Valley Aluminum to be marketed through Firestone retailers. "Olympian boats combine all the know-how of years of research and experimentation in boat design with construction based on proven aluminum engineering standards…and hard-tempered Alcoa Aluminum alloys, the finest material modern science and industry has yet developed for boat construction." Two runabouts, a 14-footer and the 16-foot flagship offered "flashy performance with minimum horsepower." Both enjoyed generous bottom ribbing and several side supports from floor to gunwale. Each had

Valley Aluminum was clearly identified by Firestone as the maker of the tire company's private brand Olympian boats.

bench seating and front seat backs. Modest aft fins gave the hulls a classic late 1950s look. The boats featured "beautiful blue Zolatone multi-flecked interiors. This finish," the brochure touted, "has a slip-proof surface, helps to deaden sound [of the pounding water at high speed], and lessen sun glare."

Orlando Boat Co. 501/503 Elwell St., Orlando, Florida. The Southern Lighting Mfg., Co., in Orlando, began producing aluminum outboard utilities in 1952. It appears that by 1955, the name was changed to Orlando Boat Co. Examples of Orlando boats sold under the name Clipper included the 12' 3" Speedster and 14' 3" Zephyr, both basic, but solid front-steered entry-level runabouts with front seat backs and rear bench seating.

OrrCraft. 110 (and then 1025) West Market St., Orrville, Ohio (1948)

Ouachita Marine & Industrial Corp. Little Rock, Arkansas. "Say Wash-A-Taw," suggested this firm's catalogs with the hope boat buyers would feel comfortable pronouncing its name. Best known for rugged (welded) flat-bottomed, semi-vee hulls, and canoes, Ouachita began in the mid-1960s. The company's manufacturing facilities were in Arkadelphia, Arkansas, where boats were finished in either forest green, olive drab, blue, white, gray, red, yellow, or orange, which gave a nice background for the marque's colorful Native American chief logo.

Persely & Riehl Mfg. Co. Port Clinton, Ohio (1956)

Peterborough Canoe, Ltd. Peterborough, Ontario (1959)

Pioneer Mfg. Co. Middlebury, Indiana. The veteran steel boat maker first marketed some aluminum utility hulls in 1951 as a sort of acquiescence to the light alloy's undeniable growing marine popularity.

Plaza Craft Boat Co. Dixon, Missouri (1957)

Polar Kraft Mfg. Co. 1237 North Watkins, Memphis, Tennessee. Entering the scene for the 1955 season with a few rowboats and an outboard utility, Polar Kraft often touted its heliarc welding techniques as making the hulls stronger than riveted ones. Admittedly, the southern manufacturer's sights were on the fishing and flat-bottom workboat market, but it did offer some traditional-looking runabouts like the 1964 Ski King. By 1968, the only boat maker with a polar bear for a logo mascot had relocated to Olive Branch, Missouri.

Randrup Fold-A-Boat from the Lonan Mfg. Co., of Walnut Creek, California, earns a spot herein for its oddity. Loosely termed a utility craft, the 12-foot (Kaiser) aluminum boat from the late 1960s weighed 125 pounds and folded into a 4-inch x 24-inch x 12-foot package. Upon unfolding, its transom and bracing were bolted into place. Publicity photos depicted the novel craft and two occupants whizzing around with a 9.8-hp Merc 110 outboard.

Razorback Boats Div., Arkla Industries, Inc. Malvern, Arkansas (1964)

Ref. Mfg. Corp. Mineola, New York. "Dart boats." It's possible that the abbreviation in this obscure firm's equally brief January 1947 *Motor Boating* listing stood for Refrigerator Mfg. Corp., which would make sense for an outfit offering welded hulls of aluminum sheeting (similar to refrigerator fabrication). Although the Long Island manufacturer probably made only an 8½-foot rowboat, as opposed to full-fledged runabouts, it is noted herein because the now-mysterious firm is one of the earliest (along with Aluma Craft, Douglas Aircraft, and Grumman) producers of small aluminum pleasure craft chronicled in the venerable magazine.

Regal Products, Ltd. Adams, Wisconsin. Starting during the early 1950s, Regal built 12-, 14-, and 16-foot open boats in stainless steel. Subsequently, aluminum might have been offered.

Rexcraft. (see Consolidated General Products, Inc.)

Reynolds Metals Co., Marine Div., 2000 South 9th St., Louisville, Kentucky. As World War II ended, Reynolds was looking to secure new consumer markets for its aluminum, and boating seemed to hold much possibility. By 1949, the firm's newly established marine division was producing a "12-foot [utility] clinker-type, semi-v concave bottomed hull stamped from one piece of tough special alloy aluminum. Only the transom [was] welded on," otherwise the rugged little boat with "assault-craft bow," aluminum floorboards, and generous foredeck, possessed no seams. Reynolds torture-tested the boat by running a 16-hp motor (probably a hefty Johnson model SD or Scott-Atwater 1-30) wide open at 25 mph and then "beaching at full speed on concrete slabs, rocks, and gravel beaches [causing] no damage." Welding the hull was recommended to owners who might encounter a puncture. "The Reynolds Aluminum Boat," as it was initially dubbed, was marketed for only a couple of boating seasons. The effort was probably primarily an exercise of a major industrial player helping to jumpstart the fledgling aluminum boat business. Along the way, the parenthetical term "Lifetime" got sandwiched between "Reynolds" and "Aluminum Boat."

Apparently, Reynolds sold its boat division to a Cooperstown, New York, outfit that then marketed the craft as "Lifetime Boats." Camp-of-the-Pines in Willsboro, New York, secured — through a middleman — several of the rugged hulls to see how they'd stand up to Lake Champlain's mercurial waters and under the novice skippering of dozens of family campers. Satisfactory results prompted the camp's owner to seek more boats, this time, though, direct from the factory. "Sorry, can't oblige," he was told. "You must order the boats from an authorized 'Lifetime' factory dealer." But when the camp operator mentioned wanting at least sixteen additional boats, the factory man immediately changed his tune and announced, "Congratulations! You've just become our newest authorized 'Lifetime' dealer!" Over the next decade or so, the boats proved indestructible — almost. Unfortunately, the camp's entire fleet couldn't withstand being bulldozed into the ground after the property was acquired by a wealthy neighbor whose wife didn't particularly enjoy the sound of frolicking campers disturbing the otherwise quiet Adirondack locale.

"If you see rust, you know it's not aluminum," Reynolds wanted boat shoppers to know when perusing alloy craft. The giant aluminum producer's "fast, sweet-handling outboard" utility was marketed to give marine aluminum some provenance in a traditionally wooden boating marketplace.

Richland Mfg. Co. Richland, Missouri. Rich Line Sea Fury boats hit the water around 1955, and by 1956 were advertised as "built to blend with motors." Actually, it was just the fleet's flagship Knight Custom Runabout (later upgraded with a motor well, like the Super Custom had) that could be ordered "in any two-tone color to match the hues of two-tone [outboard] motors." This 14-footer had a 52-inch transom to accommodate twin engines as well as upholstered seating front and rear. Though all were 14 feet in length, the Knight series could be had in five variations from the Super Custom to a stripped down Knight Runabout simply equipped with bench seats, though possessing a sexy 72-inch deck. Another interesting Rich Line runabout was Big 16, introduced in 1956 with a long foredeck, U-shaped (rear sides and center) wooden seating, and capacity for a tiller-steered (if optional wheel wasn't requested) outboard of up to 60 hp! It was subsequently available as a day cruiser with self-bailing motor well and traditional seats. For 1960, Rich Line's 11½-foot Speedster was cataloged as

Even picturing the boat without a motor, Richland Manufacturing credited "abundant pep" with causing its 14-foot Knight Super Deluxe to be the runabout "that everyone likes and wants."

a "cocky…small, but mighty craft, as frisky as a colt and with the start and go of a Kansas jackrabbit!" Rated for 25 hp, this one would be a nice find today.

By the mid-1960s (and after trying its hand at fiberglass), Rich Line shifted its focus to aluminum fishing craft, although it kept an incarnation of the 14-foot Knight in production. The 1965 Knight Special represented a good quality, entry-level family runabout value with embossed lapstrake hull, "attractive two-tone paint job and walk-through front seat with back rest." It could be ordered thorough the remainder of the decade. Along the way, Richland mentioned having additional plants in Conway, Missouri; Fort Lauderdale, Florida (probably for its glass division), and (circa 1962) an office at 526 Woodruff Bldg., Springfield, Missouri.

Rickborn Industries, Inc. 93 US Highway 46, Caldwell, New Jersey. Primarily a fiberglass boat maker and one of several small Garden State companies involved in marine glass, Rickborn cataloged a few small aluminum craft to broaden its line around 1961.

Roby-Hutton Mfg. Springfield, Missouri. The homemade-looking Aqua-Car line of aluminum pontoon runabouts was current in the late 1950s. Boxy side panels on models such as the 15-foot Sportsman provided the novel craft with tall tail fins. Don't mix up this make with the fiberglass Aqua Car, also an unusual sight.

Sabre Craft. (see Meyers Aircraft)

Sea King. (see Montgomery-Ward)

Sea Nymph. (see Aero Mfg., Co.)

Seamaid Mfg. Co., Inc. 222 South Lincoln St. (and later, West Mitchell St.), Kendallville, Indiana. Seamaid boats debuted in 1954 with an outboard utility.

Sears & Roebuck. Aluminum runabouts with the Elgin and, by the mid-1960s, Sears & Roebuck label were procured from a variety of fabricators. Sears's 1965 Fall/Winter catalog exemplifies the enigma associated with trying to determine the lineage of the big retailer's hulls. "All aluminum semi-vee boats," the description begins. "Ribbed and braced…positive foam flotation, spray rails, oar locks. Inside bottom finished in non-skid, non-glare paint." For boating historians, such detail has about as much value as a robbery witness's statement to police that the suspect "sort of looked like an average person." Armed with decades of Sears & Roebucks's corporate supplier contract records and a long winter, one could probably write a book just covering the Elgin/Sears boat origins. One occasionally present clue is small print regarding shipping that might say something like, "f.o.b. Weatogue, Connecticut," or some such locale that can be cross referenced to a boatbuilder there and then visually compared to that maker's "regular" line. That's part of the fun when researching Sears's ubiquitous aluminum utility and runabout output. There have got to be a lot of them yet to be adopted by collectors.

Seth Smith Boat Works, Inc. "Smith Craft" 2101 East Washington, Phoenix, Arizona (1959)

Smoker Lumber Co., Inc. "Smoker-Craft." New Paris,

Indiana. Primarily a line of aluminum fishing boats, Smoker-Craft debuted around 1964. By the early 1970s, the company tried its hand at offering a wide selection of embossed lapstrake aluminum runabouts including the entry-level 14-foot Lancer; the bow-rider, side console–steered 15-foot Gemini Sport "family fun boat; traditionally decked Gemini; bow rider 17-foot Sportabout." The conventionally decked 16- and 18-foot T-Bird runabouts completed the line.

Southern Lighting Mfg. Co. (see Orlando Boat Co.)

Sports-Kraft of Dallas. 3020 Sylvan St., Dallas, Texas. Also referred to as General Boat Corp., utility hulls from this maker first appeared in 1952. Grand Prairie (also home to Lone Star) was listed as General Boat's venue by 1956 when it offered "forty-five different boats to choose from, each high in quality, performance, versatility… High in everything except price." The 1957 Habana "utility-runabout" is one of the most interesting of the Sports-Kraft line. Front-steered and having a modestly angled bow, this 16-footer gains additional classic 1950s eye appeal from a set of moderately pronounced tail fins at the sides of the motor well. Each was treated to the marque's winged "SK" logo, a brand that disappeared in the early 1960s.

Squires Mfg. 609 County St., Milan, Michigan (1958)

Stan-Craft Corp. Somers, MT. A 1957 *Motor Boating* roster pegs Stan-Craft as building one-off custom boats (of any type) up to 34 feet, and indicates the western firm cataloged a 14-foot aluminum ("metal") outboard hull.

Sunray Mfg. Div. "Sunray" boats appeared in 1964 from a small West Mitchell St., Kendallville, Maryland plant.

Texas Boat Manufacturing Co., Inc. "Texas Maid Fleet." 510 South Mills St., Lewisville, Texas. A nice looking line, Texas Maid aluminum models were visually reminiscent of craft from neighboring Lone Star. Debuting around 1958, the marque featured several rowboats, as well as eight runabouts and cruisers (up to 23 feet) by 1962. The entry point in runabouts was the 14' 2" Galaxie. The 15-foot Impala was said to be "the sports car of the boat field," even though it was a far cry from, say, a 1950s Feather Craft Vagabond. Texas Boat Manufacturing Company also made a claim for its Fiesta, announcing it as "the largest selling 16-foot runabout in the industry." At 18 feet, the Tahiti (also in a moonroof hardtop — fabricated from fiberglass — version) and the 20-foot Offshore represented Texas Maid's larger runabouts. They and their cruiser sisters wore three porthole accents on either side of the bow.

Thornes Mfg. Ltd., "Thornes Boats." Listed for 1959 as being on Violet St., in Fort William, Ontario, and 1537 Mercer St., Windsor, Ontario, by 1961. 12-, 14-, 15-, and 16-foot models were offered. Runabout versions appeared to be sturdily built, entry-level affairs that one might call a beefed-up and decked-over rowboat. Windshields and two-tone paint jobs gave Thornes runabouts a bit of style. Along the way, the enterprise got listed as a division of Fabricated Steel Products.

Tonka Craft. (see Minnetonka)

Trailorboat Engineering Co. 609 Francisco Blvd., San Rafael, California. Rather than go with the term "runabout," Trailorboat dubbed its products *"Fun-a-bout."* Arguably the most fun version was the firm's cute little eight-foot, two-passenger model "designed especially for children." Probably the province of rich kids — or lucky youngsters related to a Trailorboat dealer — this nicely painted and accented tiny craft featured a windshield, full decking, steering wheel, cockpit, and motor well. The 1957 publicity photos

A great example of (probably homebrew) ad hoc runabout construction is seen in this circa 1950 Trailorboat rowboat revamped into a Class "A" stock outboard utility racer by the addition of a very modest wooden wheel deck. (Kent Hitchcock photo)

showed the diminutive runabout powered by a Johnson Sea Horse 3 jerry-rigged for remote steering, even though the throttle and magneto was activated on the motor, because OMC didn't make remote controls for its 3-horse mill. Fun-a-bouts also came in 12- and 14-foot lengths for big people. Trailorboat was initially listed as offering aluminum utility hulls for the 1951 boating season. The West Coast concern drops off trade lists by the mid-1960s.

No doubt the cutest classic aluminum outboard runabout, Trailorboat's 7' 6" model from the mid-1950s weighed just 65 pounds, sold for $200 and was meant for about 3- to 5-hp, as well as a small fry skipper.

Tubbs Mfg. Co. 2424 Wyman St., Dallas, Texas. Another of an aluminum boat manufacturing enclave that operated in the Dallas area. The company's brand name is unknown, although it's doubtful that the boating pejorative, "tub" would have been used in the nomenclature. Tubbs appears to have entered boat building around 1955.

Valley Aluminum Co. 517 P Street, Fresno, California. Valley enters the utility picture in 1954, and is listed as **Valco Boats** by 1960. Its 1967 *Motor Boating* listing shows a robust fleet from 12' 1" to 20 feet. Ten years earlier, Valley also made Olympian boats, which were private-branded for sale through Firestone tire, auto, and home stores. These boats may have continued in production into the 1960s.

Viking Boat Co., Highway 13 North, Middlebury, Indiana. Viking is noted as debuting with some aluminum outboard utilities in late 1954.

Vio Holda Mfg. Co., Inc. 844 North Madison, Topeka, Kansas. With a 1955 debut, this maker of "all welded aluminum boats" indicated it marketed utility craft.

Wagemaker Co. 506 Market St., Grand Rapids, Michigan. Better remembered as a molded plywood hull manufacturer, Wagemaker entered the aluminum field around 1955 to offer "no upkeep" craft destined to be "the lazy man's friend. Aircraft engineered with complete bulkhead and reinforced rib construction," Wagemaker's 700 Series for 1955 included 12-, 14-, 16-, and 18-foot bench-seat open boats to which optional "long foredecks and center decks can be easily [factory or dealer] installed at any time." It's interesting to note that the firm's 1955 flyer was captioned, "World's largest builder of outboards." Wagemaker didn't make motors, so the boast apparently applied to its boat output, which — even with the molded plywood output — would still seem like a questionable claim.

Ward Brothers Manufacturing Co. 430 East Gaines,

Monticello, Arkansas. The company first offered aluminum runabouts for the 1951 model year and is listed as building aluminum racing hulls by 1956. Around this time, Ward morphed into DuraCraft, an identity with which it had likely already labeled its boats.

Wards. (see Montgomery Ward)

Whitehouse Reinforced Plastic Co. Fort Worth, Texas. Even its name suggests fiberglass is its stock-in-trade, but this respected late 1950s–early 1960s boat maker also offered a pair of lapstrake aluminum craft — a utility and a runabout — in its 1960 catalog.

Winner Boats, Inc. After moving from New Jersey to Dickson, Tennessee, the pioneer fiberglass boat maker offered some aluminum utilities and runabouts around 1961. It's possible that they were badge-engineered for Winner by some other maker.

Western Auto Stores. Kansas City, Missouri. It wasn't uncommon for Western Auto to feature at least one of its Wizard outboard motors and small boats in its catalogs. While some of the hulls were "no-name" affairs — save for a Western Auto transom tag — others got branded with the Wizard label. None were from the "actual" Wizard Boat outfit in Costa Mesa, California, a pioneer in fiberglass rather than aluminum.

Chapter 4

From Plastic to Glass

FIBERGLASS RUNABOUTS, AN OVERVIEW

The fiberglass boat as we know it today owes its development to the years immediately following World War II. Fiberglass boats were, in fact, a revolutionary innovation even though the material was, at the time, viewed with skepticism. To many, fiberglass seemed like a solution to a problem that existed only in the minds of those who didn't understand what boat ownership was supposed to be all about. Yet it was fiberglass, with its ability to be molded into all sorts of shapes that, when mated with increasingly trouble-free outboard motors, paved the way for the great boom in postwar American boating. After decades of trying and failing, the marine industry had finally found the formula needed to get the typical American family into boating, an activity that had traditionally been the province of wealthy yachtsmen or middle-class enthusiasts willing to make wooden-boat maintenance an integral part of their lives.

At first, there was some uncertainty within the industry regarding exactly what to call the new material. Initially, some early manufacturers, including industry pioneer Winner, called the material "plastic." But, during the next few years, the fledgling industry began shifting nomenclature from *plastic* to *fiberglass reinforced plastic* (FRP). Still, even by the January 1955 *Motor Boating* Show Issue, the term "plastic" was still widely used. The magazine even had a distinct section entitled "Plastic Boats," which it said were "light, tight, durable, rot-proof, and emphasizing the trend towards new mediums of construction minimizing maintenance problems."

By then "plastic boat" catalog writers had decided to distance their products from the possible pejorative "plastic," which had connotations in the public mind of being cheap. Dropping the word "plastic," companies switched terminology to "fiberglass," or often "fiberglas," the official name trademarked by Owens-Corning. By the end of the Eisenhower era, even the descriptive "fiber" was often no longer used. Suddenly, runabout shoppers were looking at boats with the newly adopted marine term for space-age, carefree construction — *glass*. Now, barely more than a decade after the average boater had first heard of plastic hulls, factories turning out wooden boats began to realize what they were really up against.

"The Outboard Comes of Age" was the cover story in *Newsweek* on April 15, 1957. "It is a medical axiom that childhood diseases, when contracted by adults are

particularly virulent," suggested the magazine about pleasure boating fever. "This axiom was splendidly demonstrated [at pre-season boat shows, hot stove gatherings at the local marina, etc.,] as ten million American grownups...showed symptoms: An obsession with catalogs, an irresistible urge to hang around marine-supply shops, boatyards, and engine salesrooms."

Fiberglass's road to acceptance wasn't all due to a name change. In fact, the journey had been an uncertain one fraught with risk and even tragic consequences for some of those who pioneered the technology. At first, fiberglass innovators were typically more associated with chemistry than with mariner traditions. In fact, a few dabbled in literal plastic boat making, marketing hulls composed of resins alone. The early practitioners were originally reacting to World War II–era military needs for great quantities of strong, lightweight, and easily produced products. To cite one important example — among the Pentagon's requirements were rugged but electronically transparent "radomes" for protecting radar antennas. Fiberglass molding passed its first major field tests with such items.

Admittedly, it's difficult to precisely pinpoint when the history of "plastic" or fiberglass boating got under way, but we might also draw connections to Bakelite and Catalan plastics especially popular with industry, designers, and consumers during the 1930s and '40s. Americans developed a taste for these often stylishly molded and colored materials when radio makers used them to add bright visual elements to the aural medium. "Table radios were among the first [major] goods to be made of plastic [resins molded to desired dimensions]," noted Phillip Collins in his *Radios, The Golden Age*. "Chicago Molded Plastics built the first plastic [radio] cabinet in 1931."

Arguably, the tabletop radio vis-à-vis small boat comparison works because, before shifting to plastics, radio makers — like boatbuilders — had a tradition of constructing cabinets with wood. Molded plastic not only provided radio case designers with new opportunities in compound curvature, light weight, and integral hues, but reduced manufacturing costs and construction time previously associated with piecing together and finishing wooden cabinetry.

Even if molded larger and thicker, the inherently brittle plastics responsible for radio cabinets would never prove particularly seaworthy, although a few companies would dabble in marketing hulls composed of just plastic. They eventually realized that something was needed to reinforce molded resin the way steel rods vastly improve concrete's durability. Enter a pair of corporations looking for ways to generate some profit from what otherwise represented excess bottle production. According to company history, Owens-Corning Corporation began investigating possibilities during the early 1930s.

"Both Owens Illinois Glass Company and

Corning Glass Company had been experimenting with...creating fibers from glass — one of the world's oldest and most abundant materials. A[n Owens-Illinois] researcher named Games Slayter [sic], envisioned a glass fiber material that was not as heavy as that produced by the then-current [glass or mineral wool] technology. In 1932, a young researcher, Dale Kleist, who worked for Slayter's assistant, was attempting to weld together architectural glass blocks to form a vacuum-tight seal. A jet of compressed air [he was using in this experiment] accidentally struck a stream of molten glass, resulting in fine glass fibers. After achieving Slayter's dream [of quickly producing high quality, lightweight glass fibers], Kleist further refined the process by using steam...instead of compressed air...to attenuate the glass fiber. The result was a glass fiber material thin enough to be used as a commercial fiber glass insulation [and furnace filters]."

By 1938, Corning Glass — which had been eyeing ways to produce commercially viable glass fiber since the mid-1920s — formed a company allied with Owens-Illinois dubbed Owens-Corning Fiberglas (OCF). This new organization's name incorporated the word "Fiberglas" for which Owens-Illinois had received a trademark two years earlier. As the United States entered World War II, the company recognized that glass fibers woven to produce fiberglass cloth, and made usefully flexible via heating, could be utilized as a lightweight and strong reinforcement for molding plastic (or resin). After several others concocted crude fiberglass reinforced plastic (and even palm-leaf reinforced) dinghies, in 1944 Owens-Corning Fiberglas dabbled in canoe making. However, according to author Daniel Spurr's foundational work, *Heart of Glass,* the firm abandoned the project after the craft "collapsed during a two-mile trial. OCF [then turned its attention to cars when, the next year it helped] develop the Stout-Scarab automobile — the first automobile with a fiberglass reinforced plastic body."

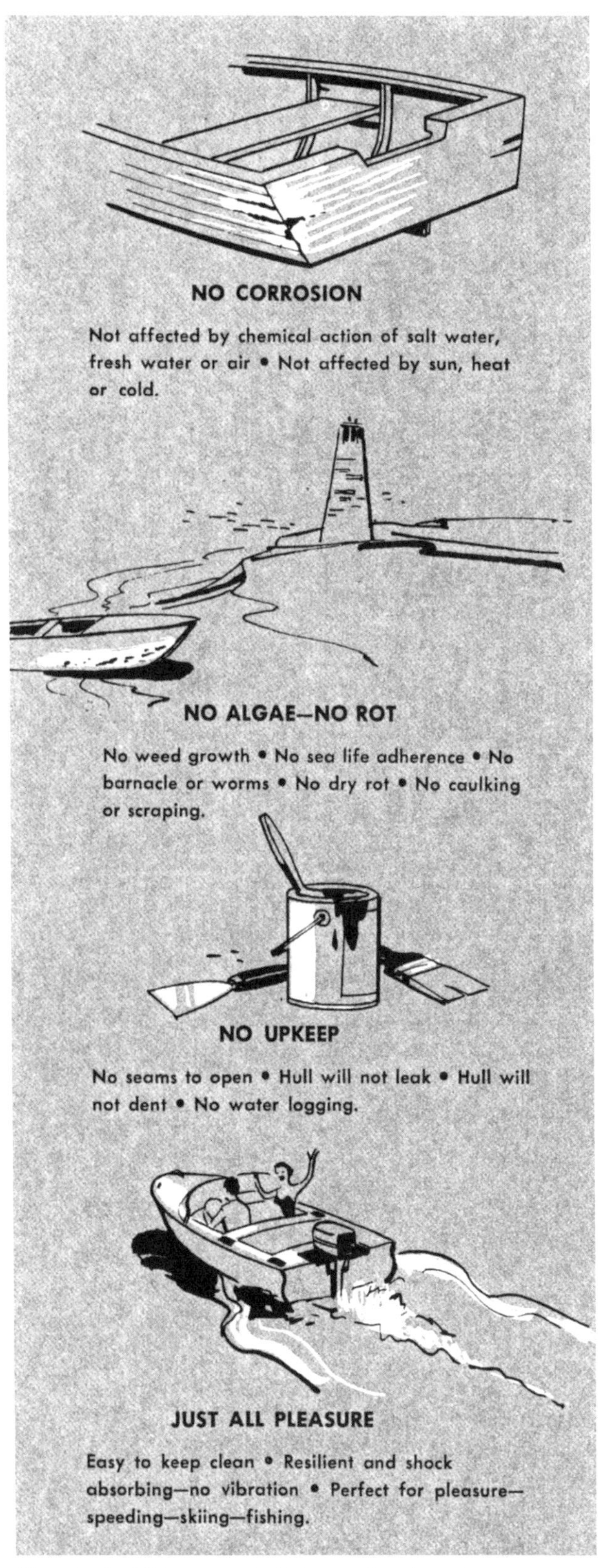

Through the 1950s, many plastic boat makers devoted catalog space to educating folks about the "miracle" of fiberglass. When some consumers' glass craft did demonstrate wear, however, the Federal Trade Commission called for companies to go easy on the promises.

This 1945 vehicle never moved beyond prototype, although the fiberglass industry's potential for acceleration was not lost on U.S. federal regulators. In 1947, they viewed Owens-Corning Fiberglas as having a monopoly over fiberglass production processes, and filed a lawsuit aimed at opening a clear, competitive roadway for those also hoping to create new product lines from the plentiful fibers and amazingly versatile resins such as polyester developed in the mid-1930s by DuPont.

In the meantime, a tiny fleet of fiberglass boats began to appear. The 1946 PlastiCraft line from West Trenton, New Jersey–based Winner Manufacturing Company probably represents the first production fiberglass boats. In a January 1967 *Yachting* article titled "Early Fiberglass Boats," author Boughton Cobb, Jr., reported that this firm "appears to have been the first volume producer of glass hulls, coming out with a small line [of originally named *Plastrend* and then quickly re-dubbed *PlastiCraft* outboard runabouts] in the years 1946 and 1947."

A distinction must be made between plastic (early on, reinforced with natural materials) and fiberglass reinforced plastic (FRP) from polyester resins. To have netted its January 1946 *Motor Boating* listing (offering nine-foot rowing and sailing dinghies, as well as outboard utilities in 12- and 14-foot versions), Winner must have had something cooking by late fall 1945, even though its mid-1940s resin type and reinforcement fabric pedigree is up for debate.

Winner Manufacturing Company's 1955 PlastiCraft catalog cover. Its spelling of "Fiberglas" was a nod to Owens-Corning's trademarked name for the plastic reinforcement.

People passing by the Winner factory in the mid 1940s probably thought it looked pretty outdated, and would likely be surprised that a futuristic boating revolution was fermenting inside.

Credit for making polyester-fiberglass hull number one, however, goes to Ohioan Ray Greene. It was Greene's love of boat building led him to embark on college science experiments by molding small craft with various plastic resins augmented by materials like chicken wire, paper, cotton cloth, and, finally, Owens-Corning's fiberglass. Spurr's exhaustive research indicates that in 1942, Greene was given "a laboratory batch of polyester resin from [someone at the] American Cyanamid Company." With this, Greene built a dinghy — the first fiberglass polyester boat.

Even before Japan surrendered, *Motor Boating*

compiled its June 1945 "Postwar Boat Buyer's Chart." Admittedly, this was a premature chronicle, but it now represents a watershed peak for the fiberglass boat industry at the very dawn of its existence. Shoppers were told that most of the noted companies were "still engaged in war production, but [could] handle inquiries at least for models listed. Orders for new boats [were] accepted only on a customer priority plan for later delivery when government permission is granted." As the sole representative of non-wooden (or steel) boat makers, Western Plastics, Inc.'s Chemold Division is conspicuous. The Glendale, California, outfit was listed as producing plastic boats in four of *Motor Boating*'s ballpark-figure size categories, from 10 to 12 feet up to 16- to 18-foot outboard runabouts. Chemold's January 1946 models (denoting late 1945 production, or perhaps just "anticipated" production) contained an impressive seven-boat line, including the 14-foot Outboard Runabout (for $325) and a $500 Deluxe Outboard Runabout 15' 11" in length. The company's material disclosure of "chemold laminated plastic," however, probably consisted of ethyl cellulose resin reinforced by a stiff muslin material, and not the subsequent fiberglass reinforced polyester plastic formula that became an industry classic.

A year after the war, and just as nascent Winner commenced making PlastiCraft hulls in heated metal molds, Gar Wood, Jr., raced to get his Oklahoma-built fiberglass *GarForm* boats into production. Setbacks with making the process consistent precluded much output before 1948, but he was reportedly able to ship about 2,000 craft by the time the first boating season of the 1950s got under way. Wood, son of the famed speedboat champion and wooden-boat builder, might have become a household name among fiberglass boat buyers had he not been beset with personal problems and manufacturing difficulties. The GarForm line shifted to an inboard emphasis (one of the first glass makers to do so), but Wood and his notable company soon faded from the scene.

An inboard version of the Chief Deluxe 17-foot Garform Plasticglass runabout. Not long after this 1955 ad appeared, the Oklahoma boat builder downsized its line to one 14-foot outboard model.

Another pioneering plastic hull enterprise, the Wizard Boat Company introduced its inaugural line of outboard boats sometime during 1947. The small California-based outfit had, during the 1946 or early '47 boating season, acquired the tooling and "male molding" (where the fiberglass hull is formed over a mold) technology of Western Plastic's Chemold Division. Before announcing its pioneering pleasure craft line in the seminal (June 1945) *Motor Boating* listing, Western had made some small molded plastic rescue hulls to be stowed aboard World War II B-17 bombers.

Now barely a marine history footnote, though central to this time line, is the small beehive of plastic boat development in the Auburn, New York, area around 1946–47. Even *Motor Boating* took notice in its January 1947 issue, identifying the Auburn-based Bo-Mer Manufacturing Company as offering eight- and nine-foot plastic dinghies. Plastic Boats, Inc., of Auburn (sometimes listed with a nearby Port Byron, New York, address) was listed as making the nine-foot Plasti-Boat. It is unknown what chemical/reinforcement process was used to form these hulls, or whether the Auburn activity had any connection with Link Aviation (a short car tip away) in Binghamton, New York, a firm that — around

1948 — developed sectional/take-apart 14½-foot canoes, 8' 11" tenders, and an 11½-foot outboard utility out of cloth-reinforced Bakelite.

Certainly among the most visionary fiberglass pioneers was Carl Beetle, descendant of a venerable Massachusetts wooden-boatbuilding family. In 1946, with the help of General Electric scientists working with polyester resins and matched metal dies in General Electric's Pittsfield, Massachusetts, plant, he began molding hulls with the plastic resin and fiberglass reinforcement. Later technology permitted Beetle to abandon the expensive metal dies and lay up hulls himself in a plant in New Bedford. Not only did Beetle produce a range of craft, from dinghy and 12-foot catboat to outboard cruisers, he also conducted one of the most consistent advertising campaigns of the early fiberglass builders. Few editions of *Yachting* or *Motor Boating* are without an ad for the then-novel BB (Beetle Boatbuilding) models.

Around 1950, Californian William Tritt, owner of a three-year-old company that made a few small sailing craft, rowing dinghies, and sailboat spars with fiberglass, picked up female molds, gel-coating techniques, and manufacturing rights from Sierra Madre–based Sea Lion Boat Works to fabricate fiberglass-reinforced craft using a newly developed polyester resin that hardened (or cured) at room temperature — as opposed to requiring high heat curing. Tritt dubbed his company Glasspar. Although boats with this brand didn't show up in *Motor Boating* annual listings until 1953, he had been offered the Sea Lion designs through a Sears & Roebuck contract for several boating seasons. Another West Coast fiberglass builder, Bellingham (Washington) Shipyard, became active in the genre during the late 1940s. Bellingham's Bell Boy line debuted in small numbers in 1947. All in all, as the World War II decade closed, boat shoppers on both sides of the country could get a firsthand look at craft concocted from revolutionary

A Beetle "BB" runabout tethered to an unseen mooring — and sans steering/throttle hookup — in a fall 1949 publicity still. Judging from the kids' coats, that day along coastal Massachusetts must have been as chilly as the public's subsequent reaction to the newfangled fiberglass craft.

chemical and glass materials.

By 1950, the venerable New York Boat Show was able to exhibit about 20 fiberglass boats. The majority were targeted to entry-level boaters also perusing outboard motor display booths. Automotive-inspired styling, remote fuel tanks, easy starting, and full gearshifts offered conveniences capable of swelling pleasure boating's ranks. Having live customers come calling to take a gander at the new, amazingly simple to operate, electric-starting, gear-shifting outboards that generated a then-whopping 25, 30, and even 40 hp was one thing. Persuading these wistful skippers to "go glass" was quite another matter in the mariner's traditional world of wood.

"It was clear," wrote Pete Smyth in *Nautical Quarterly* number eight that "to even the least savvy dealer that in order to snag fiberglass boating's biggest customer base the shiny plastic hulls would have to be perceived as a worthy partner for the motor." But, "in the early days of peddling fiberglass boats," Smyth recalled, "every customer first thumped on the hull to establish its strength [and compare it to wood]. If there was the slightest give, the customer looked elsewhere." This once-common shopper's test is a major reason why many late 1940s–early 1950s fiberglass hulls were heavier than acceptable engineering required.

Very slowly, pioneer fiberglass boatbuilders, predominantly those offering outboard runabouts, began breaking the icy reception one might expect to encounter from an industry long dominated by wooden construction. Few big name boat makers, however, saw any merit in making the transition., One Chris-Craft official reportedly lobbied his colleagues for their solemn pledge never to engage in fiberglass hull construction. He was no doubt pleased that, well into the 1950s, most boat buyers still appeared unconvinced that fiberglass was the way to go — at least not until a neighbor bought one first and could offer convincing testimony.

The Korean War didn't help, either. Polyester resin, the lifeblood of FRP production, was difficult for small start-up recreational companies to procure. Then, too, while the fledgling industry produced revolutionary boats, it had generally done so without bringing aboard accepted designers whose names might have conferred some status and prestige to this new type of boat. Small-craft expert Hank Bowman reported in his 1955 *Encyclopedia of Outboard Motor Boating* that "the slowness of the public to accept the boats has been due partially to a reactionary attitude towards anything but the commonplace wood hulls, so long in vogue, plus generally poor design on the part of the plastic

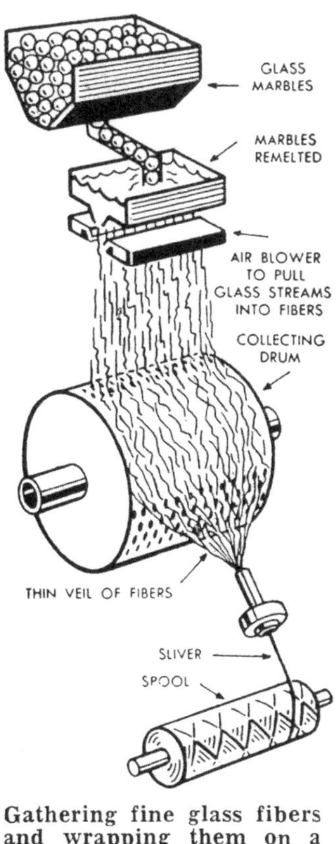

Depicted in the Rube Goldberg "contraption" tradition, this fiberglass machine made marbles into the glass fabric from which Herter's chrome fiberglass cloth was produced. Not only did the Waseca, Minnesota mail order firm build its own boats with the fabric, but it advertised cloth for homebrew application on old wooden hulls, promising "it costs the same to give your boat a coat of chrome fiberglass as it does to hire a man to sand and paint it."

boatbuilders who have largely been excellent plastics technicians but poor naval architects. In some of the early plastic production hulls [circa 1950], exposure to weather did cause deterioration. The reinforced fiberglass gradually lost its flexibility, became brittle and developed a tendency to crack."

Also reflecting upon fiberglass runabout sales of the 1950s, Arthur Liebers's *Encyclopedia of Pleasure Boating* concurs with Bowman, saying, "failure to…determine the strengths of the [wooden] hull structures they are replacing [or mimicking]…by many fiberglass boatbuilders has resulted in a rash of poorly constructed boats which have proven unseaworthy. Hence, the acceptance of reinforced plastic boats by [old-line] builders and by the general public has been somewhat retarded." Liebers believed, as the 1960s dawned, that plastic boat makers' biggest challenge was in finding willing naval architects and "persuading [them] to design the hulls so that full advantages of the material can be gained."

In fact, Owens-Corning had sought naval architects to help adapt fiberglass to boatbuilding. Not long after offering the material commercially, the recognized fiberglass leader hired the naval architectural firm Gibbs & Cox "to prepare an engineering manual for fiberglass…researched and published at great expense." Writer Pete Smyth concluded, however, that the work went for naught because "it became clear that boats built by the book simply couldn't be built economically, and even if they could [during the fiberglass boat industry's rollout years] they couldn't be sold. To obtain lab standards," he noted, "required far more precision than [pioneer hull builders on the factory floor, aka] 'hand lay-up workers' were capable of achieving economically." Because most fiberglass boat companies were small operations, unable to afford much research and development before introducing their latest model, appearance — or *dock appeal* — had to be the key selling point.

Liebers observed that "one of the greatest advantages of fiberglass is the aesthetic. The molded form can be used to create curving lines and even 'fins' on the tail deck. Since many boats [were, in the 1950s,] purchased by former landlubbers with little appreciation for the nautical aspects of a boat, a new sense of values has become applied in the boating trade. Inspired by the automobile designers, there is an attempt to sell boats by elaborate flowing lines and gaudy colors, and an obvious attempt in the fittings and decorations to appeal to the female taste."

Boats like the Reinelle Jet Flight runabout, at first glance seemingly molded from a 1959 Chevrolet body, proved the point. So did the sleek, salmon-hued Whitehouse brand speedster with plaid upholstery and top. The Cadillac Sea Lark, although built on a plywood hull, was graced with multi-colored fiberglass topsides with tall tail fins encasing tail lights. No matter which admittedly provocative design prompted Liebers's reserved compliment, the fact that women were being

If imitation is the sincerest form of flattery, then designers of the 1959 Chevrolet must have been proud to see the stern of this Reinell Jet Flight.

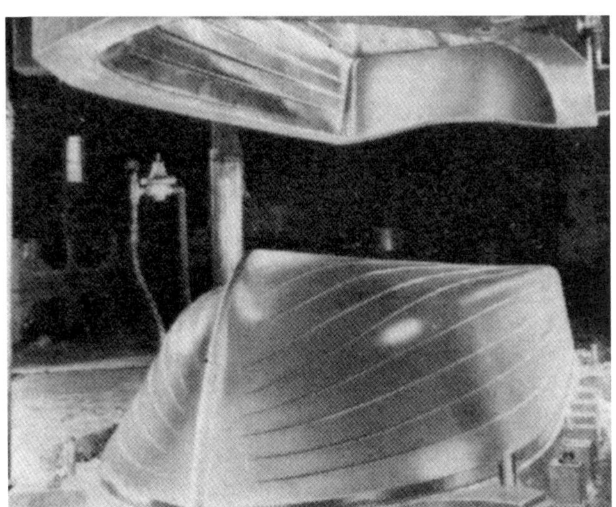

Molded Fiber Glass Company's famed and expensive matched metal dies used to "stamp out" MFG hulls. It was just one of several fabrication methods companies could utilize to fabricate glass boats.

attracted to sporty fiberglass craft was good news to fiberglass boat manufacturers — and to the millions of husbands who wanted a new boat.

By the mid-1950s, the great boating boom that the industry had been more or less predicting since the development of practical marine engines and outboard motors was finally under way. *Popular Mechanics* marveled at the number of Sputnik-era families who got into boating. Its July 1957 issue looked back on the previous year when "Americans bought 275,000 new boats and 600,000 outboard motors [and] spent more on boating than on any other recreation." Those figures climbed steadily for several years thereafter. The April 1957 *Mechanics Illustrated* conservatively noted that fiberglass was still in the process of catching on. The magazine devoted most of its "Boats and Boating Section" to wooden hulls, and noted, "price-wise, Fiberglas boats [were] somewhat more costly, but [said] the obvious appeal of negligible maintenance, molded-in color and smooth-curved surfaces appear[ed] to be offsetting this handicap."

Meanwhile, satisfied owners transmitted the "fiberglass is good" message by word of mouth. Of course, this was a slow process, though it had been given some appreciated momentum, on June 30, 1953. That's when every fiberglass boat company got help from an unlikely landlubber — the Chevrolet Corvette. By that day's rollout of the first of 300 hand-built "Vettes," millions of motorists had already been exposed to at least a few paragraphs of positive publicity about Chevy's new "plastic car." Industrial Plastics Corporation owner Brandt Goldsworthy, who in 1947 and 1948 had fabricated Triangle Boat Company's first several hundred fiberglass outboard runabouts, as well as playing a role in early Wizard boat production, was called upon by General Motors to assist with the Corvette's body construction.

"Each was virtually hand built and a lot of minor changes were made," notes *The Standard Catalog of American Cars.* While the early Corvettes were pieced together in Flint, Michigan, and later in St. Louis, their bodies were fabricated by the Molded Fiberglass Company (MFG), which later added boats to its respectable resin-related resume. Echoing GM's original mantra about the then-novel car's composition, Clymer's *Corvette V-8 Complete Owner's Handbook* (1962

For 1955, Lone Star tried a "bag-method process in Fiberglas construction [in which] Fiberglas cloth and resin 'mate' under high steam pressure to form a lightweight, seamless lifetime hull." Here, the newly minted boat is being extracted from the female "cavity" mold after the male plug has been lifted.

edition) touts, the "use of fiberglass saves considerable weight in the Corvette body as compared to production in steel. Excellent resistance to corrosion is provided. Resistance to casual damage is also outstanding. And, of great importance, fiberglass permits the lowest possible retail price in limited, high quality production."

Though other sporty autos, like the Woodill Wildfire, Kaiser-Darrin, and the G-2 from Bill Tritt's Glasspar firm had made bits of motoring news, it was the seductive Corvette supported by GM advertising that conferred widespread acceptance of fiberglass.

By 1953, even old-line pleasure craft magazines like *Motor Boating,* were happily giving enthusiastic nods to fiberglass. The "new material is a designer's [marine] dream," the respected publication stated. "It is four times stronger than plywood of the same thickness and has been tested and used for a number of years without a reported failure. [Fiberglass] makes possible the truly one-piece hull. It is easily formed into compound curves and is stronger because of them. There are no built-in tensions as in a wooden boat. The fiberglass is molded to shape and when cured resists any and all change. [Some pioneer fiberglass boat makers fired guns at their hulls to demonstrate imperviousness to such changes!] It requires as much force to continue a break in the skin as it does to cause the original fracture and repairs are easily made with the same material, because a perfect bond with the same resins can be made at any time. [And when wooden framing — or core — is used in the boat's construction], the fiberglass impregnated plastic seals the wood *forever* against absorbing or expelling moisture."

But the "forever" in *Motor Boating*'s early fiberglass praise (January 1953) was too generous. After hearing claims of new "maintenance free" boats, even the Federal Trade Commission got suspicious. Its concerns lead to hearings (in early 1961) and "Trade Practice Rules for the Pleasure Boat Industry" which barred fiberglass (and other) boat manufacturers from claiming a craft is *maintenance free* unless it "will not deteriorate during the expected life of such boat." The FTC added a note confirming that "the consensus of the industry [admits] that no boat of present manufacture is completely maintenance free under all normal conditions of use."

Besides the streamlined design possibilities of fiberglass molding, the boats benefited from the introduction of dazzling "gel coat" surface finishes. *Popular Science* described this as "the high-gloss plastic applied to the exterior and capable, in a bad boat, of covering a multitude of construction sins." Pittsburgh Plate Glass and Glidden Paint Company were among the suppliers of gel coat.

By 1957 pleasure boating icon Chris-Craft heard the buzz loud enough to grudgingly admit to coveting a chunk of the undeniably increasing fiberglass outboard runabout market. When Chris-Craft executives finally figured their firm had better learn the fiberglass "ropes," they bought a small Florida company that built craft

This 1959 Dorsett ad extolled the virtues of "functional styling," though it capitalized on famed industrial stylist Raymond Loewy's penchant for visually striking streamlining.

branded Lake'n Sea. Within months of marketing these good-looking products, however, Chris-Craft was swamped with complaints that the fiberglass came unstuck from the boats' plywood cores. In some cases, quite contrary to *Motor Boating*'s prediction, enough moisture was absorbed to sink a Lake'n Sea. And there were other less serious, but annoying idiosyncrasies like the finish fading and staining. These foibles and the catching of an unflattering nickname, Leak'n Sink, caused Chris-Craft to temporarily bail out of the fiberglass arena.

"Good riddance," thought more than a few old-timers disgusted with increasingly congested recreational waterways. One disgruntled subscriber to *Florida Wildlife* editorialized in a spring 1957 issue, "American anglers [and marine traditionalists] who nursed the boating industry through its swaddling clothes are now lost in the stampede of converted automobile fans who want their new boats to go faster and faster, and be full of gadgets, chrome, and two-tone paint jobs. A self-respecting fisherman [or old salt] wouldn't be caught dead," the letter writer ranted, "in ninety percent of the boats being turned out today!" It was an admission that things on the water were noticeably changing.

Lone Star noted, "the first step in fiberglass boat construction is the careful cutting of Fiberglas cloth and mat to the master templates."

By about 1958, the number of eager fiberglass boat buyers equaled those who purchased traditional wooden hulls, and then surpassed them a few years later. *Newsweek* admired a decidedly American entrepreneurial "boat building democracy" created by the glass boom. "While outboard engine making is concentrated in a handful of companies," the magazine observed, "the boats come from hundreds of yards (including backyards), many of them expanding fast." It is estimated that in 1960, at least 400 companies were (or had recently been) producing fiberglass boats. Several of this legion might be considered as peripheral, though, as fine print in their catalogs or in *Motor Boating* identified their craft as "fiberglass covered" wooden boats.

An unsavory sidelight to the entire fiberglass boating revolution became pronounced enough by the early 1960s for *Popular Science* to take notice. "Gyp [or "splash"] artists have moved into America's multibillion-dollar pleasure boat industry," its January 1964 issue warned, "and the magnificent molding qualities of fiberglass have made it possible for them to get away with plastic murder!" The article outlined how a crook could steal any famous hull design simply by borrowing a popular name-brand boat, "turning it upside down in a back-alley garage [and making] a fiberglass mold. Then using the cheaply made mold, he pops out carbon copies of the original. These may look exactly like a famous make of boat," *Popular Science* writer Jim Martenhoff verified, "but are inferior...sometimes with diluted polyester resin...and even unsafe." Even respected yacht maker Owens got splashed with hot water from a court judgment after some former Lone Star men it hired to put pizzazz in the Cutter runabout line Owens had acquired, used some Lone Star products as "mother boat" mold plugs.

Incentives to produce bogus boats diminished in the early 1970s oil "shortages" and resulting economic inflation. Actually, the natural downsizing had begun in

A Starcraft employee inserts wooden support stringers into a bare glass hull, later to be "glassed over," as in the bottom photo. The wood stays good unless and until water seeps through the plastic and triggers rotting.

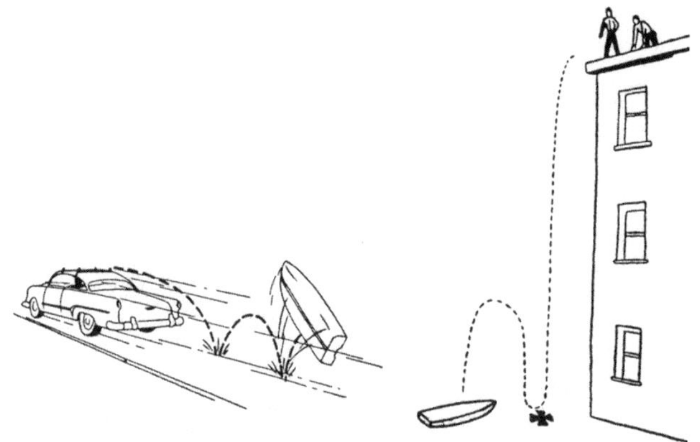

Herter's brew of chrome impregnated fiberglass (fortified with alloy stringers) gave the sporting goods company confidence to toss a 16-footer "from the top of a three story building" and eject another of its hulls from a car speeding down a highway – with no damage." Other glass boat makers pulled similar stunts to draw attention to fiberglass' ruggedness.

the late 1960s as consumer demand cooled, and ironically, the durability of fiberglass diminished the need for boat replacement. Consequently, a reasonably cared-for glass hull soon became a backward compliment to the marine fiberglass industry, with *Motor Boating*'s January 1969 issue showing that (on a nationwide distribution basis) fewer than 20 fiberglass outboard runabout makers would be vying for that genre's pleasure boating marketplace. That reduced number, though, included Bayliner, which then accounted for some 300,000 fiberglass boats sold during the go-go 1980s.

What's to be said of the thousands of fiberglass runabouts produced during the industry's early days and boom years? While at his local transfer station, *Power & Motor Yacht* columnist Richard Thiel incredulously watched a vintage 16-foot fiberglass runabout get dumped in the trash pile by a fellow who matter-of-factly jammed on his pickup truck brakes, causing the boat he was towing to go shooting into the garbage. "Fascinated, [Thiel] walked over to the boat. The seats were torn, the dash was stripped of instruments, the windshield was broken, and it was covered in grime, but [he] could tell she'd once been a pretty nice runabout. As [he] imagined Dad at the helm, Mom beside him, and a couple of kids being towed behind it, [Thiel] couldn't help but feel sad that something that had brought so much joy to its owners had come to such an ignominious end." Many old boat lovers probably feel the same way. And like those prescient plastic boat pioneers of the 1930s, 1940s, and 1950s, some are rescuing retired fiberglass runabouts so that modern generations of pleasure boaters will always have a chance to see how things looked when *glass* was new.

Chapter 5

The Glass Runabout Comes of Age

Fiberglass Boating's Major Players

"World's largest manufacturer of fiberglass boats" — 1960 Glasspar brochure

"America's largest manufacturer of fiberglass boats" — 1958 Lone Star flyer

"One of the Molded Fiber Glass Companies,
world's largest producer of fiberglass reinforced plastic" — 1960 MFG catalog

I believe it is safe to say that several volumes would be needed to contain detailed information on every fiberglass runabout offered by the companies that built these boats between the late 1940s and 1970. This chapter presents a survey of the largest fiberglass outboard pleasure craft makers of the period, and includes remarks on many of the boats for which they are now best remembered. As elsewhere, note that boat length is listed as "length-over-all" (LOA), defined as a straight line from bow tip to transom. In addition to this dimension, it was not uncommon for some makers to quoted "gunwale length," a figure always greater than LOA, because the gunwale follows a sweeping curve from bow to stern. Finally, many boatbuilders had a tendency to round up (and sometimes down) their boat lengths for simplified marketing purposes, hence a 13' 9" hull is likely to be dubbed the Funster 14 Runabout, or some such evocative, albeit inaccurate, mathematical nomenclature.

Aluma Craft (Aluma Glass, Alpex)

The 1958 debut of respected aluminum boat maker Aluma Craft's fiberglass line must have caused some lively marketing meetings in which at least a few officials considered the conventional wisdom of labeling glass hulls, "Aluma" anything. A check of boat trade names then in use shows that logical sister names for Aluma Craft's new offerings — Glass Craft or perhaps Fiber Craft — were then available. Even so, the small boating public's positive perception of Aluma Craft products won the day and the Minneapolis company's plastic output was dubbed Aluma Glass. Arguably, the nomenclature suited the boats' construction, which did use some aluminum (such as an embedded aluminum keel) to strengthen the fiberglass-reinforced plastic hull. Two models were offered, the 14' 9" Merrie Maid and 16½-foot Merrie Lady. Secretly, both runabouts came from a small boatbuilder in Pipestone, Minnesota, that contracted with Aluma Craft. A year later, however, the venerable aluminum boat company was fabricating fiberglass boats of its own. For some reason, it dropped for a time the Aluma Glass identity, and re-branded its glass hulls with the tried and true Aluma Craft name.

"If you bought the brilliant new Tripoli [18-foot fiberglass runabout for $1,595] on the basis of style alone," the 1960 catalog promised, "you'd have quite a surprise in store for you the first time you took her out." She was at the top of the inaugural glass line, featured "v-bottom with round bilges, back-to-back jump seats, flat-floored cockpit with a folding table, between-seat lockers, concealed gas can compartment, and [lots of] polished aluminum castings."

Though there was no 90-horse production outboard in 1960, the Tripoli was ready for one. The 16-foot Tangier could handle a Merc 800, 80-hp motor, in part due to its "stable-matic chines" designed by Erich Swenson. Catalog copywriters also gave a design nod (for aesthetics) to Chicago-based consultants Jack Morgan & Associates.

Dubbed, in the innocent closing days of the 1950s, the Gay Mate was the company's 15' 4" runabout offering possessing the attractive aft-decking and the exotic color combo choices of her sisters. These included two-toned "crimson lake" with "oyster white" upholstery, "sumac red," "tawny brown", and "peacock blue." The Gay Mate hull was also offered as the Skisher with "jump seats facing aft and set behind the walk-through forward seats [creating] a big, open flat-floored cockpit." Aluma Craft promoted this version for water-skiing families. Both boats were rated at 65 hp.

The smallest member of the 1960 glass lineup was the 14-foot Torino, a member of the company's mid-priced "Family Cottage Fleet" as compared to the higher-end "Yacht Club Fleet." Even at $749, though, this now generic-looking (with somewhat harder lines than the rest) family runabout cost over $150 more than the comparable aluminum Model FDR. In 1960, that might represent a couple of weeks' pay.

New for 1961, were the beefy 16' 4" Monaco and the ski-friendly 15' 4" Bali with its wisp of tail fin in the latter. But Aluma Craft's relatively late entry into fiberglass helped it avoid exaggerated space age and automotive designs that began being considered as passé in the early 1960s.

By 1964, Aluma Craft's then-parent Alpex Corporation passed a name change resolution for its fiberglass offerings. Separate brochures were now distributed for these newly christened Alpex fiberglass boats. Mid-decade models included the beamy 17' 4" Sea Aira, the sporty 15' 2" Alora Sportster ("Tailor-made for the jet set!") fitted with a ski tow bar forward of the stern light staff, and a Bali re-issue. Only Bali and the Sea Aira were still around as per a check of the 1967 Alpex outboard runabout roster, although Alora returned to the following year's line.

The Alpex nameplate was gone by 1970, as Aluma Craft Marine Products Corporation then controlled the company. That meant that Bali (then sporting, as one option, a Jade Green deck with a white hull and artichoke-colored upholstery) and Sea Aira (also in inboard/outboard form) once more carried the Aluma Craft logo. Outboard incarnations of the trihedral-hulled Jamaica came in 18' 5" and 16' 3½" lengths. Aluma Craft buffs note that 1970 marks the firm's foray into mobile housing, a natural product extension for an aluminum-oriented organization. Aluma Craft brochures indicated that company officials were "constantly looking for ways to be of service to the American Public in the field of recreation and shelter." The Tourite Mobilhome subsidiary was a result of that expansion, though apparently short-lived, as the 1971 boating catalog didn't mention it.

The 1971 catalog featured the plushly appointed 18-foot X-Press 180 and 17' 4" Sea Aira 170. Both were traditional vee-bottom craft but the trihedral offerings M-Press (18 feet), and Jamaica (16' 3") were also offered. Tradition was on the minds of Aluma Craft officials at that juncture when the firm downsized, moved to St. Peter, Minnesota, and decided to return to its roots of concentrating only on aluminum boats.

Aristo-Craft

Best known by classic outboard runabout buffs for the 12-, 13-, and 14-foot (Sea Flash, Torpedo, et al.) mahogany plywood speedsters, Aristo-Craft departed from those boats' sports car–like theme with the introduction of fiberglass hulls in 1959. Company founder Claude Turner didn't altogether abandon Detroit influences when designing his firm's debut glass hull, as it was based on Ford's 1959 Thunderbird, a stylish four-seat vehicle that had likewise veered from the original two-seat T-Bird roots. Turner wanted his new boat to be roomy enough for growing baby boomer families, while looking modern.

Turner's Atlanta Boats Works was caught short when *Motor Boating* sought information on the Georgia company's new offerings. "Aristo-Craft enters the fiberglass field," reported the January 1959 Show Issue "with a boat billed as *the most versatile we've* [Aristo-Craft] *ever built.*" But "specifications were unavailable at press time." For the 1960 edition, however, Altanta Boat Works was ready with an exotic picture of one of its 17-foot fiberglass Funliners. The runabout was shown alongside a Chinese junk. The shot, complete with a weary-looking Asian crew and their curious dog, successfully telegraphed a striking contrast between old boating ways and new.

"Aristo-Craft's Funliner hulls," the maker noted, "come fully cured and with maximum strength from electrically heated molds." The Funliner was designed for family outings. Styling included a bit of interesting tail fins, but early on, the model's biggest identifier was its permanent top, a decided mom and dad pleaser that protected against the elements. Upholstered seating for six under the canopy, as well as an aft cockpit "roomy enough to mount a fishing chair or set up a picnic table" made the Funliner a hit among day-cruising aficionados. In terms of niche, standardization, and production efficiency, Turner got a lot of mileage out of the original Funliner design, as the boat was available through 1967.

By 1963, Aristo-Craft was showing Funliners without its top. The firm's *Motor Boating* copy that January focused on the "double-molded hull and forward deck hatch as standard equipment. The hull [was] formed by fusing two hulls together under high pressure…and bonded over truss type stringers. Sleeper seats and a wider decking hatch" were also features of that era's Funliner. Back in promotional blurbs, the 1964 Show Issue was the Funliner's "fiberglass permanent top," which again distinguished the Funliner from other outboard-powered glass models.

The stern drive or inboard/outboard versions of the Funliner remain the models that most vintage boaters remember. Around 1961, they received center stage treatment in West Bend's advertising (shared with Aristo-Craft publicity folks) for the West Bend Shark-O-Matic inboard/outboard unit. Catalog shots were often snapped in front of Turner's home on a small lake he owned. For some photographic sessions, shapely

Two views of Aristo Craft Funliner 17 hardtop runabouts.

company secretaries were invited to bring a swimsuit and double as models.

By 1966, Funliner was joined by an exclusively inboard/outboard-powered sister, the 8-Teen. A slightly longer model 9-Teen followed. These 18- and 19-footers were MerCruiser-driven and came with either a stationary or sliding hardtop, the aft end of which was typically slanted inward like the rear retractable window on some 1959 Mercury cars. After another respectably long run for what was essentially a one- or two-model line, new Aristo-Crafts became a less common sight during the 1970s. Production ceased by decade's end. According to Jeffrey Beard's 1997 *Classic Boating* article, Aristo-Craft then accepted private contracts for small fiberglass hulls, most notably "the stubby little outboard-powered boats used on the lakes at Disney World."

Bayliner

Outside J. Orin Edson's gas station–size boat and motor shop was a crowd of trailed hulls and a pram or two standing on their transoms. Typically, several hand-lettered sandwich signs and a string of colorful pennants helped the boats attract the attention of mid-1950s motorists who might have otherwise passed the Seattle establishment. By 1965, sales at his Advance Outboard Marine were sufficiently robust for Edson to acquire the fledging Bayliner fiberglass boat company, which primarily consisted of a neat trade name and two fiberglass boat molds. Admittedly this original Bayliner outfit was indeed tiny, as it never appeared in *The Boating Industry* magazine's list of stock boatbuilders. The July 1991 *Trailer Boats* issue reports the entrepreneur immediately trucked the molds to Arlington, Washington, where he "set up [a revamped Bayliner operation] under the roofs of several World War II aircraft hangers and sold the [resulting] boats in his store."

Working under the radar as only a small businessperson could, Edson practiced a production efficiency and frugality that allowed him to quietly expand Bayliner through other sales outlets. By 1980, he sold his retail marine business in order to focus upon keeping Bayliner floating along in the era's sinking economy. Though the marque has been prolific, it was the 1982 Capri bow rider (a 19-footer, along with various-sized incarnations) that truly put Bayliner on plane. Brunswick Corporation bought out Edson in 1987. Several years later Bayliner became the boating industry's biggest manufacturer, and had come a long way from that little marine store on Aurora Highway.

Boston Whaler

Brass from this cornerstone fiberglass boat maker like to tell the story about the Boston Whaler that bobbed to the surface after being aboard a ship that had just sunk. The sight made surviving crew shout for joy as they climbed into the little outboard hull and waited for rescue. Some of the best free publicity in fiberglass boating came along in 1961 when *Life* magazine pictured an expressionless businessman sitting calmly in a Boston Whaler floating in a harbor while the craft was being sawed in two!

The businessman was Richard Fisher, who waited patiently while his boat was halved. Three years earlier, he'd unveiled the first of what would be decades of 13'

Since the early 1960s, many a waterside youth viewed this ubiquitous Boston Whaler publicity shot as the quintessential definition of summer "independence." With a dependable 10- to 40-horse outboard, a youngster and his Whaler could seemingly do most anything nautical.

3" Boston Whalers. Fisher told author Dan Spurr that he had experimented with making a small boat from balsa wood, but recognized that, while light and strong, balsa would quickly succumb to dents. After trying again by covering Styrofoam with epoxy, Fisher felt as if he were on the right track. Hoping to create a unique small sailboat, he sandwiched urethane foam between fiberglass "bread." It was the famed naval architect Ray Hunt who suggested that an outboard boat would be a better seller — and worked up plans based on a modified Hickman Sea Sled.

"Constructed like no other," states a 1980s-era Whaler catalog. "Most fiberglass boats are built with a single skin, which before it is stiffened with stringers, has all the strength and rigidity of a shoebox with the lid off. [Boston Whaler] starts with two fiberglass skins, which form the inside and outside of the hull. Then, before the fiberglass has a chance to cure, [Boston Whaler technicians] pour a buoyant foam between the layers, creating enough heat and pressure to fuse the two materials into a single unbreakable hull."

Fisher's original 13-foot boat remains the company's most recognizable. More appropriate to our classic outboard runabout theme, the Sports version, with center-side steering station, would still go nicely today pushed by a late 1950s Johnson or Evinrude 35. Then, too, an automatic transmission-equipped red Mercury Mark 28A would contrast nicely with the shiny white hull. Also noteworthy is Boston Whaler's 16' 7" series, namely the basic Currituck and the deluxe, "church pew"–equipped Nauset with a wooden console and windshield framing.

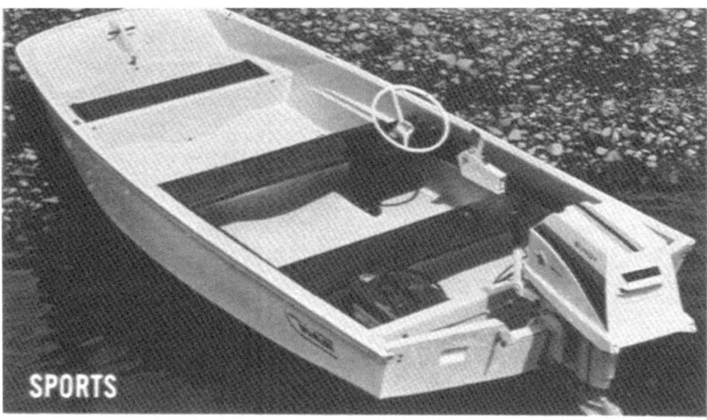

Interior of stock-in-trade 13' 3" Boston Whaler Sports is admittedly Spartan, but remarkable low maintenance was its reward. Motor is uncommon Italian Bundy, briefly imported to the US.

When seeking a name for his then unusual looking outboard runabout, Fisher came up with "Boston Whaler," though he knew that Beantown had never been very connected to those in the 19th-century whaling industry. It was simply something that sounded solidly American and seaworthy. He sold Boston Whaler in 1969 after turning it into a household name.

The Nauset featured a richly finished wooden podium control station/windshield frame/bench seat, and was long the mainstay of Boston Whaler's 16' 7" offerings.

Crestliner

Production of this Minnesota boatbuilder's inaugural fiberglass fleet was interrupted by an early 1958 labor strike. Results of "six years of exhaustive research, engineering, testing and developing the exclusive new techniques behind the new Crestliner fiberglass boats," were put on hold at the Little Falls plant until the wage dispute was settled in mid-February. That fence mended, production of 17-foot sliding hardtop Iroquois and convertible Comanche resumed.

Catalog copy seemed to reflect the union contract, as it promised "every lay-up crew is trained to work as a team and to strive for uniform product quality while maintaining production schedules. Inspectors, however, completely divorced from production and production schedules, must personally inspect and approve each of the nine stages of hull construction. Any variation, any flaw, however minute, in any one of the nine stages, forces rejection of the hull."

Compartments in the hull were built as "open and completely ventilated to prevent moisture condensation that results when fiberglass is formed into sealed, unventilated compartments." Publicity pledged, "Crestliner fiberglass hulls never become waterlogged!" Though flooring was plywood, the company's advertising stressed, "floor beams, keel, rubstrakes and spray rail are integral with the hull, and are all fiberglass." With a "snowshoe white" hull, a deck in "Crestliner red" or "crown yellow," and stern curtains of red plaid, either high-sided 17-footer made for a safe, smooth-riding family runabout — though dubbed "cruisers" in proprietary literature. A distinguishing feature on these boats was the forward "converti-seat, developed by Crestliner designers. Upholstered in rich black and white vinyl plastic, trimmed with silver piping. Both backs [were] removable and may be reversed and are used to build up [a] bunk under [the] forward deck."

By 1960, Crestliner glass boats were also being built in a Waterloo, Ontario, facility. A pair of sister plants had been established in Virginia and Arkansas, though the U.S. fiberglass line was coming from the Minnesota factory. To expand the fleet, two runabouts were added, the 14-foot Arabian and Imperial Arabian, both with balsa-cored bottoms) and the 16-foot Chieftain and Imperial Chieftain, with teakwood vinyl flooring. The 17-footers were replaced by the Imperial Del Rio "with rigid floor beams." The 1960 flyer also noted that in addition to the maker's glass line, and bread and butter aluminum craft, it offered some models in "Royalite Safety Float." This resilient substance from the U.S. Rubber Company was later found to be too rubbery to stay specifically shaped when subjected to hot, sunny summers.

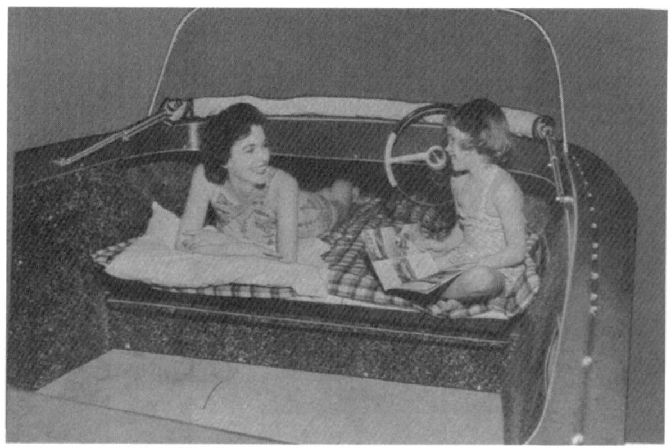

Even if somewhat of a nuisance to configure, convertible seating/sleeper beds sold a lot of mid- to large-size runabouts (such as Crestliner's Iroquois 17), as they promised memorable family camping cruises to exotic ports of call – like the craggy island several miles up the lake.

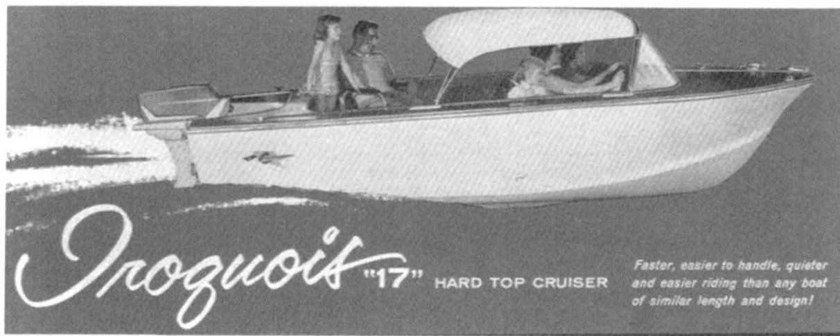

A hardtop gave the Iroquois 17 class and made her Crestliner's 1958 fiberglass flagship.

Holding company Bigelow-Sanford acquired Crestliner in 1960 and racked up a four-year tenure before selling it to MFG's parent, Molded Fiberglass Body Company. This resulted in shifting the fiberglass operation to Crestliner's Strasburg, Virginia, venue. Catalogs for 1964 footnoted a Como, Italy, licensee as producing Crestliners through a licensing deal. Among the "Fairlap Fiberglass" (molded-in lapstrake) and traditional smooth-sided glass hulls of this period was the 14-foot Ski Bird, a hard-chined, swoop-gunwale with a Jeep-style flat "fold-down windscreen." This G-3 wannabee had a "lockable tunnel for concealed ski storage, central mounted controls, reversible observer's bucket seat, handy towing mast, rakish grey canvas sun cover, and vinyl-covered side storage area." Still, this "high style beauty designed for power performance with sports car features," was probably never mistaken for the hot Glasspar that Crestliner's designers hoped to imitate. Today, however, a Ski Bird would make for a nice example of mid-1960s glass if found today in any of color options — "Bahama Blue," "Sunset Red," "Dolphin Mist," "Turquoise," or "Mist Grey."

Another small Crestliner worthy of mention is the 13-foot Mustang, introduced around the time that Ford was readying the release of its soon-to-be famous pony car. Crestliner's Mustang and a 20- to 40-horse outboard (a budget-priced, late-model West Bend 35 from some reputable dealer's reliable used motor rack would have been ideal) was aimed at the same young consumer base that Ford eyed. A stripped-down version, the Mustang Special, was added to the catalog for 1966. Admittedly, it served as a footnote to more deluxe glass Crestliners such as the molded lapstrake-hulled, blunt-decked 14' 7" Marauder; the smooth-sided 14' 9" Chieftain; the 16' 4" Del Rio smooth-hull; and the 17' 7" lapstrake Raider.

In 1969, near the end of MFG's ownership, Crestliner fiberglass designers responded to the bow rider–utility trend in family boating. Crestliners offered the proprietary "stabilized vee-wing hull, a deep-vee with stabilizing sponsons." This version of the trihedral was present in the 14-foot Muskie and the 17-foot Tiger Muskie, both so labeled to attract the angling market as well as family water ski buffs.

The brand was picked up in 1970 by the marine arm of North American Rockwell Corporation, which sold it just two years later to American Machine and Foundry (AMF). Boats from the 1973 to 1980 era were sometimes labeled "AMF-Crestliner." The name has since been owned by several successors to AMF's Little Falls boat-manufacturing enterprise. By 1990, Crestliner's ownership, which also possessed the nearby Larson plant from which the Crestliner lineage can be traced, had decided to discontinue fiberglass hulls and concentrate on aluminum. Even so, classic plastic enthusiasts agree that Crestliner fiberglass craft fabricated "with stringers, not built of narrow wood egg crate subassemblies, but made of several layers of fiberglass cured integrally to the hull," can provide for a nice restoration today.

Chrysler

Chrysler Corporation entered the marine field in 1965 with the purchase of Lone Star. As a transition measure, the venture was (for 1966) temporarily called "Lone Star boats from the Chrysler Boat Corporation" or Chrysler/ Lone Star. Along with an inherited lineup of Lone Star aluminum hulls, and a pair of newly concocted glass daysailers, were the 1966 fiberglass outboard runabouts in 13' 8"-, 14-, 15' 5"-, 15' 11"-, 16 '4"-, 18-, and 19-foot lengths. A series of stern-drive hulls with MerCruiser (or in a few cases, Chrysler power) also made the roster, though it makes sense to assume that Chrysler was most interested in pairing its boats with proprietary mills either from its auto plants or from West Bend, which it had also acquired. The West Bend logo was soon dumped in favor of Chrysler outboard labeling.

Safety represented a major theme in the 1967 Chrysler Boats catalog. "Nearly every fiberglass runabout contains flotation" the copy pointed out. "But the mere fact that a boat has flotation is virtually meaningless. Flotation can consist of a few Styrofoam blocks tucked under the floor. Or it can go to the other extreme, Chrysler Foam-Pac, a thoroughly engineered and integrated part of the hull structure. In every Chrysler runabout, the space between the floor and the hull is completely filled with specially formulated polyurethane foam. Poured in a liquid state, the foam expands and bonds to all surfaces. It sets up into a rigid structural core and produces a…sound absorption… 'sandwich' many times stronger than [the] strength of its individual layers."

With all the talk about expanding foam, several boat model designations referred to a hull's square footage, as opposed to its length — the latter always looking larger.

These figures were often joined to names borrowed from the parent company's sporty Mopar autos. For example, one of Chrysler's smaller 1967 outboard runabouts was the 14-foot Charger 118, a tribute to the then wildly popular Dodge Charger "muscle" car and 118 cubic feet of hull space. The Charger also came in 15- and 16-foot versions.

A bit smaller and basic were the 13' 8" Cadet and the 14' 9" Flamingo. A 15' 5" model, a "fun favorite at a popular price designed for sophisticated fun-seekers" was yet another runabout introduced during this period that bore the name Mustang. The Courier 229 (cubic feet) was the line's 17-foot bow rider. The Chesapeake was a rugged 18-foot lapstrake-style runabout aimed at handling Chrysler's high-profit 100+ hp outboards. Most of the bigger models were typically touted as stern-drive craft, with small print noting they could be had in an outboard format.

Chrysler's traditional vee-bottom (dubbed "Chrysler Hydro-Vee") glass runabouts occupied the opening pages of 1970 brochures, although a tri-hull graced the cover. Copy indicated that the company's proven Vee style had been patented by Chrysler to "combine safe and seaworthy deep-V design with the speed and high lift of [a] hydroplane hull…for a softer, smoother, speedier ride." This bottom design was used on the Charger series, the 17-foot Courier 229, and the 15-foot open bow rider (with center steering station) Commando 151. The entry-level 13' 7" Cadet had a generic vee-bottom that could be traced directly to 1950s Lone Star lineage.

By 1970, it was clear that Chrysler was responding to industry trends toward cathedral or tri-hulls. To that end, it offered the 16' 2" Fury and (bow rider) Sport Fury; the 14' 1" bow rider Sport Satellite, the standard decked Valiant, and the Boston Whaler-ish Sport Valiant (both also 14 1"). Mopar car enthusiasts will spot the borrowed model names.

By 1975, Chrysler was clearly classifying its outboard craft by hull type: 1) deep-vee, 2) the patented Hydro-Vee (with modest but effective side sponsons), and 3) cathedral or gull-wing tri-hull. Three outboard versions at the top of the line deep-vee Conqueror series ranged from 15' 10" to 17' 3" with cigarette boat styling and a short wraparound windshield. The smallest Conqueror is arguably one of the 1970s' most beautiful runabouts, especially when color matched to its companion Chrysler 105-hp kicker. Hydro-Vee models were all continued from previous designs. Among the new offerings in Chrysler cathedrals were 16- and 18-foot editions of the center steering–stationed Funster, and the 18-foot Sport Crown Bowrider — the "flagship of the cathedral fleet."

Chrysler models were always nicely photographed

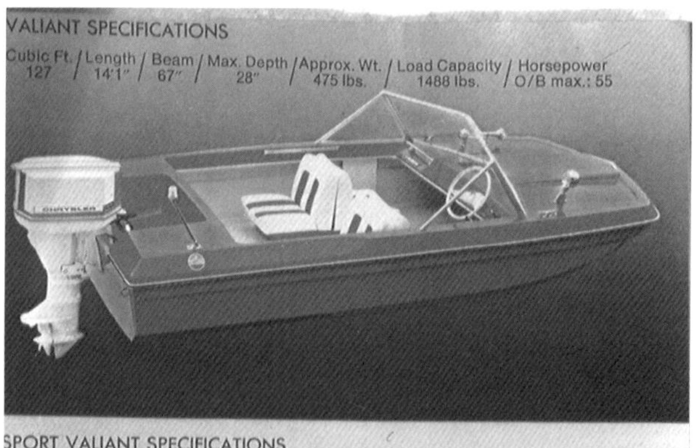

Valiant and Sport Valiant borrowed well-known model names from Chrysler's automotive line. Note the small, simple side-center steering table/deck on 14' 1' Sport Valiant. Both boats could take up to 55-hp, propelling especially the latter craft at a good clip.

in the brochures, and rear covers sometimes featured color samples for hull, deck, striping gel coats, and interior vinyl trim. By about 1970, nearly 30 such choices were offered. It may be that this presentation savvy was linked to Chrysler's seasoned automotive promotional experience. And just like every full-line car brochure saved a smidgen of space for its low-end economy model, Chrysler Marine literature could be counted upon to devote a few inches to the otherwise obsolete Cadet. "Drive a bargain!" the copy read. "Drive a sharp, 13' 6" Cadet with quick-planing semi-vee hull design." The diminutive runabout was available in either standard 15-inch or long-shaft 20-inch transoms. Any version of the Cadet series would make for a great example of a basic, lightweight outboard runabout with a notable history.

Economic woes during the early 1980s prompted Chrysler to jettison anything not central to the firm's automobile business, so Chrysler Marine was reluctantly tossed overboard to eager Bayliner. Today, the brand certainly merits attention as a quality boat representative of its era.

Crosby Aeromarine (Hydrodyne)

Abner "Ab" Crosby made his mark in the 1950s pleasure boating world by offering craft built with two materials then typically considered as flimsy — balsa wood and plastic. Baltek, the New Jersey supplier of balsa, a favorite wood of model airplane makers, caught Crosby's attention when he was seeking something light to stiffen a "plastic" boat he was planning. According to Spurr, "the first boat builder to use Baltek balsa was Crosby, [who] began using it in 1951 in a line of runabouts." The wood served as a core sandwiched between two layers of fiberglass-reinforced plastic. Mahogany was utilized for stringers. Publicity touted the "hull and glass decks [being] constructed with Crosby's unique and closely guarded method of combining wood and fiberglass for maximum strength, rigidity and flotation [and identified their company as] one of the oldest and largest manufacturers of fiberglass boats."

Through the 1957 model year, glass hulls from Crosby Aeromarine (a division of Midwestern Industries Corporation of Grabill, Indiana) wore nicely finished wooden topsides. Most models looked pleasantly generic, the kind of design a kid would depict if asked to draw a motorboat. The only nod to space age/automotive late-1950s excess was Crosby's 1958–59 Sweptfin, a two-place, sports car–like 14 footer with tail fins and a sculptured hood scoop. Brochure copy called Sweptfin the firm's "style leader with the years-ahead design and performance of advanced engineering. Rakish, custom appointments for those who prefer the ultimate in fin boats." This low-production craft is considered to be the rarest, most desirable example of the marque. Because the Sweptfin was airbrushed onto the (1958) Crosby catalog cover, there was some

speculation — before one eventually surfaced — that this model never got off of the drawing board.

More common members of the 1958 Crosby line included the 19-foot Baycomber, an indestructible-looking ski barge runabout with a motor bracket molded behind the transom. Crosby's 16-footers were the Sports Runabout available with or without a hardtop and the Capri — "the ideal boat for skiing or family pleasure, and holder of the 1,000-mile-plus Mississippi River record [run from] New Orleans to St. Louis." Both could be had with fiberglass or wooden decking. Similar wood or glass deck options applied to the 14-foot offerings in the Hydrodyne series.

After selling his first boat company to conglomerate Archer-Daniels-Midland around 1958, Crosby was made an executive of ADM's marine endeavor. He soon got into a dispute with a corporate cost cutter who approved making the newly named "Golden Fleet" boats with fewer layers of fiberglass. Shortly thereafter, Ab called in his ADM resignation and started a new firm that he named Hydrodyne. Somewhere around this time, ADM management contracted with Howard Ketcham, designer of the then-novel color telephones, to develop alluring color schemes for the 1960 Crosby fleet.

Mercury outboard's Carl Kiekhaefer had taken a liking to the Crosby designs. Kiekhaefer respected Ab's penchant for sturdy transoms and that is why late 1950s Merc brochures often featured Crosby's runabouts being pushed by a pair of Mercury four-cylinder mills or by a "tower of power" Merc six (cylinder) in-line motor.

By 1961, Ab's Hydrodyne line, which was being produced by Midwestern Industries in Harlan, Indiana, included a series of 16-, 17-, and 19-foot boats meant for pairs of big outboards, or inboard/outboard operation. A quality reputation preceded Hydrodyne so that around 1963, most of the Mercury astronauts chose Ab's new brand for their pleasure boating endeavors. One source indicates that in the fall of 1963, Jacqueline Kennedy had ordered a Hydrodyne as a gift to her husband for use the following summer on Cape Cod. According to annual November entries in *The Boating Industry* magazine, Hydrodyne (often listed as Midwestern) left the scene sometime in 1967.

Meanwhile, in 1963, the successor to the original Crosby Aeromarine operation relocated to Donaldson, Georgia. For that model year, along with the 17-foot Fish N Ski double-hulled glass family boat, this incarnation introduced "the first departure from its standard runabout class, a 15-foot fiberglass Sea Sled." Arguably, the firm had taken notice of Boston Whaler's success and hoped to give it some direct competition in a

Utility and full runabout versions of Crosby's 14-foot Hydrodyne model. Company founder, Ab Crosby would reuse the Hydrodyne name in his subsequent line of fiberglass boats.

slightly larger size. "A double bottom and foam flotation … and unsinkable" became the company mantra as it tried positioning the boat alongside Boston Whaler in consumers' minds. Color combinations were heavily promoted for the line.

Redesign was the key word for Crosby Aeromarine's 1964 fleet. A 14-foot Sea Sled for $395 occupied the group's entry-level position. Several traditional runabouts (up to 19 feet) rounded out the outboard-powered products. It's doubtful that much of this planned output ever got to marine dealers, because during 1964, Crosby Aeromarine suddenly downsized and departed to facilities at the municipal airport in Marianna, Florida. A January 1965 *Motor Boating* entry shows that the 14-foot Sea Sled (sometimes noted as "Sports Sled" 14' 11" with a 5' 1" beam) was all that this final version of the company offered that year. For 1967, the boat was called a 15-foot V-Sled. It was labeled the "unsinkable pleasure island…" The 14-foot V Sled came out the following year. Crosby finished out the 1960s with what were advertised as "new 14' 3" and 16' 2" fiberglass utility hulls built in three [seating and steering option] versions." I recall a high school classmate and fellow boating enthusiast seeing one of these craft troll by his dock. "There goes another fake Whaler," he noted. An early entry in the "bulletproof fiberglass sea sled genre," and certainly of decent quality, the post–Ab Crosby edition of Crosby Aeromarine's best-known model often seemed to be an also-ran in the soon-crowded tri-hull "sport boat" arena.

Evinrude

In the mid-1950s, Evinrude hired industrial designer Brooks Stevens to create several futuristic runabouts. These dramatic boats included a round "flying saucer" with video instrument panel and passenger seating "in the round" under a patio-type umbrella. It was powered by two outboards, mounted inboard beneath clear plastic domes. More traditional was the Lark runabout, a two-place, bucket seat–equipped "sports car of the waterways," designed to be coordinated with the colorful 1956 30-horse Evinrude Lark.

The $11,000 space-age, dramatically finned Lark made the rounds at major boat shows and a limited quantity were built under Evinrude license by the Cadillac Marine & Boat Company. These boats had a glass superstructure, but a plywood hull and were commercially available in 1957 and 1958 as the Cadillac Sea Lark. Stevens envisioned that if mass produced, his concept craft would be molded in fiberglass.

By the spring of 1961, Evinrude's parent, Outboard Marine Corporation (OMC), revealed it would begin building fiberglass boats for sale the following model year in expanded facilities on Johnson's Waukegan, Illinois, campus. These OMC-branded craft were approximately 17 feet long, but only peripheral to our study because they were stern-drive or inboard/outboard-powered. The company's first outboard fiberglass hulls would wear the Evinrude name and hit showrooms as the 1964 motors were delivered to dealers.

The rollout catalog cover noted that the "new breed" of boats' was intended simply "to match the most efficient outboard motors ever built." In addition to inboard/outboard or stern-drive versions, two 16-foot outboard models were offered, the Sweet-16 (runabout with full deck), and the Sport-16 (sport

Evinrude's gullwing hull in a 16-foot size was introduced in 1964 to sell the company's outboard engines in a boat/motor/trailer package. Despite the effort and then-revolutionary tri-hull format, the boats and marketing plan never really got up on plane.

style in a short front deck and a walk-through steering deck–forward cockpit format). Along with red accents, molded-in color options included Evinrude blue and white or Evinrude seal gray and white. Construction was described as "high-strength fiber glass reinforced plastic hull permanently bonded to a one-piece molded deck." The boats were "built of both woven fiber glass and chopped fiber glass to provide significantly greater strength than chopped fiber glass alone."

Most of the debut hype centered on the boats' "gull-wing hydraulic lift design." Sales literature touted that when confronting a wave, Evinrude hulls "slice through clean. Comes down to meet the water like you're riding on hydraulic shocks. And you are. The gull-wing design provides hydraulic lift. It harnesses the water's energy. Rather than throwing water up and away, the hull rides the spray. The deep-V keel throws water into the gull-wing troughs. It's deflected downward by the outrigger keels. The bigger the waves, the greater the shock absorbing action." Recollections from Evinrude boat owners often tell another story, one with an episode or two of some pretty rough going in choppy water.

While a matched Evinrude boat, motor, and trailer made for a visually attractive combo, the company's motor catalogs continued showing Evinrude outboards on other company's hulls, with Evinrude proprietary craft either sent to the back pages or being separately cataloged. This may have been in deference to Evinrude dealers who also sold other makers' craft and to those boat manufacturers that might easily decide to strike OMC kickers from their boat catalog pictures.

The 1966 brochure — *'66 Evinrude Motors, Boats, Trailers, Skeeters* (snowmobiles) — featured only a partial view of an Evinrude boat and motor on the cover, and highlighted just the stern-drive versions later. Hardly noticed missing from this publicity piece were the 14-foot outboard runabouts, the Ski Lark-14 and the Sport-14 that came and went in 1965. Outboard-powered models were unceremoniously dropped by the 1967 boating season. For 1968, a 16-foot inboard/outboard-driven OMC sister to the Evinrude hull was revamped with a deeper center vee in an attempt to smooth out and speed up performance in bumpy water.

Understandably, sticklers might bristle at the Evinrude (or Johnson) listing in the "major builders" chapter, as production was not nearly as robust as output from the likes of Lone Star, Larson, or Glasspar. In fact, spotting a vintage Evinrude outboard hull today is somewhat of a rare treat for most classic boating buffs. Chances are it ended up uncovered, out in the weather, and incongruently mated to some West Bend or Merc. Even so, the boats represent an interesting testament to a leading marine firm offering too little, too soon, and for too short of a run. In the mid-1960s, probably thought of as a funny looking boat, Evinrude's gull wings were ahead of the wave that would wash thousands of quasi-tri-hulls onto the pleasure boating scene just a few seasons later.

Glasspar

"I think it's from one of those early, flash-in-the-pan fiberglass companies," a 30-something antique boat museum auction attendee said of a neglected Glasspar Tacoma 100 runabout resting cockeyed on some boards. Boy, did that assessment make me feel old! I've still got the 1963 Glasspar brochure that was tacked to my bedroom wall until I headed off to college and, as I pointed out to my new-found acquaintance, Glasspar's boats influenced dozens of other boatbuilders and millions of outboarders. In fact, by 1960, the Glasspar fleet served as the very definition of fiberglass pleasure craft fabrication success.

According to a survey of *The Boating Industry*'s Stock Boatbuilders list, the Glasspar Company of 2232 Harbor Boulevard in Costa Mesa, California (just down the road from Wizard Boat's 2075 Harbour Blvd.

Though from the land of Hollywood glitz, Glasspar wasn't prone to incorporate design crazes into its hulls, as this sensible, Midwestern looking, 16-foot Avalon for 1960 quietly demonstrates.

venue), first shows up as having offered outboard utility hulls in 1951. *Motor Boating*'s January 1953 roster pegs the company's introduction of outboard cruisers, utility, and racing craft as a 1952 event.

Glasspar's founder was William Tritt, a Southern California native who, during the closing days of World War II, built a small catamaran sailboat in his off hours while employed in the production planning department of Douglas Aircraft. The catamaran project was followed shortly by Tritt's use of fiberglass while desperately trying to revitalize an old dry-rotted schooner slated for the scrap heap. The effort was successful enough for Tritt to be hired by others to perform a similar miracle on their boats. By 1949, Tritt coined the name Glasspar to denote his first product — fiberglass spars followed by a good performing but commercially unsuccessful 22-foot fiberglass daysailer.

In a roundabout way, it was Sears & Roebuck that moved Glasspar into powerboating. In 1951, Tritt and a trio of small investors acquired a modest Sears contract from an even smaller pioneer fiberglass boat maker, Bob Lyons. With the deal, Lyons threw in a couple of female molds for his Sea Lion 14-foot and 15-foot outboard runabouts, as well as instructions detailing how to best apply an attractive gel coat on the mold's inner surface. Until about 1954, Glasspar-built runabouts were marketed by Sears & Roebuck under its Elgin brand. The experience provided Tritt's outfit with cash and the confidence to set up his own dealer network in the early 1950s aimed at selling Glasspar-branded outboard hulls.

Not all of America's newly numbered Interstate Highway System was operational in the mid-to-late 1950s, making the transport of boats to showrooms a big expense. Glastron's 1975 retrospective credits competitor Glasspar with indirectly helping it solve that cost problem. "Glasspar, then the largest manufacturer of fiberglass boats, had started a program of using satellite plants to reduce freight costs." Besides the main Santa Ana plant, Glasspar's divisions included facilities in Nashville, Tennessee; Colonial Heights and Petersburg, Virginia; Sherman, Texas; Olympia, Washington; and a Michigan distribution center. It's been estimated that by the close of the 1950s, Glasspar was fabricating some 10,000 boats annually. According to Dan Spurr, that was equal to nearly "20 percent of all fiberglass boats sold in the US."

Tritt never followed the automotive fin mania that many of his competitors adopted for their boats. Consequently, a well-preserved, mid-1950s Glasspar runabout still looked contemporary 10 years later when a Glass Slipper or Lone Star Meteor appeared hopelessly out of date. Indicative of Glasspar's 1960 runabout fleet are decidedly family-friendly (colorful, nicely upholstered, sturdy, and with generous freeboard) models such as the entry-level 14-foot ($595) Lido; the 14-foot Marathon; the 16-foot Citation (featuring individual front seating and four rear jump seats); and the 17-foot Seafair, available in cabin (Sedan), open (Sunliner), and Phaeton (retractable hardtop) versions.

The G-3 Skiboat — "the agile fiber glass speedboat designed especially for water skiing" — was also offered. This model was named for a fiberglass-bodied sports car Tritt had built in limited numbers. According to the catalog, the 13' 7" $695 G-3 had "jet-like get up and go

[for] speeds in excess of 50 mph in safety and comfort. Two sets of skis fit neatly into the hull — plenty of room for a party of four." The boat had vinyl-upholstered seats, padded instrument panel trim, ski towing hardware, and a self-bailing motor well. This cornerstone Glasspar radiated a sense of "California fun." In fact, each of the Tritt-designed boats — in color options like "reef blue," white, "titan red," "surf green," "smuggler's gold," or "jet black" — possessed a clean, West Coast feel aimed at conquering the water.

In a 1960 move that is retrospectively all wet, the board of directors that Glasspar acquired around 1955 after opting for a public offering of its stock, unceremoniously dismissed Tritt while he was on vacation. Without him, Glasspar didn't introduce many new models. The 1963 catalog runabout offerings, for example, are similar to those in the 1960 brochure, save for a couple of modest dimension changes and a better appointed edition of the Tacoma called the Avalon. A bigger G-3, dubbed Super-G, appeared in 1964.

Because few of Glasspar's designs changed perceptibly and new models — such as the 18' 7" V-175 for 1966 — looked a lot like modestly changed versions of something from several years back, the line lost a competitive edge. Tired of having lost money (largely due to hefty production costs) for several model years, Glasspar brass essentially leased the company to the Larson boat organization of Minnesota in the middle of the 1966 boating season. By the end of that year,

There are some classic glass enthusiasts who just collect Glasspar G-3 Skiboats. Here's a pretty 1960 model that explains why.

At 15' 10", Glasspar's 1963 Tacoma 200 offered boaters a station wagon's worth of room aft of the basic front seating. No doubt the cargo space could quickly accommodate everything from water skis and fishing tackle to folding lounge chairs and family-size picnic coolers.

Larson bought the operation. Larson officials wanted to be associated with the California brand's top-drawer reputation and coveted its widespread manufacturing sites. Early on, most of the changes that Larson made were in producing the boats more cost efficiently. Within a few years, though, there was some crossover of Larson-like designs wearing the Glasspar name.

At the close of the 1960s, the Glasspar lineup included models of from 14 to 18 feet, among them some sport utility runabouts with walk-through windshields that seem out of the brand's mainstream. Still, the market had shifted toward the bow rider direction. Also in the 1969 flyer were several returning deep-vee hulls and modified-vee hulls. Through 1967, the latter category still featured Tritt's classic G-3. Because of a desire to build the legendary outboard ski boat less expensively, Larson reprised it in an easier-to-mold format as the G-3 Catalina. The new 14' 2" version was several inches longer to facilitate larger motors than were available when Tritt designed the G-3 in the late 1950s. Other than this sleek throwback to an earlier boating era, Glasspar models, circa 1970, were largely badge engineered.

As the 1970s advanced, Larson began experiencing

its own challenges resulting from corporate buyouts, a labor strike, and a 1975 bankruptcy. A year or so later, Larson chose not to revive Glasspar, although the G-3 Catalina remained through the line's 1977 swan song catalog. But every time someone finds one of Bill Tritt's vintage boats on a front yard or at auction, the brightest quality fiberglass runabout brand of the 1950s–early 1960s gets another chance to shine.

Note: Bill Tritt's talents also extended to automobiles, and his fiberglass-bodied G-2 car of the early 1950s and the subsequent G-3 were as well regarded then as now.

Glastron

Arlington, Texas, resident Robert Hammond is the head agent responsible for Glastron's founding. Company lore has long identified his wife, Bettye, as creator of the Glastron name (Glas for Fiber*glas* and tron because of its space-age elec*tron*ics kind of feel). Through 1959, the fledgling outfit was named Standard Glass Products in case the product line ever included plastic coffins — but that's getting ahead of the tale.

Hammond's first brush with fiberglass came while working at an aircraft plant. He translated that experience into a managerial position at Lone Star when it got into glass around 1954. Among his most dramatic Lone Star designs was the Meteor, a finned, two-toned, futuristic water car that turned heads then as now. Runabouts like Meteor were low production and even lower priority at Lone Star, when it focused on generic family craft. That's why Hammond began dreaming of an operation of his own where he'd be freer to get his unique designs off the drawing board and into showrooms. During the 1956 boating season, Hammond met with several men who could help him achieve his goal. These included successful marine dealer Bill Gaston, who incredulously watched Glasspar boats practically sell themselves at his establishment; Guy Woodward, a plastics adhesives magnate; and Robert Shoop, the casket company owner keen on making his wares with fiberglass.

The group decided to give boatbuilding a go, if Hammond could come up with a winning prototype, an assignment he quickly began after hours in a modest building the fledgling firm had decided to lease. The resulting 15-footer was torture-tested in salt water and proved more than hardy enough to spark further investment, production, and a couple dozen late-1956 sales. By early fiberglass boat standards, the little Glastron was already a hit. Orders poured in for 1957, so management felt comfortable increasing Texas-based factory space and, for 1958, establishing several additional manufacturing sites throughout the United States.

Fiberglass boat historian Kevin Mueller notes that the early incarnations of the Texas plant would seem crude by current standards, as they had dirt floors and were open on both ends to keep some air moving, especially during the hot southwestern summers. But minimum wage labor, often newly arrived from south of the border, didn't seem to mind, thus helping Glastron keep down costs and build a lot of boats. Mueller says a respectable 3,878 boats came off Glastron assembly lines in 1958. In fact this "designed by Hammond" line is recognized by classic glass enthusiasts as one of the most beautiful and well built of its era.

The flagship of the 1958 fleet was the 17-foot SEAflite, a $1,495 removable hardtop model with fins, swoops, curves, comfortable seating, "style-setting spray control bow and chrome concave Mylar side panels." Like other higher end big runabouts, its "2-engine cut-out" transom was meant for long shaft outboards totaling 120 hp. (A sister inboard version — for a 130-horse Chrysler or 175-hp Interceptor — made the catalog, too.) In common with other Glastron models, the SEAflite had as standard a "hi-gloss, molded-in color exterior and (spotted) fleck interior." Color choices ranged from a "Cascade White" hull to decking in "Matador Red," "Bimini Blue," "Tahitian Coral," and "Polished Ebony." Dealers were quick to mention that a SEAFlite easily survived a promotional "2,600 mile non-stop Texas to New York test run."

Just as alluring and charming was the 15-foot FIREflite, typically shown with a Bimini Blue topside and matching blue fiberglass-hooded Scott Atwater 40-horse outboard (although it could take a 70-horse mill). Perhaps this $895 Glastron's most notable features were its "transverse fiberglass bulkheads" covering a generous compartment just aft of the rear seating. The company's price list admitted that FIREflite served as the "bread and butter model." Sibling slices of the 1958 loaf included the 15-foot SURFflite Deluxe, which shared the SEAflite's rear seats running parallel to the sides and also serving as storage. The 14½-foot SKIflite was a more traditionally shaped Monoflite. The 14' 5" Fisherman was sold standard as an open boat, but was offered with front decking and a center wheel deck for steering. Promised for a mid-February debut was a

1965 Glastron FIREflite V-155 provides comfort and solid performance with a 55-hp Homelite 4-cycle mill.

Standard "completely restyled" as SURFflite, "including a 200 percent stronger hull, new flared rear fin styling with . . . concave side panels."

Because Bob Hammond was a skillful designer at heart, he had a penchant for regularly using these talents. That is to say, much more so than, say, MFG, Glastron regularly updated many of its models or introduced new ones. In fact, the opportunity to incorporate his ideas at will into a boat was a major incentive for him to want to run his own shop. He did harbor a drive to keep coming up with new design concepts, and a concern that whenever he did so, there'd be some who would quickly copy his creation. A mid-1970s Glastron retrospective newsletter noted that "Hammond had designed all of the boats in the early years, [but] he and [longtime Glastron associate, Mel] Whitley collaborated as the company continued to grow. Once a year they'd disappear for two weeks and create working designs for most of the next year's models."

A new Texas plant and subsequent expansions (an Indiana division would be short-lived) continued keeping Glastron up on plane as it sped into the 1960s. A smooth riding vee-bottom, dubbed the Aqua-Lift Deep Vee-Hull, went from Hammond design to production in 1962. By the end of the following year, Deep-Vee Aqua-Lift models represented over 50 percent of Glastron's dollar sales. This success spawned dealerships in every state, including the two newest ones, Alaska and Hawaii. Manufacturing licenses were also sold to boatbuilders in South Africa and Spain, with UK and Europe to follow.

Among attractive runabouts of this era was the 1963 JETflite with hatch/tonneau covers. In fact any two-place JETflite outboard model, or even a 1970s vintage four-seater makes for a truly classic runabout. Besides the original Aqua-Lift, another soon-to-be-wildly popular Glastron bottom type would be on the market in 1967. The Aqua-Lift II cathedral hull was introduced in craft like the Swinger V-176 and 1968 GT-160. Arguably, the company's bright contrasting color schemes and accents, which really started to come of age during this era, drew buyers to the brand as effectively as did the hull designs. The public's quick embracing of these and other bow riders, makes this style the most prevalent of all older Glastrons found today.

Much less common from the late 1960s–early 1970s are Glastron-Carlson high performance boats like the CV-16 and CH-16, either one being at home with a tall, powerful Merc outboard. After establishing a professional relationship with noted speedboat designer Art Carlson, Hammond made a similar deal with Angelo Molinari, which resulted in some winning Molinari/Glastron tunnel hull racers. Understandably, these were limited production craft, not significantly contributing to the count that would reach the "100,000 Glastron boats produced" mark achieved in 1970.

"During the '70s," records the company's historical newsletter, "the V-156 bow rider became the highest unit volume fiberglass runabout produced in the United States for many years, even with dozens of copies. [No competitor] could match the quality and price made possible by Glastron's high volume of this model. Five thousand, seven hundred and four were sold in 1973." That's the year that Glastron received its best publicity, thanks to the James Bond movie *Live and Let Die.* Glastron had built and sold 26 Glastron, and Glastron-Carlson boats to the film company. The director selected a GT-150 mated to an Evinrude 135-hp outboard for the movie's major stunt. He had the boat "modified with two wooden rails attached to the bottom to provide lateral stability while on a specially constructed ramp. [It] was jumped over 100 times to find optimum speed and ramp design to achieve what became a world record 110-foot jump" over two police cars.

The resulting eight-minute 007 secret agent chase scene served to promote Glastrons to millions of Bond buffs the world over. This added popularity pushed the main Austin plant to pop out a new Glastron every 5.6 minutes! In the process, indicated the company newsletter, "over four million square feet of plywood, an equal number of board feet of dimension lumber, a million gallons of polyester resin, 3.5 million pounds of fiberglass mat and cloth, 1,617,00 lineal feet of aluminum and nearly four million feet [of] marine vinyl" were consumed.

Perhaps Glastron's 1970s kudos from *Live and Let Die* and its status as largest fiberglass boat maker caused Bob Hammond to consider his future at the once fledgling firm he helped create from a 15-foot boat design, and logically think "been there, done that." For whatever reason, he left Glastron in 1974. (See his subsequent listing under Hammond Boats in the following chapter.) Into the next decade, Glastron would continue as the biggest boat maker, until being surpassed by Bayliner. Enthusiasts can still see Hammond's first Glastron, as the prototype is displayed in a company facility. Reportedly, though, many of the old hull "molds and engineering test boats that didn't meet standards" have long ago been bulldozed into the Texas ground.

Johnson

Kissin' cousins of the OMC stern-drive hulls that debuted in 1962, Johnson outboard-powered boats were introduced the following model year. At just over 17 feet in length, the fiberglass boats were true tri-hulls. The January 1965 *Motor Boating* described Johnson's "three-point bottom design [as] provide[ing] two tunnels to deflect spray and three sponsons for stability." Neither Johnson nor Evinrude appeared to push their outboard boats as hard as they did stern-drive or inboard/outboard versions of these respective lines. By 1967, they'd quietly discontinued the outboard-driven craft.

When shown in a Johnson motor catalog, the co-labeled boats were typically depicted with a light blue deck (green was also available) on a white hull pushed by a V-4 formatted 75- or 90-horse Johnson. Reportedly, these craft rode more smoothly than related Evinrudes, possibly because the Johnson boat sprang from an OMC designed to handle the added weight and speed of hefty inboard/outboard engines. Like their Evinrude relatives, though, the hull marque was a rather uncommon — though certainly pleasing — 1960s sight, and restorable examples should be considered a decent find today. This is especially true while similarly serviceable examples of related motors are still kicking around at reasonable prices.

Larson

"Got any mid-fiftyish Larson brochures?" I asked the literature vendor.

"Man, those are tough to find," was the reply. The vendor figured it had something to do with Larson's roots as a regional marque, fueled primarily by lots of neighborly word-of-mouth advertising.

From about 1915 when Paul Larson began building a few boats for customers in the Little Falls, Minnesota, area, through much of 1950s, the Larson Boat Works wasn't particularly focused on printed publicity. With his products' excellent reputation long established, the Minnesotan had about all of the business his factory could handle. Still, the chance to branch out always beckoned, and increased promotions began around 1958, just four years after the quality wooden boat maker got into fiberglass with a redux of its most unusual models — the Falls Flyer.

First marketed in 1938, Falls (as in Larson's locale, Little *Falls*) Flyers quickly earned a reputation as a fast, sleek, sporty outboard runabout with as many contours as cedar strips and canvas covering would allow. The model was occasionally updated to retain its futuristic

Larson's trademark waterline "spear" or "mermaid kiss" is especially evident on the 16-foot, 1967 All American 166 with V-4 Johnson outboard.

edge, and at one time came with a bubble compartment that fit over its motor.

All incarnations were noticeably narrower than most runabouts. Larson sacrificed beam for speed, as he wanted to make the best use of the approximate 25-hp ceiling of period outboards. Revamped with chubby aft fins for 1958, the Falls Flyer sported side trim similar to a Pontiac's of that year. In 1959 advertising, however scant, the maker recognized the 15-foot $1,025 Falls Flyer as "an unusual boat with an outstanding stock racing record." Glass editions, with operating turn signal tail lights, rival novel craft like the Lone Star Meteor, and are now especially prized — much more so than during their original run.

Technically the company had offered quasi-FRP craft in 1953, giving buyers the option of ordering their wooden Larsons with a fiberglass skin on the hull. The debut 1954 fiberglass Falls Flyer, however, was a true FRP boat, having been molded in top and bottom sections. Its good looks drew attention to Larson's Laker line of fiberglass models. The real Laker star, though, would be less flashy and begin her long reign with runabout buyers about two years later.

Noticing the growth of other marine companies moving in the FRP direction, and realizing that local employees trained to work in the new medium would be apt to ply their new-found trade at his firm, Paul Larson recognized that fiberglass held the key to Larson Boat Works's future. According to Larson historian Lee Wangstad, in 1957 the founder had been boatbuilding for over 40 years and envisioned his future with a little more leisure time. To that end, Larson "sold an interest in Larson Boat Works to Earl Geiger [who possessed] expertise in handling national accounts. Not long after, Chuck Gravelle came to Larson as director of sales and marketing. Together," cited Wangstad, "these three formulated a plan to take Larson from [being] a regional builder into the national market."

To position the company for coast-to-coast plant acquisition and regional distribution without having to outlay funds for brick and mortar, it was decided to license Larson designs to existing builders in Ontario, California; Nashville, Georgia; Casper, Wyoming; and Cornwall, Ontario. The latter locale could instantly cover Canadian production, as well as distribution there and in northern New York and throughout New England. The management trio recognized that the expansion would require an all-fiberglass line. Vital, too, was the ability to offer a medium-size, family-friendly outboard runabout for a dollar figure an average American (or Canadian) family could afford — and then throw some useful extras in the deal (like side curtains, convertible top, lights, windshield, and decent seat upholstery) without jacking up the boat's reasonable suggested retail price.

Larson's ticket to the boating boom's biggest batch of buyers was introduced in 1956 and named the All American. With the roster of accessories that came standard, it could have easily been labeled the All Inclusive. Offered until 1994, in several sizes and many editions (delineated by an LOA-related numerical suffix, that is, All American 152), this bread and butter runabout was one of the Larsons built with the output of the Rand chopper gun, a unit capable of spraying chopped up glass fibers and associated resin onto a mold. One of several such devices to be embraced by some fiberglass boat makers because it saved time over the hand lay-up process, the Rand Gun got the name because its inventor was working with Ingersoll-Rand when he developed the device around 1954. Larson was an early participant in I-R's program to get the gun into the market for industrial uses like fiberglass hull spray-up production.

While deliberately as generic as cola, the All American did have a distinctive look imbued by its molded-in lapstrakes lines below the chines. Larson called this its "Lapline Hull," essentially a smooth-sided craft with a lapstrake bottom.

Why this design? "Listen to the sound of a Larson hull running," the company's ads would simply challenge. "Hear the air cushion effect of Paul Larson's 'Million Bubble Ride' working when you run in a chop. The hull makes a 'schuss-schuss' sound as waves are flattened. Millions of bubbles are trapped under the lapline hull [as] they compress and roll back from bow to stern."

Besides its laplines, the All American was distinguished by the Larson name tastefully scripted in its aft teardrop logo. The boat could be ordered with a stylized stripe that ran the entire length of the boat. Some call the design a spear or arrow, but take an abstract view of it and you might agree that the marking looks like a lipstick impression — the boat having been kissed by a beautiful mermaid.

A 14-foot All American was introduced in 1957. She and the 16-footer were fitted with wooden decking, but went to all glass (except for the cedar stringer reinforcement network) the following boating season. That's when Larson got a call from the Goodson-Todman TV people. For the fall of 1957, NBC had given the game show producers a primetime slot for their *The Price Is Right* program and they wanted prizes that'd resonate with a national audience. As master of ceremonies Bill Cullen asked what was next for contestants to price, and the curtain parted, announcer Johnny Olsen enthusiastically described the virtues of a glossy new 1958 All American. The studio audience went wild. Their reaction — while admittedly staged by the flashing "applause" prompt lights — no doubt provided Larson with priceless publicity.

Handsome is the word for the 1957 Thunderhawk, a 16-foot runabout with a six-foot beam. Its girth, generous molded topside that formed stubby aft fins, a rear seat back and motor well, and front seat backs–walk-through center deck contributed to a solid 1950s appearance reminiscent of a '57 Pontiac Convertible. Surprising to classic glass buffs, it didn't sell very well and was gone from the line when the 1960s arrived.

During 1960, Larson's name came up in Brunswick acquisition meetings. The firm wanted a boatbuilder with a solid reputation for quality fiberglass runabouts so that it could extend its marine holdings beyond the Owens Yacht Company and Cutter Boats (an Indiana-based Owens division producing entry-level fiberglass craft) lines it had already purchased. By the fall of 1960, Brunswick bought Larson for stock shares with an estimated value of more than $3,000,000. The deal included a new, regional Larson plant in Alliance, Ohio, that Brunswick closed in 1961 when much of the boat making operation shifted to a Warsaw, Indiana, factory.

There were lots of changes, fits, and starts associated with the acquisition. One of the fits was reportedly thrown by E. Carl Kiekhaefer, who'd sold his Mercury outboard enterprise to Brunswick and gotten a board of director's seat in the 1961 deal, along with Brunswick stock. Believing Merc profits would be jeopardized by Brunswick's ownership of boat companies not necessarily marketed by most Mercury dealers, he loudly lobbied for the divestiture of the boat division.

For some reason, rather than make the recently stellar Larson line especially attractive to corporate raiders, Brunswick division management didn't do much that was new in 1962. *Motor Boating*'s January show issue reported that the only new fleet member was the Tradewind, an 18-foot cruiser "Comboard" (presumably for <u>com</u>bination out<u>board</u> runabout and cruiser). Central to the line were All Americans in 16- and 17-foot versions and the 13½-foot Playboy ski-boat. Although hardly in the Glasspar G-3 league, this is a cute little speedster rather unsung in its day, but would now make for a fortunate find.

The 1963 *Motor Boating* "Outboard Boats" section identified Larson as "Brunswick Corp," and simply noted "there are three 16-footers for 1963 from Larson Boats, built by Brunswick Corp., Warsaw, Indiana." Other than an All American with a raised convertible top, no other boats appeared; not even one of the low budget Cutters with Larson badge engineering was included. Marine industry observers had little doubt that Brunswick was distancing itself from the very brand it so dearly coveted several years earlier. Amazingly, Paul Larson (by this time in his early 70s) and a local investment group were able to buy back the Larson Boat Division with a check for a relatively miniscule $160,000. Brunswick took a multi-million dollar hit on Larson in terms of its 1960 purchase price and subsequent operating costs, but directors such as Kiekhaefer seemed happy to be rid of what they viewed an albatross, not central to Brunswick's focus. Ironically, much of Brunswick's 2005 revenue came from the boat and motor operations it focused upon in many waves of subsequent buying sprees.

Larson's "new" hometown ownership and handful of staff didn't have time to get copy to *Motor Boating* in time for the January 1964 Outboards article. But chagrined dealers contacted the plant hoping to find out what happened to the Larson product they had so easily been able to sell. When the plan to slowly reconstruct

Notice the stylishly convex deck and windshield on the 1967 18-foot All American.

some kind of sales network was explained, the dealers' response was typically, "Well, then count us in and send a load of All Americans!" That trusty model — in 152, 162, 166, and 167 suffixes — served as the bulk of Larson's rebound output for 1964.

Two years later, the company turned 50, with *Motor Boating* noting that the celebration included giving buyers "a two-year warranty against theft, physical damage and defects in workmanship." The jewel in the commemorative crown was the Medallion 166, a 16-foot All American hull with impressive bells and whistles such as full helm instrumentation and an 8-track stereo tape player. Maybe somebody put a happy sounding cartridge in the slot when management announced that Larson had just managed to purchase the Glasspar line.

By the end of the decade, Larson output included 14' 7", 15' 1", 16' 4", and 18' 4" Shark sport utility runabouts (fun, open boats with wheel deck center steering) and, of course All Americans in 14' 3", 14' 7", 16' 4", and 17' 11" versions. The two larger ones had outboard or inboard/outboard options. Also cataloged was the Volero deep-vee 17-foot outboard (or inboard/outboard) runabout.

By now located in St. Paul, Minnesota, Larson announced "a new construction technique that makes its boats virtually impossible to capsize. Larson's Life/Guard bonds a high-buoyancy plastic foam between inner and outer hulls of fiberglass to produce a hull that will neither sink nor turn turtle when completely awash."

In 1970, Wilson Sporting goods — owned by Pepsi-Cola — acquired a controlling interest in Larson. By 1973, this interest was sold to General Boats Partnership. Serious labor unrest precipitated bankruptcy in 1975. After some rough waves, the marque went to Genmar, which later picked up nearby Crestliner, another famed boat company started by Paul Larson.

Lone Star

Lone Star fiberglass boats were only built for about a decade, but during this period Lone Star's FRP influence spread directly to two other significant boat brands and influenced many others. In fact, Cutter, a small Indiana runabout builder, was found by a court to have been too enamored with some glass Lone Star designs, and sentenced to pay royalties. Founded in 1945 in tiny Grand Prairie, Texas, as an aluminum hull fabricator, Lone Star reportedly had rowboats on the market sometime the following year.

As the aluminum line expanded into runabouts and cruisers, Lone Star research and development people began considering fiberglass for the firm's next step. By 1953, the catalog included a pair of 14-foot FRP craft, the Ranger rowboat, and the Texan runabout. "For sometime now," claimed the 1953 brochure, "Lone Star has been experimenting with this newest of boat building materials — Fiberglas." The 1954 sales literature noted that "The unusual boats are manufactured by a careful, patient method of 'sandwiching' layer upon layer of Fiberglas matting and woven Fiberglas cloth on a master form. Each layer is impregnated with polyester resin and color pigments. After 'setting,' these hulls are sanded to a permanent glass finish...smooth [enough to] increase speed up to 20 percent."

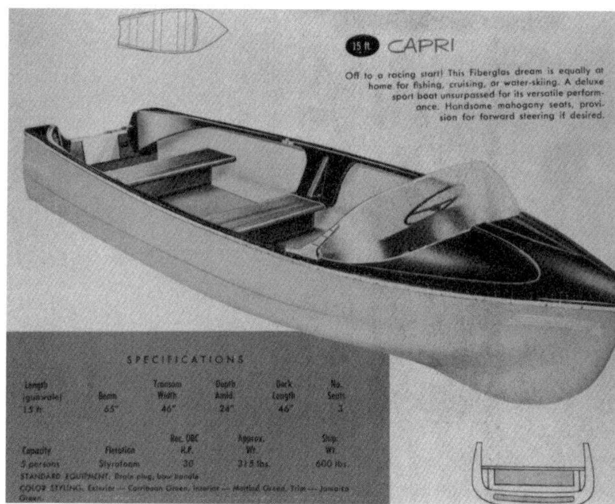

"Imaginatively conceived, brilliantly executed, these boats sweep the field with their 'years-ahead' styling and flashing performance," noted Lone Star's 1956 ad copy for its glass craft like 15-foot Capri, subtitled "a Fiberglas dream."

With curvy contours (especially on the slightly convex, double-cockpit topsides), the Texan exhibited a generic plastic look that would cause some observers to dub the two-tone Seafoam Green (hull)/Forest Green (top) craft and other early FRP incarnations like her, "Tupperware boats." But, with a garden-variety Johnson Sea Horse 25 on her transom, the Texan could really step out, even with five folks aboard. Specifications for the $495 model FG-200 claimed she could handle one of Evinrude's hefty, rope-start, 33.4-horse, opposed four-cylinder Speedifours. The rating was wisely reduced to 25 hp in 1954 for Texan's second and final offering. That year, too, a lighter Jamaica Green was used on the topsides. For 1955, the Texan was revamped into a more deluxe, windshield-equipped Challenger, a 14-footer

Lone Star said its 1955 Challenger was "built like a rocket, a beauty in action or at the dock." Even in the mid-1950s, though, the sight of such 14-footers orbiting the local lake would have been rare.

with molded seating (as opposed to the Texan's marine mahogany seats) pigmented in "Mottled Green."

NBC *Today Show* host Dave Garroway was a sports car buff who'd wondered about the strength of fiberglass bodies. He suggested to a producer preparing for a *Today* segment from the 1955 New York Boat Show that telecasting a fiberglass hull being dropped onto the Armory floor might make for compelling TV. Nobody, except a Lone Star publicity official, took the challenge seriously. Reportedly, he agreed to allow a 14-foot Challenger to be fork-lifted some 15 feet high, and then closed his eyes as the RCA video cameras captured its fall. "No damage at all," *Today* viewers learned.

The gamble resulted in free advertising on national television, arguably one of the first coast-to-coast exposures for a fiberglass boat. It should be noted that some sources peg this tale as involving a 15-foot fiberglass Lone Star runabout. If true, that would move the incident to 1956 when the fleet's two glass runabouts, the entry-level Capri (with wooden seating) and deluxe Constellation (featuring twin cockpit and motor well plus molded fiberglass seats) were cataloged. Both 15-footers appeared with front steering, though a molded center console through which motor controls could be positioned came only with the Constellation.

Before departing in 1956 to begin what would become Glastron, Bob Hammond directed Lone Star's fiberglass endeavors. He told *Boating World* columnist Lee Wangstad about sketching a futuristic fantasy runabout based on the 1951 Buick Le Sabre show car dreamed up for that year's GM Motorama display. Although thinking the drawings could certainly result in a wild boat, Hammond never figured the design was suitable for mass production. But some Lone Star execs who saw the concept art wanted to make at least one for boat show display. A prototype for Hammond's Meteor was fashioned in time for the big New York display, where the designer recalls it being "quite a hit." Spectators and the media crowded around both this craft and Brooks Stevens's similarly far-out Lark runabout commissioned by Evinrude. Well-heeled admirers of each boat clamored to submit orders, but it was the Lone Star that got produced in larger, albeit modest, numbers during 1956 through 1958.

The Meteor's upholstery, lighting, and custom metal trim, as well as the precise fitting together of the boat's many accent pieces made Meteor production costs well above the family runabout norm. At $1,600, the 1956 Meteor cost more than a pair of Lone Star Constellations and a good used 25-horse outboard — combined! Still, even if the company earned nothing on each Meteor sale, the related publicity when another one hit the water did wonders for Lone Star's brand name.

To the casual observer, all Meteors look the same, but company engineers worked hard getting the boat to shed some weight and just over 300 bucks in the retail price. Oddly, during its three year run, the eye-catching craft did not net space in many of the firm's catalogs. Lone Star's main 1956 booklet and 1958 "Carefreedom Fleet" folder serve as examples. The former mentions nothing about it. The latter literature does note the 1958 Meteor price of $1,295 "FOB Grand Prairie Only," but shows no pictures. In a day of fast changing automotive styling, the Meteor, sensational in 1956, would have seemed an anachronism just four or five years later. Mercifully, Lone Star let it rest after those small-print 1958 mentions.

Though Bob Hammond had already been building his Glastrons for a couple of model years when the 1958 Lone Stars were unveiled, Hammond's design influence was unmistakable in second-generation 15-foot Lone Star glass runabouts, the basic Skylark and the better-appointed Continental. Along with modest tail fins, a hint of gunwale swoop in the lines just aft of the front seat might cause boat shoppers to see connections between the two Texas-based company's products. Also evocative of Glastron was the wave-deflecting dolphin-like nose on Lone Star's 19-foot Caribbean runabout sedan. The bow style was more modestly incorporated into the front of Hammond's Glastrons like the 1958 FIREflite.

A third generation of fiberglass Lone Star runabouts was offered by 1960. That year's catalog talked about the manufacturer's "marine scientists" conducting "continuous engineering and year-round endurance tests [and working on a new hull] master mold, which required thirteen months to develop." The family-friendly 13' 8" Capri (with simulated seam embossed deck) and 13' 9" Monterey had higher sides, a softer-riding hull, and a larger ("Panoramic") windshield than most of their older sisters. The 14' 9" Flamingo was said to be the "model that's stealing the heart of boating America." Presumably that's because it offered a bevy of seat options, hydraulic "Starguide" steering, a custom-fitted vinyl canopy, and various optional customized touches. These and other Lone Star models were now being built in plants in Grand Prairie, Texas; Bremen, Indiana; Tallahassee, Florida; and McAdoo, Pennsylvania. Seating and color options were especially plentiful during this period.

An oft-confusing matter of choice for Lone Star and other circa 1960 runabout buyers was navigating the small print regarding transom lengths. As outboards were getting more powerful, most of the larger models required mounting bolts instead of or in addition to thumbscrews. Shaft depth increased five inches to accommodate deeper transoms. But some hefty outboards could be had either way. A boat shopper had to determine whether his hull and motor would be mated forever or if a newer, larger mill might be in the offing should the fiberglass hull do as advertised and last indefinitely.

An 18-foot early 1960s Lone Star runabout that made such decisions easy was the Belle Isle, available only with a long-shaft transom. Except for the entry-level 14-foot Monterey, the 1961 glass runabout fleet graduated to a long-shaft school. These included the 14-foot Riviera, 15-foot Deauville, 16-foot Bermuda, and 17-foot Fleetwood. A notable feature of the 14-

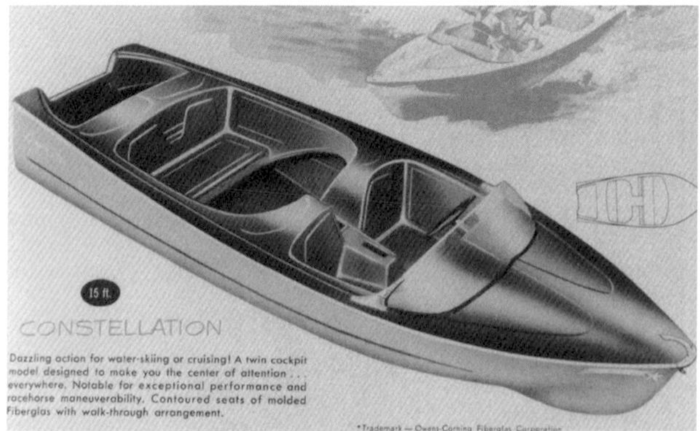

The 1956 Lone Star Constellation is quintessential in its two- piece "snapped together" plastic look present in many early fiberglass runabouts. Note the molded-in storage (between seat backs) compartment and outboard motor control mounting cavity through which the levers could rise like a sports car stick shift.

and 15-footers was the embossed seam deck accent. The Bermuda's lines retained the Hammond "swoop" and modest tail fins, described as "graceful styling."

Molded-in lapstrake entered the Lone Star fiberglass line in the 1962 16-foot Biscayne, a nicely upholstered model that was based on a modification of the previous year's Bermuda molds. The coral-colored 16' 8" Fleetwood was designed for the then new Merc 1000, 100-hp outboard, and came with a 12-gallon fuel tank, deck gas cap, and fuel gauge. A second tank could be added. The Fleetwood and several of the fleet's other comfy seat models (as opposed to the less generous padding in basic 13' 8" Capri's seating) wore an interesting stylized star design on their seat backs. This light brown and tan Lone Star asterisk was centered in a sort-of-TV screen, a design that'll surely be tough for restorers to reproduce today.

As Lone Star brass considered ways to best survive a general slowdown in boat and motor sales, they introduced a couple of neat runabouts for 1964. The 15' 5" Triton appeared to be the Texas company's answer to the popular Glasspar G-3. Comparisons of the Triton's main publicity shot in the 1964 Lone Star–published *Boats Illustrated* magazine shows it running neck and neck with a seaplane. There's little doubt that the idea came from Glasspar's 1963 catalog cover sporting a G-3 alongside a similar aircraft! The Lone Star version incorporated something dubbed the "remarkable quad-chine hull, utilizing auxiliary planing surfaces designed into the hull alongside and forward of the load-bearing planing area to give exceptional stability on turns and straight-away."

With a maximum 75 horses, it'd be fun to see a Triton racing a G-3 capped at 60 hp. Most money would likely be on the Glasspar, though the Triton was a decent craft and would make a nice find now. A second unique glass Lone Star for 1964 was the 14-foot Mystic with a small windshield and rear bench seating running down the middle of the floor from the back of the front seating to the motor well. Under the long cushion, there was room on what Lone Star promoted as a "unique, plush runabout," to stow a pair of six-gallon fuel tanks and a tool kit. Slatted floorboards and aluminum grip rails on the gunwales made this quasi-blunt-decked sportster a great fair-weather ski boat or gentleman's hotrod, especially with a 50-horse Merc 500 to max out the transom rating.

In 1965, discussions began with suitor Chrysler Corporation. Perhaps to make the fleet look more versatile, a 13-foot fiberglass sailing sloop was added, as were some larger stern-drive craft. In the meantime, the outboard runabouts were reheated for 1965 consumption. Marine analysts who helped Chrysler negotiate a purchase offer for Lone Star assets pointed out that most of the molds for the 14- to 16-foot runabouts would provide Chrysler with at least several years of attractive bread and butter FRP output.

Molded Fiber Glass (MFG)

According to company history, Molded Fiber Glass (MFG) sprang from the idea of Robert S. Morrison "to mass produce the first commercial products using polyester resins and fiberglass reinforcements." To that end, Morrison opened up shop in 1948 at Ashtabula, Ohio. He was no stranger to business, having run (from the mid-1930s) Morrison Motors, a successful Ford dealership in Ashtabula. *Composite Age* newsletter recalls that his response to the World War II cessation of new automotive production was to "offer reconditioned or *Morrisonized* cars." He didn't like to see things sitting around in no shape for service.

After the fighting stopped and Detroit was again busy shipping him vehicles, he sold a fleet of trucks to a pulp products outfit that later got into financial trouble. As a creditor, Morrison arranged to quietly acquire this moribund egg carton plant. Envisioning parallels

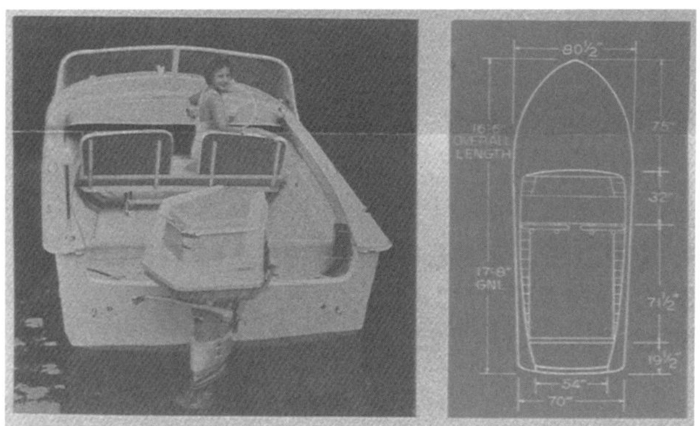

MFG's 16' 6" open runabout wore simple aluminum-braced front seats and could handle enough horsepower to ski tow most of your bunch and the neighbor kids, an important criteria for more than a few 1960s-era cottagers.

between pre-forming pulp into hard paper products, and molding things out of newfangled fiberglass, the entrepreneur shifted the small firm's emphasis to the latter material. Because few then understood the versatility and value of fiberglass-reinforced plastic or FRP, Morrison dedicated his early tenure to securing markets for his firm's capabilities. FRP firefighting helmets and bread trays represented early output. Typically, with each new line, Morrison would create a "division" (and in some cases a separate factory, such as the MFG Tray Company at Linesville, Pennsylvania) for what soon became the MFG Companies.

Chevrolet's decision to put the "plastic" Corvette into production provided a catalyst for Morrison to get into a major product area with General Motors. "During a series of meetings," *Composite Age* says, Morrison "was able to convince GM that MFG could build a facility that could produce the car body out of fiber glass reinforced plastic. The resulting "Vette" contract quickly spawned the MFG Body Company, an outfit that "ten months later was in production" fabricating the sporty car's fiberglass exterior.

Owens-Corning had a stake in the Chevy project, too, knowing that if it flopped, the average person might think of O-C's trademarked *Fiberglas* — used in the Corvette — as flimsy. The glass company wanted an extra gun aiming at the venture's success, so it tapped Brandt Goldsworthy, who'd already built some fiberglass auto bodies for a minor sports car maker, to help MFG. Though we can only speculate here, it seems logical to assume that while consulting in Ashtabula, Goldsworthy mentioned his experience of having fabricated reinforced plastic boats for West Coast marine concerns Triangle and Wizard.

While generating a lot of work for MFG, the GM deal gave Morrison pause to consider what might happen if Chevy didn't sell sufficient numbers of what many motorists viewed as a niche vehicle. Another product line was needed. Brainstorming resulted in MFG Body locating a Lyman outboard runabout and using it to make a mold that could facilitate a fiberglass copy. The resulting craft — essentially an FRP Lyman lapstrake hull — was proudly transported over to Lyman's Sandusky, Ohio, headquarters where, much to Morrison's surprise, officials at the venerable wooden boat manufacturing organization promptly rejected it. *Composite Age* reported that Morrison also approached other companies. "His initial talks with boatbuilders were met with much skepticism. They showed little interest in [anything made from] the new material."

Back in Ashtabula, the lone hull sat in the MFG Body plant. Perhaps if Morrison had been a boater

Could that be a powerful six-cylinder 1957 Mercury Mark 75 on this little 15-foot MFG? Lucky kid!

he'd have some seats put in the hull, used it summer weekends, and chalked up the failed venture to the everyday fiscal risks of research and development. But, as MFG historian Jim Coffman points out, Morrison had "no true interest in boats." His idea had simply been to pop out bare plastic hulls for an established pleasure craft company like Lyman that would pay MFG for each one delivered to someone else's factory and sales force. Eventually Morrison authorized the fabrication of more hulls, as well as decks, seats, and other parts to get them on the marine market. Many enthusiasts can't help but wonder if Lyman ever reacted to seeing these clones. Perhaps some design use agreement had been reached between the two companies? And might Morrison have breathed a sigh of relief if some Lyman bigwig bumped into him at a boat show and said, "OK, you've made your point. Let's talk about how we'll really get into this new fiberglass boat industry, together." But no such cooperation from the veteran boat maker materialized.

One of the new MFG venture's earliest listings is found in *The Boating Industry* of January 1955. Admittedly uncharted waters for Morrison's publicity people, the boat business publication entry (likely initiated no later than Thanksgiving of 1954) only read "Molded Fiber Glass Body Co., 4601 Benefit Ave., Ashtabula, Ohio, Robt. Morrison." During 1955, a Union City, Pennsylvania, plant was put into operation so that by the time influential *Motor Boating* magazine's January 1956 show issue hit the newsstands, the new MFG division was included.

"Known as Molded Fiber Glass," the magazine reported, "the new 15' 7" fiberglass boat with lapstrake design molded in, is said to offer greatly increased longitudinal strength and increased stability. The hull of the new boat is molded in one seamless piece in matched metal dies, and reinforced with bonded-in crossribs of fiberglass parallel-strand reinforced plastic." Period ads claimed that the prototypes were "torture-tested for hundreds of hours in the rough waters of Lake Erie...prov[ing] pound-for-pound, the most rugged boat built."

Rather than have his staff do all of the mold-up process by hand, Morrison invested in expensive matched metal dies that would allow for rapid mass production. In fact, MFG used what was known as "the world's largest matched metal die." When Art Liebers was researching his *Encyclopedia of Pleasure Boating*, he got a bird's eye view into MFG fabrication. Liebers noted that, while yielding a stronger boat than possible using hand layup, the costly dies lock manufacturers into a particular design because "any change would require a large capital outlay." Even so, "the construction is simple," he noted. "Matched metal dies, constructed of frame hardened steel, telescope within each other to place the resin under 700 tons of pressure and a constant temperature of 240 degrees Fahrenheit in the same way that fluid is compressed by the piston in a hydraulic cylinder, and guarantees a uniform molding of fiberglass into the hull. The method makes the hull stronger than steel of the same weight and thickness."

After removal from the dies, the newly created fiberglass hull was fitted with stringers or floor braces, originally wooden but later aluminum to guard against hull degradation in the event of water seepage. Completed hulls were turned upside down and lowered onto the deck where adhesive and gravity combined to create a tight bond. For all the company's emphasis on fiberglass being "very easy to care for," the early MFG line had a lot of transom and topside wood. However, the "simulated lapstrake" and nicely varnished "natural" decking made for a very sensible transitional craft in the eyes of many mid-20th century boaters.

"Available in three models," *Motor Boating*'s introductory 1956 MFG details reported, "the new boat is trimmed in solid mahogany and presents the appearance of a conventional wood boat. However, color is molded in and the hull never needs painting. Keels, keelsons, and floorboards are treated with wood preservative, and maintenance is thus reduced to a minimum."

Each MFG model was named for some community in the MFG Boat factory region. The Union, "an all-round fishing and utility boat, features a 54-inch mahogany deck, open cockpit, two full-width seats and starboard corner seat. The Cambridge model is a family boat with [a] 54-inch deck and choice of solid or split center deck. Erie is a deluxe boat with [a] 63-inch mahogany deck, two cockpits with full width seats and back rests, split center deck and rear well for outboard motor, gas tank, etc."

The first MFGs were rated for 30 horsepower, and then for 40 horses by 1958. When subsequently bought in the used market, it wasn't uncommon for one to be mated to larger mills. Early on, tiller steering was typically shown, but control quickly moved up front.

MFG lost little time in going big on advertising. The February 1956 edition of *Outboard* serves as an example. MFG bought the magazine's entire inside cover and paid extra for three shades of color, airbrushed in to jazz up what was originally black and white photography. The headline boasted the MFG as being the "only boat of its kind in the world…molded in one piece in the world's largest matched metal dies [by] the world's largest producers of fiber glass reinforced plastics." All those international superlatives aside, however, the bold publicity wasn't too proud to invite inquiries from potential MFG dealers.

By 1960, Morrison's boats were enjoying wide distribution, positive name recognition, and a devoted following. MFG catalogs that year touted an expanded model line that included four basic sizes. The original 15-footers (14' 10" LOA) included deluxe upholstered double seat Oxford; the Waterford with upholstered front seats and, like the Oxford, a fiberglass deck; and the basic Celeron, sporting wooden seating and decking. MFG's "big 13-footers" (12' 8" LOA) were all called versions of the base Corry. The Corry Carefree was all fiberglass with vinyl seating. The Corry Suburban had mahogany deck and seats. The Corry Utility was, as the name suggests, an open-hull version.

The 17-foot models (16' 6" LOA) included the all glass Edinboro and wooden decked Albion. The only MFG of the period not to be produced in the brand's famous matched metal dies was the 19-foot (18' 10" LOA) Seaway. Its "lapstrake hull patterned after the [13- and 17-footers] was designed in consultation with Owens-Corning Fiberglas Corp. who have as consultants, Gibbs & Cox, Inc." This all-glass craft could be purchased as a big open runabout, a fiberglass hardtop, or, in a 19' 8" LOA version, with a flying bridge cabin cruiser body. Brochure copy suggested powering any of the largest MFGs with either a tall, six-cylinder Mercury or a pair of OMC-produced 75-horse outboards.

Matched metal die fabrication still grabbed the lead sentence in MFG promotional copy for *Motor Boating*'s January 1965 boat show edition. The 12- and 14-foot trihedral-hulled utilities were touted along with the 14' 4" Niagara "sport runabout with bucket seats." Red, blue, and green deck coloration was still available, as were matching upholstery hues. MFG flyers mentioned (seemingly as an asterisk) the availability of "aluminum boats painted with baked-on acrylic colors in 14- and 16-foot lengths. Three are runabouts with features similar to the fiberglass hulls." These obscure Molded Fiber Glass aluminum craft were likely output from Crestliner, which MFG acquired in 1965 and quietly owned for some seven years. Any MFG-branded alloy hull would represent an uncommon find today. On the FRP side, the Crestliner connection combined with the Ohio boat maker's main marine output helped MFG claim the title of "world's largest producer of fiberglass boats" by 1971.

The dies were being phased out by the late 1960s when MFG continued shifting into the trihedral hull avenue with boats like the 16-foot Beachcomber Utility, 16' 7" Chevron, and 17' 9" Convair. Even so, a new deep-vee runabout was offered for 1969. The Caprice 197 had been designed for MFG by Jim Wynne (credited with inventing the stern drive) and John Gill as a gentleman's offshore racer. The 18-foot boat was available as an outboard format, though most were probably equipped with inboard/outboard power. Even in a changing pleasure boating market fascinated with tri-hulls and deep water competition, diehards struck with the simplicity and classic lines of MFG's original designs. In the 1980s, after the pleasure craft industry experienced several tumultuous shakedowns, MFG decided to dry-dock its boat division. Even so, it's not unusual to see one of the famed company's vintage hulls still cruising along. Each of these Lyman-inspired fiberglass craft serves as an icon of outboard boating history.

Sea Ray

This famous marque gets its name from founder Cornelius Ray, who entered boatbuilding in 1959. That year, his Ray Industries of Oxford, Michigan, picked up Carr Craft, a tiny Detroit area firm dabbling in fiberglass runabouts. Though these boats handled adequately, Ray wanted to make them look sportier. He found an automotive stylist who helped revamp the runabouts and also worked with Ray and a former Carr designer to come up with new styling ideas. In addition, the consultant suggested deep-vee hulls to give a smoother ride in rough water.

By January 1963, Sea Ray netted a listing in the *Motor Boating* show issue, though inboard/outboard runabouts and cruisers highlighted the 19-model fleet. The following year, Sea Ray shifted publicity focus to its "fiberglass outboard runabouts of 14-, 15-, 16-, and 18-feet built in standard and deluxe versions with lights, hardware, cable steering, ski fittings, upholstered paneling, vinyl carpeting, foam bucket seats, and windshield." By 1966, the better-equipped models, from what had now become the Sea Ray Boats Division, were admired by family boaters who wanted style, comfort, roominess, safety, and the day's biggest outboards. A sample is the 1966 model 18' 10" SRV180, capable of cruising, picnicking, and water skiing.

Sea Ray 700, a 16' 6" early 1960s model helped establish the brand as offering roomy, comfortable, family-friendly runabouts.

When *Trailer Boats* did a 1988 retrospective on the then most successful boat makers, the magazine cited Sea Ray as an early innovator in using "high-tech composite materials for boat construction." The magazine lauded Sea Ray for "creating sleek-finished interiors and highly stylized boats known for excellent performance and a high resale value." Ray left the company around the time of that article, following his 1986 sale of Sea Ray to Brunswick Corporation/Mercury Marine. By then, Sea Ray brass had relocated to Knoxville, Tennessee, in what *Trailer Boats* called "truly a showcase of free enterprise [because] the island on which Sea Ray's headquarters sits is surrounded by majestic bluffs and the far-reaching Tennessee River — an immediate proving ground for the boats produced in Tennessee, where the company has three major manufacturing plants."

By the mid-1980s, more than 15,000 craft were produced by Sea Ray facilities during a typical annual production run. Although a late comer — in terms of this work's time frame — and well known for craft larger than 20 feet, Sea Ray's prolific nature and wide marine consumer acceptance makes many of its outboard runabouts of interest to enthusiasts with an eye toward "future gold." An especially nice example might be a late 20th-century Sea Ray with color-matched Sea Ray-branded (Force) outboard motor.

Starcraft

After initially misjudging the public's appetite for aluminum boats rather than steel or magnesium, it's likely that Starcraft officials didn't want to make a late call on fiberglass, too. So, for 1958 the line included a trio of glass hulls. Two, the 12-foot Scatback and the 14-foot Wanderer, were open (or rowboat) models, while the Royal Star served as Starcraft's flagship. Curiously, although pictured as the 1958 brochure's cover-boat, this "15-foot fiberglass runabout complete with accessories" received no further attention in the company's pocket-sized folders. Arguably, the aluminum Jet Star had been slated to be the fleet's crown jewel until the decision was made to go glass. The last sentence in the Jet Star's description noted, "Specifications for the fiberglass Royal Star, shown on the front page are similar to those of [the] aluminum Jet Star."

In fact, though shot individually, both boats had been photographed at the same dock on the same fall 1957 day. Starcraft historians can examine the pictures and sense the catalog editor's deadline. Even as a last-minute entry, the $815 Royal Star was worth the wait. Likely molded from her aluminum sister, she possessed the $750 Jet Star's "flared Clipper-style prow and unobtrusive tail fins," but wore them with "feminine contours not as conducive to metal fabrication." Lucky classic boaters who find a first edition Royal Star will have a famous name milestone craft worth restoring and powering with any period 10–50 horse (like a colorful 1958 Evinrude "fat-fifty") outboard.

The Rocket, a 13' 4" entry-level boat was positioned by Starcraft as its 1961 "bargain...pace setter among small fiberglass runabouts." For angling duties, a 10-horse motor would do, said the manufacturer, though the 40-hp Johnson mated to her here made Rocket's model name more realistic.

In 1959, the Goshen, Indiana, boat maker offered a separate catalog for its fiberglass models. The Wonder Star led the pack of "stay-in-style boats built to last a lifetime." Presciently, that declaration envisioned a not too distant time when automotive styling excesses would calm down and take runabout design along for a more sedate ride. To that end, the tail accents on 1958's Royal Star were absent in Wonder Star, as Starcraft "eliminated costly cosmetics [like] gaudy 'dime-store' type fins and other protrusions that hit docks or other boats." Consequently, the Wonder Star and her sisters' "gently curving contours and wide flaring bow" would

The Seasport is an interesting little 1969 trihedral that exhibits Starcraft's incorporation of the hull design in a traditionally decked runabout format. Collectors often seek models that bridge styling genres.

allow the runabouts to look contemporary decades after their christening.

The three glass runabouts for 1960 included the richly appointed 17-foot Commander, the 15-foot Voyager, and the 14-foot Rocket. With a mid-size outboard — preferably a white with black-and-red-accented Johnson Sea Horse 40, if a solid white hull was selected — and a pair of brightly colored Cyprus Garden water skis, the Rocket could serve as the prototypical jet setter's ski boat.

A 1961 swinger earning the then handsome sum of maybe $15,000 a year might have opted for the new 17-foot Capri and a Merc 800 (80 hp). With such a six-popper, the roomy hull would be the life of a ski party. The 15-foot Vagabond, with "interior sides cushioned in soft half-inch-thick foam rubber and then covered with striking gold and white vinyl," could handle a 75-horse mill and took the place of the previous year's Rocket, a model designation newly assigned to a 13' 4" entry-level runabout. Each glass offering had double bottoms, unitized hulls, strengthened decking, gunwales, spray rails, and "extra layers of fiberglass matting and woven roving at every point of stress…in keel, prow, and bottom." A one-year guarantee was offered.

To garner publicity, Starcraft once hired the respected boating writer Hank Bowman to fill one of its runabouts with lake water and try sinking it. "I selected a model at random," he reported, "and pulled the plug. The boat supported not only its power plant, but six concrete blocks. I was particularly impressed with the generous amount of flotation. [And] entrapped air under the foredeck did not escape. This impressed me with the tight seal between hull and deck molds." Bowman's sincere attempt to send that Starcraft to Davy Jones's locker provided marine salespeople with a great selling point. "We were going to get a beautiful mahogany Hi-Liner runabout," a boyhood friend lamented, "but then the dealer showed my dad those Hank Bowman pictures and he got sold on safety and Starcraft."

Starcraft's 1971 V-140 Modified ski boat measured 14' 4" and was rated for 65-hp. Check out those plush bucket seats!

Seventeen feet of sleek, near rectangular hydroplane styling made the 1971 Starcraft T-170 Eliminator look like rival G-W Invader. Its transom invited 140-horses.

As a memento of the sincere publicity gesture, the manufacturer had the accomplished boater and writer highlight his findings in a free booklet titled *Hank Bowman Previews the 1964 Line of Starcraft Boats.* "Read this before you buy any boat!" small ads in the likes of Popular Mechanics requested. Find out what a "boating expert…likes and dislikes about the Starcraft fiberglass and aluminum cruisers, runabouts, fishing boats, canoes and new sailboat. No punches pulled!" Bowman's honestly positive appraisal proved beneficial to Starcraft for years.

During the early 1960s, sales of the quickly popular brand — sparked by its aluminum line — were brisk enough to annually expand the fleet to the point where mention of each fiberglass model would fill a book. By 1964, a molded-in lapstrake hull design was standard on all but one offering, the 14-foot entry-level Fury. With "classic lines and smartly simple décor, this debonair sandalwood tan sportster [was designed to prompt] an appreciative gleam in the eyes of little girls and their bigger sisters [while] making men become fascinated by the brute strength of its hull, its superb handling, and its quiet, dry ride."

Other models included the lapstrake style of the 13' 10" Cobra and Siren, the 15-foot Bahama and Del Ray, the 16-foot Belle Isle,and the 17-foot Riviera with a hatch deck and front/ski observation seats that folded down into beds. For 1965, the 13' 10" Mustang was yet another boatbuilder tie-in with the wildly popular Ford Mustang introduced just as the 1965 Starcraft catalog was being planned. Pictured suspended near a red Mustang car, and with unmistakably automotive copy urging, "Take the wheel and unleash the speed and dash only Mustang can give," Starcraft's version was adroitly positioned for the same fun-loving, but practical demographic.

As the 1960s progressed and many of the company's glass runabouts got bigger (like the 1966 18½-foot Imperial V), more comfortably appointed, or both, Starcraft embraced a deep-vee hull and high freeboard approach. To be sure, some of the older semi-vee designs remained as stalwarts for the boaters with modest needs, but were all from lapstrake molds. The 15-foot Explorer Deluxe served as Starcraft's nod to the emerging trihedral hull phenomenon. The boat had center steering, was billed as a sports runabout, and paved the way for many such Starcraft utility fishing/cruising/skiing boats to follow.

By decade's end, boats were just one of the company's "great escape machines" which also included campers, all-terrain vehicles, and snowmobiles. Trihedral bow riders and vee-hulls were about evenly represented as the 1970s became established. Starcraft of interest to our study — for 1971 — include the 14' 4" V-140 Modified (the foot-longer Deluxe), a classic California ski boat and the T-170 Eliminator, a 17-foot hydroplane rated for up to 140 hp. For waterside bicentennial celebrations, patriotic boaters might have enjoyed Starcraft's American S-19, an arrow-like 19' 4¼" wraparound windshield runabout treated with chrome accents, cushy upholstery, and a red metal flake deck. Several smaller (18-, 16-, and 15-foot) incarnations were available, although not nearly as stylized.

The manufacturer ended the 1970s and celebrated its 75th anniversary with the announcement that it had snagged *Powerboat* magazine's 1978 styling award. One of the few glass outboard runabouts left in the catalog was bow rider Tri-Star 15. (Refer to Chapter Two for additional information on this brand's subsequent history.

Winner (PlastiCraft)

Winner Plasticraft's late 1940s 14-foot utility runabout.

"The Winner Manufacturing Company, Inc., has produced PlastiCraft Boats commercially, on a volume basis," an October 1950 flyer noted, "for over six years." While this math dates those pioneer hulls to the fall of 1944 during the World War II production prohibition of such consumer goods, Winner easily wins the title of

first mass producer of reinforced plastic boats. The West Trenton, New Jersey's fledgling late 1945 line was early enough to qualify for the pioneering distinction.

But there's an asterisk in the story, though it doesn't threaten Winner's crown. *Yachting* editors had gathered information on Winner sometime before publishing the magazine's January 1946 issue. Their late-fall research found PlastiCraft boats being fabricated with "special plastic resins...in combination with tough, fibrous material [and producing] a smooth interior surface. Cured under heat and pressure, this one-piece hull, including transom, is seamless." As is often the case in such matters, some conflict involving timing exists. A circa 1960 newspaper clipping reported that "it took until January 1947 before Winner engineers were satisfied and the first production fiberglass boat was introduced to the public at the New York National Motorboat Show."

Arguably, Winner's hesitation was caused by the "sisal" plant fiber reinforcement used to stiffen the pre–1947 boats. "Learning that Owens-Corning had developed a strong glass fiber," the newspaper article continued, "Winner began experimenting with it. It worked [better than sisal], but then there were the problems of getting the new material into economic production, getting it to release from the mold, hiding its natural dirty yellow coloring, and answering the basic translucence of glass, which tended to make consumers wary." One can imagine the factory's frantic pace and late nights precipitated by the January boat show deadline.

Taylor Winner had begun his marine-related business during the early 1930s and within a few years was a leading producer of aquaplanes, surfboards (including a model with outriggers and outboard motor mount!), water skis, and balsa wood swimming belts, as well as pool accessories and lifeguard rescue gear. Snow skis, poles, bobsleds, ice cream vending boxes,

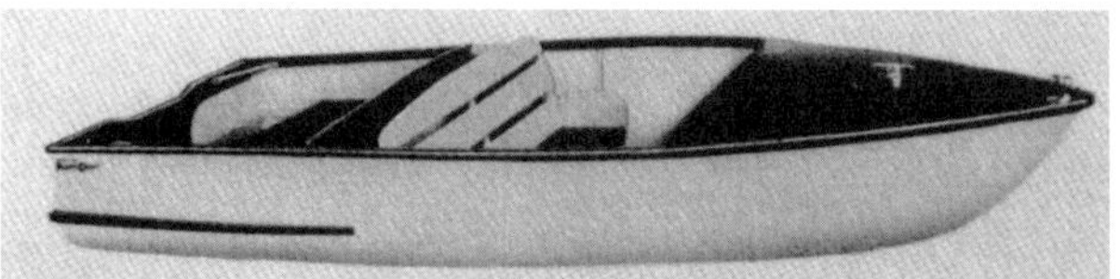

The 12-foot Winner Plasticraft utility runabout hails from about 1950 and features wooden slat front seat back.

advertising novelties, balls, and pontoons represented some of Winner's other prewar product offerings.

Even after PlastiCraft was getting firmer sea legs in the late 1940s, Winner secretaries would insert a water sports, beach and pool, and life-saving pamphlet in the envelope addressed to a boat shopper requesting PlastiCraft information. The back cover of many of the firm's early fiberglass boat brochures touted Winner water skis, and often also contained a layman's guide to understanding glass fibers and the benefits of their use in plastic molded hulls. The icon of the debut-era PlastiCraft was the line's only wheel-steered runabout, the sleekly contoured 14-foot Deluxe, for $395. At 335 pounds (compared to a 140-pound, similarly sized Aero-Craft model DD), it's noted in 1948 literature as having seating for seven and a rating for up to 33 hp.

Most accompanying publicity shots show the Deluxe pushed at 40 mph by a massive opposed four-cylinder Evinrude Speeditwin. The open utility version of this 14-footer also had a 33-hp rating. Others in the fleet included a 12-foot utility rated for the big Evinrude 22.5 or Johnson 22 opposed twins, and a pair of 10-foot rowing or sailing dinghies.

By 1951, a 12-foot Deluxe runabout with center wheel deck was added. The catalog indicated that the 14-foot Deluxe had been lightened, though made 20 percent stronger "than previous models." As if to start distancing themselves from references to plastic, 1955 Winner copywriters positioned a caption box containing the Owens-Corning trademarked "Fiberglas" over every PlastiCraft heading. Taylor Winner had, around 1947, run into some trouble with O-C when he sought a patent on the fiberglass boatbuilding process. O-C successfully argued that experimenter Ray Green came up with the idea during World War II. An improved relationship followed and Winner saw the wisdom in aligning his publicity with the company most people thought of when hearing the still-novel term "fiberglas." After all, in the 1950s, "plastic" still had connotations of being cheap.

Winner's mid-1950s runabouts included the 14' 3" Super Deluxe with windshield and wheel deck control, the 14' 3" Deluxe (rated for 25 hp) having a center deck but no wheel or windshield, and the 12-foot Deluxe equipped like its bigger sister. Open or utility versions made the catalogs, too, which by this time were being mailed from the company's new Trenton address (although the boats remained F.O.B. West Trenton). Shortly thereafter, the PlastiCraft label was dropped. The 1958 Winner models had more evocative names than "deluxe" or "utility." They included the nicely appointed W-12 Warrior and the more basic W-12 Wasp, tidy little front-steered 12½-foot runabouts suggested for use with 10– 15-horse motors. The 15-foot runabouts, in descending order of price and amenities, were the Seafire S-15, Seahawk S-15, and Seawolf S-15. The 17' 2" Voyager, Viking, and Valiant constituted the V-17 series. Winner molded in a hint of aft fins for the V-17 and two S-15 models.

A circa 1979 *History of Winner* identifies 1960 as the year "Winner introduced the first version of its Modified-V or Gull-Hull design. By bringing the center section of the hull deeper in the water, Winner was able to provide greater stability, a softer ride, and good mid-range speed without sacrificing top end performance. Winner called its new deep-vee design the 'Quadralift' and built an eighteen-foot prototype for the tortuous Orange Bowl Nine Hour Marathon in 1964. Quadralift was one of eleven finishers out of a field of eighty-one."

In the meantime, around 1959, California-based Wizard Boats Inc., acquired Winner and during 1960, moved the operation to a Wizard facility at Dickson, Tennessee. For 1961, Winner and Wizard shared several models, such as the outboard cruiser Baronet 18. Winner runabouts in 1963 came in 13-, 14-, 15-, 16-, and 17-footers. One of the last such boats with classic PlastiCraft styling was the 1964, 13-foot Sprite, a Glasspar G-3-like gentleman's racer sporting a touch of aft fins.

By 1967, bigger boats with stern drive were crowding traditional runabouts out of the Winner line. A few exceptions, like the 15-foot Cobra, remained, but even that had an inboard/outboard option. For its November 1966 *Stock Boat Directory* ad aimed at attracting new dealers, Winner dragged out of factory storage a 1947 PlastiCraft that had been tossed on the moving truck several years earlier. Though it wore a long-expired New York registration (perhaps from Hudson River stock outboard marathon days), the vintage wheel deck runabout was quickly fitted with a contemporary 20-horse Merc and cruised past a waiting photographer. "You have a future with Winner Boats," read the accompanying copy. "We have the past to prove it."

As a nod to 1967's trends, the company put its version of tri-hull technology into the 15-foot Tiki Utility and 18½-foot Cougar bow riders. As Winner moved further from its outboard runabout roots, late 1960s brochures promoted a 23½-foot fin-keel sloop. The wind had died down for Winner sales by 1977, when a Nevada-based subsidiary of Thompson Boats acquired "the Winner name, all molds, the patent rights, and the inventory of Winner Boat Corp. Thompson closed the Dickson, Tennessee, operation a year later, but used the Winner name for boats it made elsewhere. Reportedly, in the early 1980s, a small group of erstwhile Dickson Winner employees opened up shop in town and built some boats sporting the Winner (of Dickson,

TN) logo. Though the name continued for a time, that's where we'll end the story of the company that helped move fiberglass boating from novel to normal.

Wizard

Likely dubbed "Wizard," for the seemingly magical, infinitely moldable, and indestructible qualities of reinforced plastic, this brand originated in 1946. That's when a machinist and entrepreneur named Curtis Herberts bought the plastic hull tooling and formula from the Chemold Division of Western Plastics, a company that had concocted some small plastic craft for the military. Western reportedly co-opted the fabrication process from a couple of young experimenters who'd whipped up a crude plastic dinghy (reinforced with shredded vegetation) and then showed it to the plastic company's owner. Herberts based his resulting Wizard Boats, Inc. in Costa Mesa, California.

Because the 1958 Wizard catalog touts, "Some Wizards, now in their eleventh year, are still performing as good as new, and some of the original [Chemold] plastic boats made in 1944 are still in use by military forces," we can assume that the earliest boats in the Wizard line appeared for the 1947 model year. In fact, that 1958 flyer revealed, "Wizard was organized in June of 1947." Resins bonding the manufacturer's pioneer hulls were reinforced with muslin cloth, and were hardened or cured at temperatures over 200 degrees. In the early 1950s, however, Wizard embraced the emerging standard of polyester resins and fiberglass matting supplemented with spray-applied chopped-glass fibers. Along the way, Wizard's flamboyant publicity included brochure snapshots of workers tossing one of the company's smaller craft off the factory roof, blasting a rifle at the poor thing, and treating it to an aggressive sledgehammer.

In 1958, pioneer plastic boat maker Wizard claimed its 13' 10" Holiday Deluxe was "among the most popular Fiberglas plastic boats ever built." The model's high sides and pronounced non-trip chines were typical of most Wizard craft aimed at the family "all around sport boat" market, a clientele soon largely lured away by newer names in the glass game.

THE 13½′ UTILITY RUNABOUT

Relatively high sides and generous deck overhang were characteristic Wizard features seen in this 1958 Utility Runabout.

For some now forgotten reason, during the late 1940s–early 1950s, Wizard specifications in *Motor Boating* were all over the place in terms of model length and hull material. That is to say, the Deluxe Outboard Speedster grew to 16 feet in 1949, shrank to 11' 1" the next year, and down to 11 feet for 1951. Some models were denoted "plastic" and others "fiberglass." This is especially curious because the adjacent Winner Manufacturing (PlastiCraft) entries were consistent, typically bearing the magazine's code letter "F" for fiberglass. Maybe the plastic boats had the muslin or some reinforcement other than pure fiberglass.

Wizard's founder passed away in 1954, leaving vice president Harold Hautflaire at the helm. Within

Some speculate that Wizard's '58 Golden Wasp (also simply called Wasp) might have been the inspiration for Glasspar's 1959 G-3, also from a southern California company.

four years, he'd added plants in St. Joseph, Michigan, and Dickson, Tennessee. (The latter would also house Winner Boats after being bought and moved there by Wizard around the fall of 1961.) According to company literature, "More than 17,000 Wizard boats [were by 1958] in service all over the free world, from the steaming jungles in Africa to the icy seas of far northern Alaska and Norway." Euphemistically, the copy assured boat shoppers that there were "Wizard dealers in virtually every city, town, and hamlet in the United States and many foreign countries." This surprised a number of vintage outboarders who grew up in medium-sized waterfront communities and told me they'd never seen a Wizard hull, not even a 1957 Holiday 14-foot runabout aimed at the broad middle-range family boating market.

For folks wanting to make a statement, Wizard offered its most beautiful in the line of "laminated fiberglas plastic boats." Gracing the 1958 catalog cover was the 13' 2" Wasp, often referred to as the Golden Wasp because of its "Fire-Gold glittering deck." Meant for a 35- to 40-horse outboard, the 1958 Wasp had front and rear upholstered seats (a previous edition just had front seating) and a "central plastic housing for the controls." Tasteful fins and a stylized windshield made this $1,055 boat evocative of Studebaker's Golden Hawk.

More traditionally styled boats in the late 1950s Wizard fleet included the 13' 5" Utility entry-level runabout, the more richly appointed 13' 10" Holiday with walk-through center decking, the 14' 10" Resorter molded with a "new semi-vee bottom with spray deflecting chines," and the 15' 11" Marlin with generous freeboard that could be ordered as a standard runabout, hardtop sedan (with sliding windows), or permanent bulkhead cabin model. The 19' 2" El Dorado cabin cruiser topped the era's Wizard roster and was often shown in two-tone pink and coral mist. Among the other color options that helped make Wizard a 1950s style icon among pleasure craft buffs were "canary yellow," "platinum gray," "buckskin tan," "dark green," "mist green," "dark blue," "cirrus blue," white, and red.

Wizard entered the 1960s with Baronet, an 18-foot high-freeboard runabout/daycruiser/ski boat combo, and a 14-foot Wasp for 1961. The latter hull underwent "particularly high-speed tests to prove its maneuverability and accommodation of a 40- to 50-hp outboard motor," up to 10 extra horses than the debut Wasp. Wizard was absent from *Motor Boating*'s 1962 show issue and went missing from *The Boating Industry*'s "stock boatbuilders" tally by late 1963. In fact some of the Wizard design lived on in the Winner line, a competitor Wizard bought around 1959 and moved to Tennessee. Because Winner had the more recognized handle, the Wizard-Winner operation opted to simply do business as Winner.

Finally, it should be noted that Western Auto Stores sold outboard motors under Western Auto's Wizard trade name and similarly identified some of its boats, such as those built for it by Aristo-Craft in wood from 1949–53. It doesn't appear, however, that our study's Costa Mesa firm ever had any connection to Western Auto's Wizard hulls.

Chapter 6

A Multitude of Brands

Fiberglass Boatbuilders, The Minor Makes

"The situation [of so many boat makers] is due to three factors:
1. The boom in boat [sales],
2. The development of new hull designs that can [be] easily copied, and
3. The excellent sculptural qualities of fiberglass which permit low-cost, complex hull designs."

— *Popular Science*, January 1964

A quick count indicates that there were at least five times more fiberglass boat makers than the 100 or so marine aluminum concerns. Detailed study of the enterprises' start dates and locales often reveals an "enclave" or "clustering" pattern in which small companies spring up near established fiberglass builders (in California and Texas, for example), as well as a fascinating migration from the (1940s–50s) greater Los Angeles, metropolitan New York–New Jersey, and Southeastern Massachusetts–Rhode Island areas to second generation (1960s–70s) glass boat entrepreneurial colonies in spots like Hialeah, Florida.

Some observers estimate that there were literally dozens upon dozens of tiny, local, flash-in-the-pan fiberglass boat companies, as well as surprising numbers of moderately financed but quiet regional makers that flew under the radar of *Motor Boating* annual "outboard boats" rosters. If and when detected, this legion could swell our listing to a couple of thousand entries. In brief entries for which little additional detail is available, the firm's approximate first year of having cataloged fiberglass hulls is enclosed in parentheses. It's certainly possible that glass builders sold some early production boats a year or so prior to having gained a listing (or bought advertising) in any national boating magazines. Such a scenario makes inaugural pinpointing difficult.

When the general trade name for a company's line is not apparent in its corporate identity, the name is noted — if known — in quotation marks following the corporate handle. Because some records begin the chronology the year *after* a company had sold 25 boats through dealers, while others (typically published near year's end) introduced the upcoming model year, debut dates should be given leeway. An additional caveat relates to the term "plastic" often used in *Motor Boating* and *The Boating Industry* documentation prior to 1951 as a descriptor for any resin-related composite hull. On one occasion, a company pegged in the annual rosters as producing fiberglass plastic craft was found — in its own tiny magazine ad — to tout a fiberglass-covered plywood process. It may be that a handful of early and obscure brands herein were, in fact, fabricators of craft that might not pass the "true fiberglass" boat test even by late 1950s' standards — meaning FRP.

Other issues must also be noted. Stamford, Connecticut's Botved Boats exemplifies the conundrum of identifying fiberglass manufacturers. The artist's advertising rendering of Botved's 1956 Coronet "fiberglass hardtop Sedan," earned the craft a berth in the following listing, until small print revealed that the 19' 4" boat possessed a glass top, but only a "fiberglass covered hull." To be sure, neither the word "wood" nor any type of lumber was mentioned in the company's ad, but the craft's construction didn't feature enough fiberglass for qualification as a legitimate FRP boat.

Finally, some companies got into the mix although they probably only served as temporary subcontractors for an "actual" marine manufacturer possessing a boat trade name. In any event, please accept the following chronicling as a snapshot of what boating boom runabout buyers could have encountered at a bustling boat show in the good old days.

A.R.A. Mfg. Co. Grand Prairie, Texas (1961)

Admiral Boat Co. Tampa, Florida. A quarter-page generalized ad in *The Boating Industry*'s June 1961 "Boat Names Guide" is among Admiral's early surviving publicity. There, it heralded an "exciting new boating idea: competing with the best quality, competing with the best price." In announcing its "value" strategy (on all sizes from 8-foot dinghy through 18-foot Cruiser) the Florida firm offered a picture of an unidentified fiberglass runabout of about 16 feet LOA. The deck was accented with a painted black arrow, while spear motifs graced the hull sides. The boat looked like a Larson All American, then one of the industry's best sellers and certainly a worthy craft for Admiral to imitate. By 1962, the manufacturer was noted as an Oldsmar, Florida, concern.

Admiral Fiberglass Corp. "Valiant." Gloucester, Virginia (1962)

Advance Engineering Co. "Glassport." 5045 South 2275 West, Roy, Utah (1960) **Aero-Craft Boats Div. of Harwill** "Aero-Glas." St. Charles, Michigan. Pioneer aluminum boat maker Aero-Craft/Harwill was offering fiberglass hulls (like Neptune 16) by 1960 under the Aero-Glas banner. Another Michigan pleasure craft company, Water Wonderland, also marketed product with the Aero-Glas name.

Aero-Nautical, Inc. 154 Prospect St. Greenwich, Connecticut (1967)

Airide, Inc. Washington St., Hudson, Massachusetts (1961)

Albright Boat & Marine Co. "Albright Boats." 520 Penman St., Charlotte, North Carolina (1959)

Alexandria Boat Works, Inc. Highway 52, East Alexandria, Minnesota (1958)

Allcock Mfg. Co. "Adirondack." North Water St., Ossining, New York (1960)

Allison Products Co. 14 Park St., Roseland, New Jersey (1960)

John Allmand Boats. 471 NE 79th St., Miami, Florida (1964)

Allstar Mfg. Corp. "Allstar Fleet." 591 2nd Ave., North Lewisburg, Tennessee (1962)

Aluminum Boats & Canoes, Inc. "Princecraft." 100 Maple Ave., Princeville, Quebec (1957)

Aman Plastics. "Aman Boats." 1520 South Dixie Highway, Hollywood, Florida (1960s)

American Boatbuilding Corp. (Successor to Beetle Boats) Greenwich Bay Shipyard, East Greenwich, Rhode Island (1958)

American Fabricator, Inc. "Amfab Boats." 261 Seminole Ave., Orangeburg, South Carolina (1964)

American Fiberlast Co. Atlantic Ave., Boothbay Harbor, Maine (1955)

American Marc, Inc. 1601 West Florence Ave., Inglewood, California. Along with Scott/McCulloch, and the Outboard Marine Corp. group (Evinrude/Johnson), American Marc was one of the few outboard motor makers to also offer a like-branded boat line. To be sure, the West Coast company only earned a footnote in outboarding history, but an interesting one in the form of a 9¾-horse diesel kicker dubbed AMARC 10. Its rollout was slated for 1959 in a promised line of diesel outboards from 7½ to 22 hp, but only a few (in several nuances) of the AMARC 10 motor ever materialized. The engines were advertised with a sizable armada of AMARC fiberglass boats from 14 to 30 feet long. These included an outboard runabout (typically pictured only as an artist's rendering rather than as an actual photo), as well as sailboats and inboard runabouts and cruisers. Enigmatically, a single plywood sailboat got thrown into the lineup (at least on paper) for 1961. American Marc was gone from *The Boating Industry* index by 1962. Collectors finding both an AMARC 10 and American Marc glass runabout would be considered great hunters — or incredibly lucky!

American Marine Industries, Inc. 311 East Alexander, Tacoma, Washington (1964)

American Molded Fiberglass Co. 65 Governor St., Patterson, New Jersey (1957)

American Multi-Craft. Here's an early 1980s fiberglass twin-tunnel hull utility that can be nicely outboard-powered with about 75 hp, or thanks to a presto-change-o setup, converted to a sailboat.

Amfab, Inc. Kingsdown Road, Orangeburg, South Carolina (1968)

Amphibious Boats, Inc. "Falcon" and "Amphibian Boats." 1815 Shady Oaks Drive, Denton, Texas. For 1960, the company (noted as being in Dallas) unveiled amphibious craft (in sizes from 15 to 19 feet) that looked like many competing fiberglass outboard runabouts, except for a set of retractable wheels underneath the rear seat area. This "airplane type landing gear," said publicity, "eliminates the need for a boat trailer." These boats could also be ordered as members of the Falcon line without the wheels.

Anchor Plastics, Inc. Gatesville, Texas (1965)

The Anchorage, Inc. 57 Miller St., Warren, Rhode Island. Producer of the famous Dyer line of dinghies (beginning in the early 1950s) and powerboats, the Anchorage was also included in *The Boating Industry* as offering plastic outboard craft —a 14-foot utility and a 16-foot fisherman — in 1951.

H. H. Anderson Co. 810 East 8th St., Superior, Wisconsin (1959)

Anheuser-Schantz Mfg. Co. "The Lauderdale Line." 108 SW 21st St., Fort Lauderdale, Florida. Distributed through the Lauderdale Marina, by 1956, Lauderdale's outboard fleet included a 16-foot runabout (Caribbean), as well as a 15-foot utility.

Ankor-Craft. Also noted as **Scott Boat Company, Inc.** 801 4th St., Tell City, Indiana. From a corrugated metal building with a little office area and a big shop, workers laying up fiberglass boats here could see the Ohio River. Ever present were big pieces of Styrofoam used to sculpt the latest design into what would become a hull or topside mold. The marque's 1977 brochure of "Quality Boats" featured over a dozen outboard craft, most of which were tri-hulled bow riders.

Anthony Powercraft, Inc. 6032 Shull St., Bell Gardens, California, and South Gate, California. This brand was offered in glass by 1960. The Starfire 14 for 1961 was influenced by the Glasspar G-3, and got similarly dubbed "ski-boat." It was rated for motors from 30 to 60 hp, but was pictured with a 70-horse Merc. Those appreciative of generous aft fins might even choose a Starfire over a G-3.

AquaCraft, Ltd. 11 Harding Ave., North Arlington, New Jersey (1959)

Aqua-Craft Boat Co. 19141 East Arrow Highway, Glendora, California (1960s)

Aqua King Corp. 2490 N.W. 151st St., Miami, Florida (1968)

Aquanautics, Inc. 1066 Linda Vista, Mountain View, California (1967)

Arkansas Traveler. A pioneer aluminum boat maker chronicled in Chapter 2, this Little Rock-based manufacturer added glass for 1959 with models like Rocket 14-G, 15 and 16-footers in its Sports series, several utilities, and an 18-foot day cruisers. During the early '60s, Sears contracted with Traveler to fabricate boats wearing the Elgin name.

Arena Craft Products, Inc. 130 Buchanan Circle, Pacheco, California (1968)

Arrow Glass Boat & Mfg. Corp. "Arrow Glass."1764 Chelsea Ave. (and later, 1371 Farmville Road), Memphis, Tennessee (1964)

Ash Craft. (formerly, Wagemaker Co.) Cadillac, Michigan (1962)

Associated Naval Architects, Inc. "A.N.A. Skiffs." 400–500 Washington St., West Norfolk, Virginia (1951)

Astra Industries, Inc. 853 Dundee Ave., Elgin, Illinois (1959)

Atlantic Boat Works. 11374 Atlantic Ave., Lynwood, California (1958)

Atlantic Marine Industries, Inc. "The Newport Line." Arney's Mount and Fort Dix Roads, Pemberton, New Jersey. "Boating is play, the Newport way!" promised Atlantic Marine's 1959 brochure. Who's to say, but the Newport 15 (14' 5" LOA) and Newport 17 (15' 9" LOA) models appear influenced by Winner runabouts from a neighboring Garden State factory. Utility versions had front deck dashboard steering and a front bench seat but were otherwise open, while Deluxe editions wore molded seats fore and aft, a walk-through center deck, and a motor well. Both came with a white hull, but could be had with aquamarine, maroon, black, or mandarin red topsides.

Aztec Boat Corp. 298 W. 24th St., Hialeah, Florida (1961)

Badger Boat Builders. "Badger Boats." Couderay, Wisconsin. Debuting in glass for 1950, Badger can be considered a quiet pioneer fiberglass boat company that operated into the mid-1960s, long after most of its earlier contemporaries had left the marine industry.

Badger Boat Corp. Black Creek, Wisconsin (Successor to above?) (late 1960s)

Baker, Jewell, Inc. Orrville, Alabama. This obscure

1957 listing was juxtaposed in another source and may actually be Jewell Baker, Inc. Little has surfaced about the firm's boats.

Balco Yacht Co. Dundalk, Maryland. This firm marketed some outboard utility and runabout kits in fiberglass, circa 1959.

Barracuda Marine Co. 33 South LaSalle St., Aurora, Illinois (1959)

Bass Boats, Inc. Hurst, Texas (1967)

Bauman-Harnish Rubber & Plastics, Inc. 410 North Lee St., Garrett, Indiana (1958)

Becker Products. 202 South Lyons Ct., West Atlantic City, New Jersey (1965)

Bedell Engineering Co. Port Washington, New York (1953)

Bee Boat Co., Inc. 302 North Market, Paxton, Illinois (1961)

Bee-Line Mfg., Co. 2411 Walker Road, N.W., Grand Rapids, Michigan. The 16-foot Luxury Sapphire represents this small glass fabricator's brightest gem. "Features hydro-dynamic design for fast planing, smooth riding and exceptional maneuverability," claimed Bee-Line's tiny 1958 ad. "Complete with wide choice of colors, lights, all hardware, steering wheel, windshield, speedometer, step plates and mirror." Sapphire gets the nod for biggest, pointiest fins!

Beetle Boat Co., Inc. 19 County St., New Bedford, Massachusetts. "Beetle wasn't the first to use fiberglass," *Trailer boats'* Larry Carpenter recalled, "but its extensive line of outboard hulls, inboards and sailing craft marketed for over a decade served to break the ice for the armada of fiberglass boats that would follow." Carl Beetle met a General Electric Company employee who told him about plastic covers (or "radomes") that GE was making to protect radar antennas from the elements. Beetle was so enthusiastic about the possibilities, as was GE, that he cashed in his most famous wooden sailboat design (the Beetle Cat) and invested the dough in creating a line of fiberglass craft. Among the processes he and GE people (in Pittsfield, Massachusetts) used were matched metal dies to make early Beetle fiberglass dinghies and small sailboats. Beetle took some to the 1947 New York boat show.

After Carl Beetle sold his pioneer glass boat company, the new owners adopted a beetle logo to serve as the firm's "front man."

The next year the "BB" (Beetle Boat) line of "Impregnated Fiberglass" models included sturdy outboard runabouts. For 1950, they were 10' 3" BB-Skimmer, the 12' 3" BB-Flyer, and the 14' 3" BB-Clipper. "All 'BB' lifetime boats are molded in one seamless, leak-proof piece by the famous 'BB' process," the ads exclaimed. "All are permanently colored and never need painting. All are rot-proof, worm-proof, corrosion-proof, and have tremendous strength and toughness, and will stand amazing abuse. They are safe, seaworthy and permanently buoyant. They are unaffected by heat or cold, fresh or salt water, they will

A freshly minted, 14' 3", 1950 "BB-Clipper" gets a workout in New Bedford, Massachusetts, not far from the Beetle Boat Company

not deteriorate."

In retrospect, while Beetle's claims were indeed correct, to boaters resigned to annual hull maintenance, the ad copy probably sounded like a commercial for some miracle diet that doesn't require any exercise and calls for eating large quantities of ice cream and chocolate cake. A true pioneer FRP boatman, Beetle worked hard to shift boat buyers from wood to glass (taking out expensive, full page ads in *Motor Boating*, for example), but the public's perception that wooden boats were *the* real boats wasn't to change until the late 1950s. Beetle sold the company in 1951 and passed away a year or so later.

The "BB" outboard cruisers were especially rugged, but earned a bad rap in the aesthetics department. "Sure it's seaworthy," one old salt admitted of a faded green, beaten-up Beetle imbued with almost exaggerated contours, "but the darn thing looks a discarded rubber shoe." Carl Beetle may have been just a bit ahead of the curve when it came to fiberglass boats, but any one of the rare Beetle outboard boats would make a great addition to one's boat collection or to a maritime museum's most prominent display area. As this is written, Mystic Seaport Museum has just acquired a BB Swan catboat.

Bell Boy Boats Div., Bellingham Shipyards Co. Squalicum Waterway, Bellingham, Washington. As early as the late 1940s, Bellingham was fabricating plastic craft under the Bell Boy banner. Though production and local distribution began around 1952, the consumer trades picked them up in the mid-1950s when the line's small, colorful outboard cruisers garnered a reputation for seaworthiness and ease of maintenance. To be sure, Bell Boy built sleeker boats, too, one of which (the 20-foot Bikini runabout) was designed by racing hydroplane maven Ted Jones for possible 1957 sale. It could really exceed 50 mph, but wasn't stable enough for Bell Boy to confidently market the boat to the general public.

Exaggerated tailfins on the 1958, 14' 6" Bell Boy are big enough to serve as easel for a spread eagle wing motif.

After being brought under the United Boatbuilders, Inc., restructuring, the line was acquired by Sabrecraft in nearby Tacoma around 1964.

Bell Boy Corp. Columbia City, Indiana. Sometime in 1957, Bellingham Shipyards established a midwestern plant to fabricate its Bell Boy boats. A New York facility was subsequently added to better service the East Coast.

Bellecraft Industries Ltd. 1150 River St., Kamloops, British Columbia, (1960)

Bemidji Boat Works (and **Bemidji Boat Co., Inc.**). "Corecraft." Bemidji, Minnesota. At first glance, this company's trade name appears to read "Correct-Craft," but is spelled and pronounced "Core Craft," which makes it different from the famed Florida ski boats. It surfaced in the trades around 1958.

Best Fiberglass Products. 306 East 2nd St., Dundee, Illinois (1962)

Bilt-Well Boats, Inc. Route 2, San Antonio, Texas (1961)

Roy M. Bloom, Inc. 274 Madison Ave. New York, New

York (1962)

Blue Mfg. Co. 2221 North Main St., Miami, Oklahoma. In 1958, the Blue Star aluminum boat people got into the glass game, but only remained until about 1963.

Bluewater Products, Inc. 410 North Spring Garden Ave., DeLand, Florida (1956)

Boat Distribution, Inc. "Starliner Boats." Lisgon St., Clinton, North Carolina. Nearly every sentence in this maker's 1959 brochure shouts, "Bargain!" Oddly, there is no boat on the cover, just a swordfish. But inside, each pictured craft is captioned with fiscally conservative statements like "Budget-priced Starliners make boating a pleasure," and "Starliner's budget prices make buying a pleasure, too." Though the line was said to include glass boats, only plywood hulls are evident. Small print on the back cover indicates, "Starliners are also available in all fiberglass models." It may have been that a plastic order would send Starliner workers fabricating a mold from one of the wooden boats.

Bock Boats, Inc. "Bock," or "Bockster Boats." 3600 Summit St., Toledo, Ohio. The 18-foot Bockster was a unique outboard (up to 50 hp) runabout/sailboat combo. From 1960, it was made of fiberglass and aluminum.

Bo-Craft Plastics Company. 523 Rice St., Little Rock, Arkansas. Everett Bowman, president. (1960)

Bowman, Inc. also Bowman Mfrs, Inc. "Ply-Glass Boats." 1823 Woodrow St., and subsequently, 713 Izard St., Little Rock Arkansas. Introducing a glass line in 1955, Bowman used a Goodyear Aircraft Division's one-piece plastic hull with mahogany topside finished in cardinal red enamel for its 1956 flagship, the Havana. By 1957, Bowman product offerings truly ran the gamut with the company touting "Plastic, *Plyglas* [glassed-over plywood], Aluminum, and steel boats." It was one of several firms to use "plastic hulls made under 1,000,000 pounds of pressure by Goodyear Aircraft Corporation."

Bo-Mer Mfg. Co., Inc. Auburn, New York. (1947)

Bonito Boats, Inc. Orlando, Florida (1968)

Otis C. Borum Boats, Inc. 129 East 21st St., Jacksonville, Florida. After starting in the 1950s as a wooden builder, and going glass around 1960, Borum (as renamed Borum Mfg. Corp.) moved to Folkston, Georgia, and returned to plywood by late 1961.

Bowers Fiberglass Fabricators. "Bowers Boats." 121 Heard St., Elberton, Georgia (1961)

Melford F. Brandenburg. 130 Dore St., San Francisco, California (1953)

S.S. Brandon Mfg. & Engineering Co. 2905 SW 2nd Ave., Fort Lauderdale, Florida (1964)

Brevil Boat Co., Inc. Harbour One, 17201 Biscayne Blvd., Miami, Florida. That's the way the company name got spelled in *The Boating Industry* for 1964, although, it was listed in 1965 as Breuil. Rosters for 1967 and 1968 say, "Brueuil."

Bristol Boat Corp. 1258 West Gaylord, Long Beach, California (1960)

British Marine Products. 80 Shore Road, Port Washington, New York. Probably an importer rather than a manufacturer at about the time of its 1957 *The Boating Industry* listing, BMP also marketed small J.A.P.-powered Sea Chief outboard motors brought in from England.

Bronson Boatbuilding Co. 4301 South Union, Tacoma,

Washington (1959)

Brownie Boats. 191 Oakwood Drive, Avon Lake, Ohio (1957)

Brunswick Corp. During the late 1950s and early 1960s, this billiard and bowling concern branched out into marine endeavors through its acquisitions of boat makers such as Owens, Cutter, and Larson, as well as Mercury outboards. Interestingly, while much of Brunswick's early 21st-century revenues are generated by its pleasure craft–related holdings, the firm's initial round of boat maker purchases — Larson, for example — resulted in fiscal and managerial strife. Classic boaters who look closely might find a rare Owens or Cutter hull branded with the Brunswick name. The 1961 Brunswick/Owens 13-foot Brisbane would make a great find, as the sporty ski-boat was fitted with "Ride-Guide steering [from co-owned Mercury], back-to-back upholstered seats, rear view mirror and speedometer."

Bryant's Marina, Inc. 1117 East Northlake, Seattle, Washington. Begun as a modest 1930s Johnson Outboard dealership, Bryant's blossomed into a major marine sales and service organization and Evinrude distributor with multiple locales by the 1950s. Bryant-branded boats (typically built in wood by the Morris Brothers of Everett, Washington) included a line of glass hulls, starting in 1958.

Buccaneer Fiberglass Boat Co. 3707 NW 49th St., Miami, Florida (1955)

Burnham Products, Inc. 4203 West Harry, Wichita, Kansas (1960)

Bylsma Boats. 505 Crofton St., SW., Grand Rapids, Michigan. George Bylsma, owner. (1955)

Cadillac Marine & Boat Co. 110 7th St., Cadillac, Michigan (1956)

Canots Cadorette Canoe Co. "Cadorette." 320 12th St., Grand Mere, Quebec (1960)

Cape Cod Shipbuilding Co. Narrows Road, Wareham, Massachusetts. One of several venerable New England boat makers to embrace glass early on, Cape Cod jumped into plastic outboarding by 1952. Perhaps most coveted by non-wooden runabout buffs is the firm's Class AU (American Power Boat Association stock outboard utility) family runabout. The 10-footer had been designed by racing boat expert Fred Jacoby. A larger and more conventional use Cape Cod runabout was the 15-foot Stormy Petrel of 1954, appropriate for big water and motors to 25 hp.

Stormy Petrel from Cape Cod Shipbuilding was built with salt water day cruising in mind.

carAqua. Unlike their juxtaposed namesake, Aqua-Car, carAqua was no landlubber. Instead, the late 1950s water-mobile simply looked like a big Detroit vehicle. Automotive grillework (on the blunt bow) and headlights probably generated a lot of lakeside double takes. Most versions used outboard power, though one featured a Fageol-Crosley engine plant positioned in carAqua's "trunk." An open edition (with no rear seats or motor deck) dubbed "Station Wagon" could also make one's dock look like a used car lot.

Carlson High Performance Boats. 11645 Anabel

Ave., Garden Grove, California. A pioneer in tunnel hull design, Art Carlson introduced a small lineup of high-performance craft. By 1971, he was associated with Glastron, where his designs began being marketed under the Carlson/Glastron banner.

Carolina Fiberglass Products Co. "Shearwater Boats." 510 East Jones St., Wilson, North Carolina (1960)

Carter Craft Corp. Panama City, Florida (1960)

Carver Boat Corp. Pulaski, Wisconsin (1960)

Catamaran Corp. of America. 2324 Summit St., Kansas City, Missouri. This firm marketed several glass outboard utilities, runabouts, and catamarans in kit form around 1961.

Cathedral Yacht Corp. 220-222 SW 27th St., Ft, Lauderdale, Florida. This late 1960s company built several cathedral-hulled utilities, the smallest of which (for 1969) was a 16-footer.

Central Boat Works. "Lamar Boats." 101 Highway 348, La Marque, Texas (1959)

Century Boat Co. 1860 Broadway, New York, New York (1960s)

Challenger Marine Corp. 13301 Biscayne Blvd., North Miami, Florida (1958)

Chemold. (see Western Plastics, Inc.)

Champion Boats. 1923-25 N.E. 150th St., Miami, Florida (mid-1960s)

Chaparral Boats. Built in a former Larson plant in Nashville, Georgia, a 15-foot tri-hull was William Pegg's 1965 debut craft. He got a taste of the glass boat business when his family's fiberglass fabrication shop was contracted to make some boat molds and crank out a few boats per week.

Chesley Mfg. Co. 1219 East Florence Ave., Los Angeles, California (1953)

Chestnut Canoe Co., Ltd. Fredericton, Newfoundland (1960)

Chetek Boat Corp. Dovre Road, Chetek, Wisconsin (1958)

Chris-Craft Lake'n Sea (see Parsons Corp.)

Clyde-Craft Plastic Boat Mfg. Co. Richmond, Virginia (1956)

Coastal Fiberglass Products, Inc. Rt. 2, Hart Road North, Fort Myers, Florida (1967)

Cobia Boats. Sanford, Florida. By the late 1960s, Cobia's "easy-riding catamaran-type hulls" were the line's stock in trade. For 1967, they came in 15-, 17-, and 19-foot versions.

Commando Boat Co. 2121 South Union, Tulsa, Oklahoma (for 1961, and by 1962, as a) Div. of Claude Miller Enterprises, Inc., 3301 Charles Page Blvd., Tulsa, Oklahoma

Commodore Boats, Inc. New Bern, North Carolina (1965)

Continental Boat Corp. "Squall King." 1815 NE 144th St., North Miami, Florida (1961)

Continental Plastics Corp. "Starline Boats." 2011 Placentia, Costa Mesa, California. Around 1960, and hoping to follow in the footsteps of nearby Wizard and Glasspar, Continental also made Costa Mesa its home.

Corl Boat Co. US 6 East, Nappanee, Indiana (1961)

Correct Craft, Inc. Pine Castle Branch, Orlando, Florida. Famous for quality inboard and inboard/outboard ski-boats, Correct Craft began offering some fiberglass outboard runabouts around 1959.

Corsair Boats. Industrial Park, Cortland, New York (1964)

Costello's Boat Works. Lake Blue Drive, Winter Haven, Florida (1967)

Crest Fiberglass Industries, Inc.

Craig Systems, Inc., Marine Div. "Craig Craft Boats." 360 Merrimack St., Lawrence, Massachusetts, and Cedar Rapids, Iowa (1961)

Crownline Boats, Div. of Duo Marine. Decatur, Indiana. (mid-1960s)

Crownline Mfg. Co. Onarga, Illinois (1957)

Cruisers, Inc. (1963)

Custom-Craft Marine Co. 1700 Niagara St., Buffalo, New York. Boat kit purveyor Custom-Craft branched out toward the fiberglass market around 1956, three years before rival Luger. Most fondly remembered is the marque's Ray series of stylized runabouts. During the early 1960s, these included the Tiger Ray, Manta Ray, Delta Ray, and Sun Ray. The boats featured sculptured automotive accentuation like tail fins and (fake) tail lights. Some wore headlights (just under the bow), as well as a hardtop. A "modified catamaran type hull" not only added to the sleek appearance, but helped Custom Craft move right along. Models such as Sun Ray were sprayed-up with the Rand chop gun, allowing for intricate shaping, but only providing for the same strength as a fiberglass shower stall. At just under 14 feet, Manta Ray was prone to sponson damage when

Custom Craft's catamaran Manta Ray was built to accommodate a 100-horse Mercury, though shown here with a smaller Merc.

carelessly beached. Of course the general condition of Custom-Craft found today depends largely on owner care and how well the original buyer assembled it in the first place. It should be said, though, that these boats are worth restoring.

Customglas Plastics, Inc. (Formerly, Johnsen Boats, Inc.) Leesburg, Florida (1962)

Cutter Boats, Inc. Troy Road, Tell City, Indiana. This brand came on the scene around 1957, initially thanks to Owens. Several years later the brand was under Brunswick Marine's ownership and Cutter became its parent organization's entry-level outboard runabout line. Some looked like badge-engineered Owens craft while others were intermingled with Larson lineage after Brunswick acquired the Larson line. Marine historian Lee Wangstad recalls Owens getting into some trouble when starting Cutter. Management hired some ex–Lone Star people to get things going, but didn't know Cutter's molds would be copied from Lone Star designs. "There were hundreds of others that were pirating [fiberglass boat] designs from other manufacturers," Wangstad notes, "but none with the financial backing that Owens had. They were an easy target. The court ordered Owens to cease producing [the Lone Star knock-offs] and pay a royalty on each one they had built." To avoid even the appearance of being a copycat, Owens quickly employed designer Brooks Stevens (fresh off the Evinrude concept boat project) to style some distinctive hulls for the Cutter and Owens brands. A trio (including the 15-foot Jet de Ville) was ready for the 1958 model year. An additional designer was hired to develop some bigger runabouts to be rolled out around 1959. A deluxe erstwhile Owens 17 with those big tail fins and a sliding hardtop entered the Cutter's 1960s line. For 1961, Cutter's 16½-foot Tornado (with convertible top and back-to-back seats) provided a nice entrance to pleasure boating.

A 1962 Cutter Scamp with back-to-back (aft set popularized for water skier observation) seating represents the early '60s runabout genre's next step up from open aft area/entry-level models.

Dakota Boats, Inc. Britton, South Dakota (1964)

DaLarco, Inc. "Dar-Ling Boats." 9425 6th Ave. North, Minneapolis, Minnesota (1959)

Dargel Boat Works. Route 1, Donna, Texas (1968)

Davidson Mfg. Co., Ltd. 1872 West Georgia St., Vancouver, British Columbia. (1953)

Dawes Products Co. 2350 Mountain View–Stevens Creek Road, Los Altos, California (1961)

Delaney's Sporting Goods. 285 South Pacific Highway Woodburn, Oregon. Listed for 1961 in *The Boating Industry* as a maker of fiberglass canoes, outboard utilities, runabouts, and houseboats, this firm may have sold private-branded boats, as opposed to being an actual manufacturer. It appeared in 1962's listing but evaporated by the following year.

Desert Marine, Inc. "Oasis Boats." 2319 Fairview Ave., Boise, Idaho (1958)

De Soto Boat Co. (aka Jake Newsome Boats) Bradenton, Florida (1962)

Dixie Boat Works. "Dixie Boats." 321 Newton Bypass, Newton, North Carolina (1959)

Dixiecraft Boat Co. Magnolia, Arkansas (1961)

Dolphin Craft, Ltd. 220 Richmond St., West, Toronto, Ontario (1953)

Don Deed Craft. 1214 Gates Ave., Brooklyn, New York (1964)

Dorsett Plastics Corp. 1973 Lafayette St., Santa Clara, California. First noted in a 1956 listing, the company is categorized, by 1961, as Dorsett Marine Division of Textron Corp., the maker of Iso-Glass Boats. Their claim to visual fame was highlighted in an early promotion that stated, "Styled by [legendary industrial designer] Raymond Loewy."

Built-in fuel system, removable stern seating and spring-supported front bucket seats were among the nice standard features of the '62 Dorsett Eldorado, a lot of style in a 13' 8" package.

Ed Douthit & Son Boat Works, Inc. "Edson Boats." 5933 Old Redwood Highway, Santa Rosa, California (late 1960s)

Driscoll Bros. Boat Works. San Diego, California. A plastic hull pioneer, this organization is reported to have begun offering fiberglass boats in 1947, although it first appears in *The Boating Industry* listings for 1954.

Dudley Marine Crafts. Mountain View, California (1955)

Duo-Marine, Inc. "Duo" Decatur, Indiana. First hitting the water around 1961, Duo established a decent reputation in the crowded fiberglass outboard boating scene. By decade's end, the line included deep-vee runabouts from 15 to 21 feet long, and several tri-hulls. Duo's snub-nose deck served as a distinguishing feature. So did its stylized three-blade propeller logo, part of which formed the "D" in Duo.

Durabond Corp. (Mid-1950s)

DuraCraft Boats, Inc. Monticello, Arkansas (1959)

Duraplane Boats. Old State Road, Cayce, South Carolina (1960)

Duratech Mfg. Corp. Route 202, Peekskill, New York. A veteran aluminum boat maker, Duratech first entered glass by building craft for Glass Magic, and later in 1959 sold such boats under its own name. Not long into the 1960s, though, they re-focused on aluminum.

John Ek Boat Works. Clinton Harbor, Clinton, Connecticut (1953)

Elgin Boats (see Sears & Roebuck)

Endura-Craft. Div. of Dorsett Plastics, Inc. This trade name was reportedly used by Dorsett starting around 1955 but was dropped in favor of "Dorsett" some three years later, in an effort to identify with the corporate identity.

Enfab, Inc. 1955 Lafayette, Santa Clara, California (1955)

Fabri-Glass. 4900 Seventh St., Moline, Illinois (1961)

Fabuglas Co. 312 Jefferson St., Nashville, Tennessee. Introduced around 1960, Fabuglas later relocated to Nashville's 6401 Centennial Boulevard. For 1969, the bulk of its outboard fleet consisted of 14' 2" and 15' 7" vee-hull runabouts, as well as trihedral Trident utilities in 15' 4", 17', and 21' 10" versions.

Fairbanks Engineering & Mfg. Co. 3611 SW Archer Road, Gainesville, Florida (1964)

Fantasy Boat Div., Hydrocraft, Inc. 804 Lake St., Huntington Beach, California (1961)

Feather Craft, Inc. 450 Bishop St., NW, Atlanta, Georgia. As a leading aluminum boat maker, Feather Craft probably thought long and hard before deciding to get into glass. The foray was begun in 1958 with the 15-foot La Sirena, "a superbly appointed, custom-molded fiber glass runabout." On my copy of a promotional flyer meant to encourage dealers, the fiberglass rhetoric is crossed out, possibly signifying a false start. By 1959, Feather Craft glass was available, but the boats never made the positive impact on company revenues that aluminum had a decade earlier.

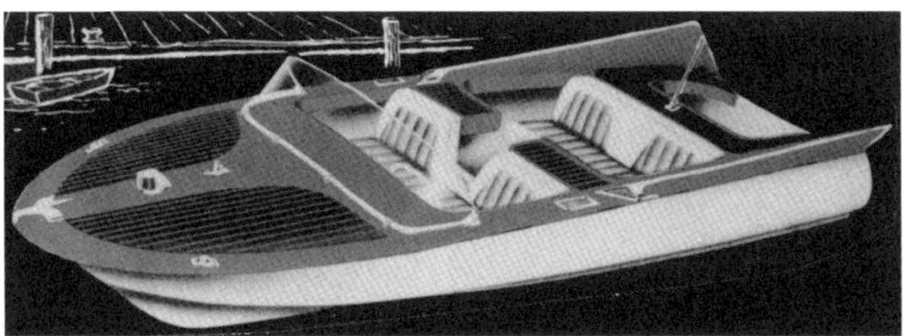

The mysterious 1958 La Sirena, Feather Craft's debut fiberglass offering. Then again, maybe she never made it past the drawing board that year.

Fiber Craft, Inc. 1820 NE 146th St., North Miami, Florida (1956)

Fiberform Plastics Mfg. Co. There is some confusion regarding this name because it showed up at several times and in various venues that might not be related in any way. During the early-to-mid 1960s, a Fiberform Products existed at 14049 South Marquardt, Santa Fe Springs, California. By 1970, **Fiberform** appears as a division of U.S. Industries, Inc., Building 20, Spokane Industrial Park, Spokane, Washington. This was admittedly a regional builder, as its brochures stated "Fiberform [represented the] most copied boat in the west." As was customary industrywide around 1970, deep-vee and tri-hulls were Fiberform's stock in trade. Among the former, the 14-foot Custom served as an entry-level runabout, while the trihedral bottom made a good showing on the 15' 2" Surfer. Common in affordable fiberglass hulls was coring or strengthening with a lot of plywood embedded in the resin. This worked well unless the boat owner wasn't careful to check for any holes or cracks in the glass that could allow water to seep in and rot or delaminate the core. Canadian Fiberform, Ltd., operated out of Kelowna, British Columbia.

Fiberform Products. "P-14," "P-17," and "Fiberform Boats." Santa Fe Springs, California. A mystery company from 1961 with no clear connection to its Washington namesake.

Fifteen-foot Fiberform Surfrider possessed the tri-hull/bow rider characteristics considered "hot" by many young 1970 boaters.

Fiberglass Boat Co., Inc. Highway 6, Waverly, Nebraska. Debuting for 1957, this organization is subsequently listed as Fibra Glass Boat Co., Inc., and could be the predecessor to the Fibra Glass outfit later seen in Arkansas.

Fiberglass Boat Co. Somerset, Pennsylvania. Around 1961, notations appeared regarding this firm's "Waterspeed" Deluxe and Super Deluxe outboard runabouts. It's not known whether there had been any connection to the similarly named company out of Nebraska.

Fiberglas Forms Industries. 9032 Charles Court, Twinsburg, Ohio (1959)

Fiberglass Company of Alabama. LaPine, Alabama (1960)

Fiber Glass Engineering, Inc. Route 2, Old Verona Road, Madison, Wisconsin. (1959)

Fiberlay, Inc. 1158 Fairview North, Seattle, Washington (1962)

FibraGlass Boat Co., Inc. Highway 6, Waverly, Nebraska. This conjoining of Fibra and Glass might simply represent a corporate name change for 1958.

Fibra Glass Boat Co., Inc. "Guardian." Kay & Nevada Sts., Hot Springs, Arkansas. This listing either represents a 1959 acquisition of the above Nebraska firm or an inadvertent name duplication. Because one seems to disappear as the other surfaces, though a company contact's name carries over, the buyout possibility seems to provide the most plausible explanation on this mystery of fiberglass runabout minutiae.

Fibre Glass Boat Corp. Coral Gables, Florida. "Woodson" sure seems like an odd identifier for a fiberglass fleet, but this Florida firm saw fit to dub their trihedral runabouts and utilities accordingly. Among the 1968 line was Vagabond, a 15-footer available as a utility "with seating for two, walk-through windshield and forward well, or [delivered as a] sport runabout with seats for four that convert to lounges." The options reflected the fishing versus cruising dichotomy that started driving the outboard pleasure craft market by the mid-1960s.

Fillip Mfg. Co. Rt. 4, San Angelo, Texas. As its debut 1961 offering was dubbed Bass Buggy, the small Texas boat maker probably focused on the angling market.

Fisher-Craft, Inc. 4635 S. Harlem Ave., Berwyn, Illinois. Frank J. Fisher, president (1956)

Flare Fiberglass Boat Co. 1311 Greenwood St., Lakeland, Florida. The ocean influenced Flare's model names, as the inaugural 1961 fleet had models like Sea Lancer, Sea Lark, and Sea Scout.

Frank Fisher Enterprises. 4635 South Harlem Ave., Berwyn, Illinois (1955)

Fleetcraft, Inc. Woodbine Airport, Woodbine, New Jersey. (1959) Here's one of several cases where a name is used by more than one concurrently operating company. The New Jersey version of Fleetcraft appears to have offered only a small line (such as its Fleetcraft Sea Skiff), while subsequently noted California-based Fleetcraft surnamed its bevy of over a dozen models Fleetliners.

Fleetcraft Marine Corp. "Fleetliner Boats." Los Angeles, California. This marque appeared in 1961, though there had been a Fleetcraft Marine Sales, Inc., 1235 East Florence Ave., Los Angeles, listed in January 1955's *Motor Boating,* apparently reflecting a corporate name adjustment.

Fleetform Corp. Fort Worth, Texas. Among the most beautifully contoured of all 1957 fiberglass runabouts was Fleetform's 15-footer. With a one-piece hull shaped into distinctive lines, it looked like a true "sports car" of the waterways.

Florida Fiberglass Products. "PlastiCruiser Boats." 329 River St., Palatka, Florida (1955)

Florida Fibre Glass Corp. 4535 Ponce de Leon Blvd., Coral Gables, Florida (1967)

Flotilla Corp. "Fleetcraft" and "Deepwater Boats." Airport Road, Woodbine, New Jersey. A 1965 startup with a possible connection to Fleetcraft.

Flyin' Cat (see Masco Corp.)

Flyin' Flivver Co. New Prague, Minnesota. *Boat Sport* writer Hank Bowman got one look at these 8' 2" fiberglass shingles and thought it might be a hoot to stage an informal race with some of his pals and then report on the antics. He was surprised at how well the novel boats handled and how fast they'd go with a motor of about 15 hp. Introduced around 1957, Flyin' Flivver had the potential to capture young boaters' imaginations the way the Jet Ski would 30 years later, but for some reason the craft never went much further, on a national scale, than in Bowman's article.

Flying Finn, Inc. 527 Lexington Ave., New York, New York (1961)

Folboat Corp. 42-09 Hunter St., Long Island City, New York. An admittedly dubious 1953 entry as this canvas folding boat outfit was curiously denoted as offering a fiberglass outboard runabout over 14 feet. It's doubtful the thing could be folded.

Ford Moulded Fibre Corp. "Ford Sportliner." 60 North Rose St., Mount Clemens, Michigan. Noted on a leaflet from dealer and possibly distributor, W.L. Masters & Son, Inc., of Chicago, the 12' 9" Ford Sportliner nicely represented early fiberglass in a center wheel deck utility runabout style. It is believed the craft debuted around

The makers of Flyin' Flivver figured its eight-foot-and change outboard-powered bedpan would spark a personal watercraft cottage racing craze, but the little fiberglass craft never caught on. That's why, today, finding a Flyin' Flivver would be fantastically fortunate.

1951.

Forester Boats, Inc. 725 Bruce St., Wyoming, Minnesota (1968)

Fort Dodge Boat Co., Inc. (Possible connection with Glass Craft?) Expo Park, Fort Dodge, Iowa (1959)

Frontier Fiberglas Industries. Air Port Station, Cheyenne, Wyoming (1959)

Gad-A-Boat Mfg., Co. 15211 Joy Road (later, 1205 Telegraph Road), Detroit, Michigan (1955)

C. C. Galbraith & Son, Inc. "Galbraith Boats." Maple Place and Manchester Ave., Keyport, New Jersey (1959)

Garform Industries, Inc. 225 South Main St., Wagoner, Oklahoma, and later, 816 Daniel Building, Tulsa, Oklahoma. Gar Wood, Jr., had early versions of his plastic boats in the water by late 1946, but production problems delayed the nationwide rollout until about 1948. Author Dan Spurr estimates some 2,000 of Wood's novel boats had been sold by 1950. A half-page January 1955 *Motor Boating* ad noted, "Garform plasticglass boats were designed by one of the nation's greatest boating authorities [likely, Gar Wood and/or Gar Wood, Jr.] for waterproof, warp-proof, weather-proof [boating and] speeds over 40 mph." The lion's share of Garform Plasticglass output was of the inboard engine type, though the pioneering firm did offer outboard hulls.

Gay-Craft Boat Co. 1202 Grand Ave., Schofield, Wisconsin (1962)

General Marine Company. "SpeedLiner," and "Sunliner Boats." 6 and Oak Sts., St. Joseph, Missouri (1957)

Geneva Boat Co. 2699 Geneva Highway, Manitou Beach, Michigan. Later, 109 Mechanic St., Hudson, Michigan (1958)

Geneva Marine Products. "Geneva Boats." Lake Providence, Louisiana (1959)

E. Gitt & Sons. "Minnow Boats." Springfield, Pennsylvania (1961)

Glas-Craft, Inc. 705 Pemberton St., Fort Worth, Texas (1955)

Glass Craft Co., Inc. Fort Dodge, Iowa. Though also debuting in 1955 listings along side Glas-Craft, this is a separate company. It's likely, however, that Glass Craft Co., Inc., is related to the Glass Craft Boats, Inc., noted for 1960 as being headquartered in Humboldt, Iowa.

Glass Fiber Products. "Electra Boats." Brennan Road, Columbus, Georgia (1958)

Glassflite Company. 7345 Edna, Houston, Texas. W. H. Zinnecker, co-owner. (1956)

Glas Foam Corp. 1071 East 52nd St., Hialeah, Florida. Glas Foam Boat's two 1960 models bore the name Foam Flyer.

Glasgow Boats, Inc. 625 Maple Ave., Burlington, North Carolina (1962)

Glassco Boats, Inc. 2845 Bryan, Fort Worth, Texas (1960)

Glass-Go Co. Browns, Alabama (1958)

Glass-Magic, Inc. 2759 Loudelle St., Fort Worth, Texas. In addition to this marque's Texas-produced hulls, some were made under agreement for eastern consumption at Duratech's New York facility. The debut (1958 model year) sales pitch involved something called a "Plus 33" performance rating. In order to "break the performance barrier of boating," Glass Magic tested their designs "for performance at speeds above 33 mph, the performance barrier of [other boats] for boating fun and safety." With the era's garden variety Evinrude or Johnson 25- to 35-horse mill, 33 mph was considered pretty fast, a rate perceived to yield rather bumpy results in any kind of chop, or due to proposing in calm water. Actually, bouncing around at 10 mph is not much fun either (especially after a picnic lunch on some island), but the company must have liked the way "33" (then, a greater speed than most boaters had gone on water) looked in its publicity. Glass Magic designs incorporated what its Texas designers termed a "reverse-vee bow to cushion the ride [and deliver] rakish styling to enhance beauty." In 1961, Glass Magic's headquarters was noted as 2730 Ludelle Street in Fort Worth, with a midwest plant in Elkhart, Indiana.

Likely a prototype, this "mystery" fiberglass speedster was pictured in Glass Magic's 1958 catalog promoting its eastern boats being built by Duratech, but didn't get specifically identified.

Glassmaster Plastics Co. 5600 Shakespeare Road, Columbia, South Carolina. Debuting around 1959, the Glassmaster line represented solid value. By 1967, Glassmaster had relocated to Lexington, South Carolina. One industry observer called the boats "a meat and potatoes brand," meaning well built, but not overly fancy. I recall a couple of 60-something fishing-buddy types who each did his own version of splurging on a runabout in the late spring of 1966. One went all out and bought a high-end Glastron and 110-hp Mercury, while the other got a deal on a shorter Glassmaster and 35-horse Merc. Though the boats now have different owners, both can still be seen navigating Lake Champlain on summer weekends.

Glasspar Co. 2232 Harbor Blvd., Costa Mesa, California. This legendary fiberglass boat maker's first listing in *The Boating Industry* appeared as noted in January 1952. Anyone serious about delving into the fledgling marine plastic industry would have been wise to make a pilgrimage to Glasspar's Costa Mesa address. The legion of neighboring fiberglass hull manufacturers would also have made such a trip extra worthwhile.

Glass Slipper. (see Marlin Marine Div. of 13 Co.)

Glastex Co. "Speed Queen Boats." 6101 West 147th, Tinley Park, Illinois. A single 14-footer served as the 1955 debut Speed Queen. Glastex touted its "RIJ-A-BRIJ" construction, which primarily consisted of five molded bottom stringers for hull support. The smooth-lined, twin-cockpit (plus motor well) runabout looked like it was influenced by Winner PlastiCraft hulls of similar size. Typically sold in all white, molded-in two-tone coloration could be ordered for an extra hundred bucks on the $875 base price.

Speed Queen by Glastex photographed at speed on reflective water as calm as glass. The smooth-sided low slung runabout moved right along with her 40-horse Mercury Mark 55, also introduced in 1955.

Glastek by Chetek Boat Corp. Chetek, Wisconsin. In 1958 wooden boat builder Chetek entered the glass game with the 15-foot Del Ray. Its "hull, flotation chambers, flared transom, and trim [were] all 100 percent molded in a color-fused fiberglass material." Tasteful aft fins give this front-steered runabout an appropriate period feel. Any of the late 1950s colorful outboards (up to 40 hp) would make a great match for the debut Glastek, a marque seldom seen today.

Glen's Boat Shop. "River Boat." 913 SW "H" St., Grant's Pass, Oregon (mid-1960s)

Goodyear Aircraft Corp. Akron, Ohio (early 1950s) *Motor Boating* listings (in 1956 and 1957, for example) show Goodyear as building and marketing craft like the 16-foot fiberglass Bowman Havana outboard runabout. Similar to GE's 1940s glass molding efforts with Carl Beetle's Beetle Boat line, however, it appears that Goodyear was simply looking to manufacture fiberglass hulls and wholesale them to established boat works like Bowman Manufacturers, Inc. of Little Rock, Arkansas, where they'd be finished and marketed. Bowman said Goodyear plastic hulls were molded "under a million pounds of pressure," hinting at a sophisticated matched metal die and hydraulic press system that a well-heeled organization like Goodyear could better afford.

Grady-White Boats, Inc. "G&W Boats." 714 Albermarle Ave., Greenville, North Carolina. By 1966, this venerable wooden boat maker offered "lapstrake skiffs in both wood and fiberglass in lengths from 16½ to 20½ feet. The 17-foot Riviera with "upholstered back-to-back seats" is an example of the early glass output. The 1971 catalog of GW "fiberglass boats with fun and quality built in," notes Grady-White output as a product of National Boat Works, Inc., in Greenville. That model year, the smooth-sided 16½-foot Sting Ray represented the company's outboard runabout entry point. That said, the boat's rich appointments included full-length, quilted side storage shelves, so this family ski and cruising boat was hardly a basic economy hull. The firm emphasized its 160,000-square-foot production area where "all hand layup with alternating layers of [fiberglass] roving and mat" was employed. The brand's GW logo featured a propeller motif (inside the "G"), and should not be confused with the G-W of G-W Invader fame, which was not related to the Greenville-based company.

Gray Craft Fiberglass Boats, Inc. Routes 14 and 15, Ravenna, Ohio (1961)

Gray-Wooldride. "G-W Invader." Sharpesville, Indiana. For most young (and young at heart) outboard boating enthusiasts, from the mid-1960s through the early 1970s, the G-W Invader fleet simply meant, "Oh wow!" The cornerstone of the line was a little slice of fiberglass hull that checked in at just over 10 feet, though rated for outboards up to 55 hp. To be sure, the firm offered bigger conventional boats, including trihedral bow riders, but its high performance craft were clearly "designed for the now generation [and] rugged individualist. The G-W Invader has won hundreds of races from coast to coast," noted company brochures, "The race course is our testing ground. If you want performance, you want G-W Invader." Though by today's cautious safety standards, a 55-hp rating would not be allowed on a new 10-foot boat, G-W Invaders with such power handled remarkably well. Consequently, most G-W owners are used to telling admirers, "No, it's NOT for sale!"

Great Lakes Industries, Inc. 302 East Superior St., Duluth, Minnesota (1953)

Ray Greene & Co. Byrne at South St., Toledo, Ohio. The founder of this company is credited with making the first modern (fiberglass and polyester resin) fiberglass boat in about 1942. A sailboat enthusiast, Greene put most of his energies into fabricating dinghies and sailing craft, even though it was listed in January 1953's *The Boating Industry* as having produced some fiberglass outboard runabouts and utilities in 1952. The foray lasted for about five years, when all of his company's focus was devoted to offering sailboats and "hulls to be finished."

Grew Boats, Ltd. Penetang, Ontario (1959)

Gulf Craft, Inc. 2418 West Eighth Court, Hialeah, Florida (1967)

Gull Fiber Plastic Products, Inc. "Gull Boats." Missoula, Montana (1960)

Hammond Boats. After leaving Glastron, its co-founder and chief designer, Bob Hammond, founded a company on which he could best focus his creative energies. Most of the resulting craft were of the high performance–richly styled genre.

Hampden Wood Products, Inc. 155 River St., West Springfield, Massachusetts. Perhaps this was a glass-covered wood maker that inadvertently slipped into early 1960s *The Boating Industry* fiberglass boat manufacturer directories. Among its model names were Sea-Liner, Sea-Mate, and Water-Bike.

Hands Shipbuilding Co. 7207 East McNichols, Detroit, Michigan (1959)

Hains Industries, Inc. Winter Haven, Florida (1967)

Harvey Boat Works, Inc. "Scanoramic" and "Harvey Boats." 21460 Tualatin Valley Highway, Aloha, Oregon, and later, 120 North State St., Oswego, Oregon. Among the 1959–60 models in Harvey's brochure were the likes of Ski-Whiz and Sea-Scanner. A name change to The Harvey Corporation occurred in 1961.

John F. Hebert Co., Mobilcraft Boats Div. 9629 East Valley Blvd., Rosemead, California (1955)

Henderson Plastic Engineering Corp. "Teal Craft." R.R. 2, Highway 60 South, Henderson, Kentucky (1960)

Henry Boats, Inc. Plain City, Ohio (1965)

Herbert's, Inc. Alhambra, California (see Mobilcraft)

Herblin Boat Corp. 37 Orchard Beach Blvd., Port Washington, Long Island, New York. Featured in *Motor Boating*'s January 1954 fiberglass photo essay was Herblin's 11½-foot Panther runabout. Notable properties included a contoured support ridge running atop the deck from bow light (and under the windshield) to dashboard, center/front-mounted steering wheel, and bench seating plus a pair of aft jump seats. The Panther could perform with outboards "of 5 to 25 hp," the latter yielding "top speeds as high as 35 mph."

Herter's, Inc. R.R. 1, Waseca, Minnesota. By 1956, the venerable Herter's sporting goods mail order outfit cataloged fiberglass runabouts. Much of its magazine advertising of the period showed what looked to be an Aluma Craft rowboat while touting a "guaranteed world's finest quality 14-foot fiberglass boat at less

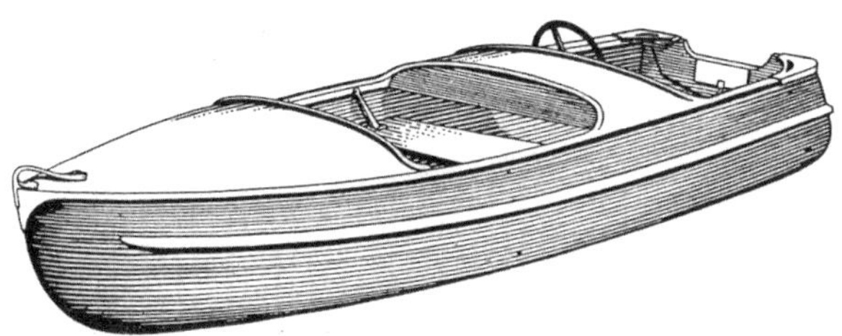

"We will produce only a very few Mark III [as shown, 14'-] and Mark IX [16'-] runabouts in 1956 as we produce them only to keep our good employees during off seasons," said Herter's of its limited edition wheel-decked Chrome Fiberglas utility runabout models.

than wholesale prices [that could] take up to a 40-hp motor." In fact, the boat appears to be a glass version — with lots of aluminum bracing — of an Aluma Craft. Even if, at a distance, these Herters resembled another firm's hulls, they were indeed unique. Herter's novel "chrome fiberglass boats" were fabricated from glass with chrome molly tubing for support. Additionally, the prow deck, dashboard, gunwales, spray rails, seats, and transom plate were aluminum (or "duraluminum," as the company noted).

While most sporting goods concerns that sold boats private-branded them from other makers, Herter's made their own. And, the full-fledged Herter's runabouts were some of the most eye-catching of the 1950s "fin era." Quintessential Herters sported lots of fins and accessories like a cigarette and lighter holder. The cast-aluminum tail of the 1956 Chrome Fiberglass Duofoil and Flying Fish Runabout were cataloged as "of the Cadillac Eldorado design." The 15-footer's aft bottom got advertised as using "the design principles the English [jet] Bluebird boat." Actually, the 1956 version could be considered subdued compared to the tail fins on Herter's 1957 model. This one was fancifully dubbed "Herter's chrome fiberglass duofoil world famous walk-through deluxe model *flying fish* runabout." It was flamboyantly "guaranteed the fastest runabout of its length made in the world." And if that weren't enough self-inflicted kudos, Herter's stated that the revolutionary "new design [made] this high speed boat usable as a fishing craft." With cast aluminum tail fin and tail light backs sufficiently tall to hide most outboards, and a nicely molded and upholstered interior, who'd want to put some string of slimy sea bass in the two-toned fashion statement? A Watermaster Deluxe Flying Fish for 1959 offered additional flamboyancy in fins and chrome. Like its older sisters, the boat's noticeably round bottom could yield an equally noticeable roly-poly ride. With a bit more conventional bottom design and bow angle, the Eldorado Rocket runabout, a 13' 4" two-seater with a rear seat molded into the topside, made the 1957 catalogs. It, too, had big wings or fins, although Herter's literature show several "standard" versions of its gregarious boats like Flying Fish in economy mode with bench seating and no fins.

The 1962, "twin-hulled [catamaran] hydroplane, Fantasy 15 by Hydro Craft measured just over 14' 3", and loved big kickers like that 80-hp Merc 800.

For 1957–58, the14-foot Mark III (for only $290), and 16-foot Mark IX gave Herter's boat buyers entry-level runabout opportunities. Both were rated for 75 hp, even though the notion of rigging one with the day's big 60-horse Merc was probably speculative fodder for the dreams of young speedboaters with a Herter's catalog and some outboard motor brochures in their hands. It's incredible that waterways weren't teeming with Herter's crafts, because the firm's prices were remarkably low, even by the standards of the day. For example, completely decked out in super deluxe form, the Flying Fish was only $586, or just $457 with a less lavish interior. At twice the price, though, any "Chrome Fiberglas Herter's" would be worth the investment. That metal framework, by comparison to competitors' wooden support reinforcements, probably means that a surviving Herter is still quite serviceable. Classic boaters who find them seldom have an interest in resale. Herter's runabouts were available new into the 1960s.

Hi-Way Products, Inc. "Seaswirl," and "P-14 Boats." Canby, Oregon. Here's one of several incarnations of the interesting "P-14" hull. The firm was noted in a 1967 *Motor Boating* roster. (see Seaswirl)

Holiday Plastics, Inc. 1301 Fairfax Trafficway, Kansas City, Kansas (1959)

Hollywood Boat & Motor Co. South 42nd & Union Ave., Tacoma, Washington (1960)

Honey Creations, Inc. 407 Commercial Center, Beverly Hills, California (1961)

Howard Boat Mfgrs. Later called **Howard Fiberglass Boats, Inc.,** Wrentham, Massachusetts. Howard Ladig, partner. (1958)

Hunt Mfg. Co., Inc. "Huntline Boats." 857 West 19th St., Costa Mesa, California. Here's another relatively early Costa Mesa-based fiberglass boat outfit. *The Boating Industry*'s January 1951 issue first identifies Hunt as offering outboard craft in both "plastic" and "fiberglass." Unless one finds one of these boats and takes a scientific look, it's difficult today to specifically state exactly what composite elements went into this brand's "plastic" products.

Hupp Engineering Associates. 216 West Jefferson St., Bloomington, Illinois. Also called Hupmobile (no connection to the old-time automobile maker), the novel "H" shaped hull (actually more like an "A" with blunt head) that Hupp introduced around 1958 was dubbed the Flying H. Note that during the early 1960s, there was also a Hupp Corporation that owned Aluma Craft Boats, though it was not related to Hupp Engineering.

Hurricane Fiberglass Products Co. Cypress Gardens, Florida (1961)

Hustler Boats. McHenry, Illinois

Hydro-Cycle, Inc. 375 Umbarger Road, San Jose, California (1968)

HydroSwift Corp. (formerly Ludlow Townley Co.) 3045 West 21st South St., Salt Lake City Utah (1961)

Ideal-Aerosmith, Inc. 3913 Evans Ave., Cheyenne, Wyoming (1958)

Impala Crafts, Inc., Div. of Impala Oil Corp. Enid, Oklahoma. Avenger was this company's 10' 3" speedster. No doubt, sports-car inspired, the Avenger had plush bucket seats, stick shift controls, and a foredeck that looked like an automotive hood with headlights. It was a design element more in keeping with the 1950s rather than the late 1960s, when the diminutive outboard runabout was marketed.

Imperial Fiberglass Products Corp. 174 West 25th St., Hialeah, Florida (1965)

Inboard Marine Corp. "Fleet Form Boats." (circa 1960)

Industrial Fiberglass Products Corp. Ludington, Michigan (1967)

Industrial Marine Corp. (1963)

Inland Boat Co., Div. of Inland Lakes Boat Works. Madison, Wisconsin. Long a marina as well as a boat works, Inland built a line of fiberglass craft for regional distribution from about 1955–72. Anyone restoring an Inland will need to find her a companion Merc, as Inland's owners, the Coats family, has long been associated with promoting Mercury motors.

International Shipbuilding. "Scottie-Craft." 1815 NE 144th St., North Miami, Florida. (1958; see Scottie-Craft)

International Yacht Sales. 604 Kerr Bldg., Detroit, Michigan (1959)

Invader Boat Co. Also listed as Invader Mfg. Corp., Giddings, Texas (1960)

Iola Molded Products, Inc. West Lincoln Rd, Iola, Kansas. After its late 1950s Midwest fabrication/distribution contractual relationship with Red Fish Boats ended when the original Texas-based Red Fish fell on hard times, Iola secured the rights to continue making Red Fish craft.

Island Maid Boats. Camilla, Georgia. For 1967, Island Maid offered Sea Hawk, a "high-performance, 15' 2" deep-vee runabout," that could be fitted with a 150-hp outboard, or a 155-hp in an inboard/outboard. It wore a blunt-nose deck. The craft's publicity shot featured just a 35-horse Merc — sans controls or steering hook-ups — quickly clamped to the transom for the photographer.

Islander Craft Corp. "Islander Boats." 2895 46th Ave., St. Petersburg, Florida (mid-1960s)

J & R Plasticraft Corp. Reeseville, Wisconsin. Initially listed for 1957, it's doubtful that the midwestern firm's boats were connected in any way to Winner PlastiCraft.

Jayhawk Marine, Inc. 17th & Elliott, Parsons, Kansas (1959)

Jet Boat, Inc. "Jetra." 11238 South Western Ave., Chicago, Illinois (1961)

Jet Stream (1961)

Johnsen Boats, Inc. "Starfleet" and "Star Fisher Boats." Highway 441 East, Leesburg, Florida (1961; also see Customglas)

Kaysea Kraft Boat Co. 1706 Euclid Ave., Cleveland, Ohio. M. E. Rogat, owner. (1956)

Kenner Boat Co., Inc. "Ken Craft." Knoxville, Arkansas (1959) Kenner's late 1960s' offering included several editions of the tri-hulled Ski Barge utility.

Kenway Boats, Inc. Palermo, Maine (1961)

Kelson Engineering Co. 1002 West Philadelphia St., Whittier, California (1949)

Kentucky Molded Boats. Main St., Burgin, Kentucky. Robert Culton, owner. (1956)

Kettenburg. 2810 Carleton St., San Diego, California. Paul A. Kettenburg, owner. (1959)

Kingfisher Boats. Clarksville, Texas. From about 1963 to the early 1990s, the former Red Fish factory served as home and catalyst to the Kingfisher line.

King-Meier Corp. 422 West Ponce de Leon Ave., Decatur, Georgia (1958)

Kippin-Ker, Ltd. Georgetown, Ontario. Debuting around 1950, here's one of Canada's pioneer "plastic" boat outfits.

Kiski Plastics Co., Inc. Saltsburg, Pennsylvania (1957)

Kober Kat Boats. 934 West Foothill Blvd., Monrovia, California (late 1960s)

Kolb Boat Co. 109 West Gale St., Angola, Indiana (1955)

Kury Plastics, Inc. "K-P Boats." 1st St., Charlotte Park, Punta Gorda, Florida (1960)

Laby Engineering Co. 16028 Blythe St., Van Nuys, California. Jordan M. Laby, owner. (1955)

Lakefield Boats, Ltd. Queens St., Lakefield, Ontario (1961)

Lake-Flite Plastics, Inc. Sycamore Drive, Knoxville, Tennessee (1965)

Lakeland Boat Co. 221 East Commercial, Lebanon, Missouri (1962?)

Lakeland Boats, Ltd. (1962)

Laminated Plastic Products Co. 19666 South Harbor Blvd., Costa Mesa, California. This is yet another Costa Mesa–headquartered pioneer "plastic" boat maker. Outboard utilities and runabouts over 14 feet long were available by late 1949.

LaPierre Boat Works. Lower Main St., Belfast, Maine. Wm G. LaPierre, owner. (1956)

The Laurel Corp. Shippensville, Pennsylvania (1961)

Leavens Brothers, Ltd. "Leavens Boats." 3220 Dufferin St., Toronto, Ontario (1956)

Lee Craft Boats, and **Lee Craft Marine, Inc.** Flathead Lake, Somers, Montana (1958)

Link Aviation. Binghamton, New York (late 1940s)

Linzmayer Fiberglass Corp. 4230 Austin Blvd., Island Park, New York (1956)

Long Beach Glass Boat Co. 1520 Seabright Ave., Long Beach, California. Charles Cobb, owner. (1956)

Los Altos Marine, Inc. "Sidewinder Boats." Los Altos, California (late 1960s)

Love Corp. "Sportsman Boats." Henderson, Texas. Baseball great Mickey Mantle had a connection with the company that built these craft. In a 1961 publicity shoot, Mantle and his family mugged for the camera while cruising by in the 16-foot Sportsman Hercules runabout.

Ludlow Townley Co. (see HydroSwift)

Luger Industries, Inc. 9200 Access Road, Minneapolis, Minnesota. Brothers Orm and Ren Luger opened up their kit boat business in 1952. Seven years later, they added do-it-yourself fiberglass craft to the catalog. Central to the brochures was a down-home, family-friendly atmosphere in which many satisfied customers

When most classic boaters think of Luger fiberglass, the Minnesota company's seemingly ubiquitous pulp magazine ads featuring this model come to mind. While Luger designs were patented, its early glass runabout looks a bit like the Lake'n Sea of Chris-Craft notoriety.

shared their Luger boatbuilding experiences and snapshots of the finished product. That honest approach and the boating boom caused the company to prosper thanks to a large clientele that either couldn't afford a factory-built boat or simply wanted to build their own boat. The Luger kits required final assembly only as the molded color pieces were ready to go.

"Only required a few short hours to assemble a 17-foot runabout," Luger catalogs noted. "And best of all, anyone can do it.... Absolutely no experience is needed!" None of 12 construction steps (one of which was getting the boat into the water for a trial run) seemed like rocket science. Fashioning a cradle from discarded pieces of the shipping crate was probably the only time the builder was on his own. Otherwise step-by-step directions did the trick. As a testament to the company's many proven designs, it should be noted that none of Luger's glass boats looked particularly homebrew.

Luger was one of the few runabout makers offering fiberglass craft in kit form. The 14-foot Ski-Whiz hails from the mid-1960s.

Lunn Laminates, Inc. Huntington Station, Long Island, New York (1959)

LuToCo, Inc. 1750 South 8th West, Salt Lake City, Utah. Ray S. Ludlow, president. (1958)

Lyn-Craft Boat Co. "Seabreeze Boats." Rt. 2, and later 1661 County Line Road, Sarasota, Florida (1962)

Mac Bay Boat Co. 5605 Airline Road Muskegon Heights, Michigan (1960)

Magnolia Boat Mfg. Co. Highway 61 South, Vicksburg, Mississippi (1959)

Marine Aid Products, Inc. Lake Park, Florida. (mid-1960s)

Marine Fiber-Glass & Plastics, Inc. "Totem Craft." 6707 220th St. SW, Mountlake Terrace, Washington (1961)

Marine Corp. of America. 200 Klumac Road, Salisbury, North Carolina (1965)

Marine Plastics, Inc. "Glass Magic Boats." 2751 Ludelle St. Fort Worth, Texas. Prior to being dubbed Glass Magic, Inc., this was the circa 1956 corporate identity for what was being planned as the Glass Magic line.

Mariner Boats Div. of Midwest Marine. (1967)

Marlin Boat Co. Fort Myers, Florida (1955)

Marlin Marine, Div. of the 13 Co. (see The 13 Co.)

Marlin Fiberglass Boat Co., Inc. Boca Raton, Florida, and Owosso, Michigan. There could be a connection to the earlier Marlin Boat Company, also based in the Sunshine State. The Boca Raton venture first appeared during 1959. That's when its 14-foot Scat-Cat Overnighter fiberglass catamaran hull generated some boating news for mariners with big families. Not only could it seat eight (four in each of two generous seats) and sleep four, but with a pair of 70-horse Mercs, the craft was said to hit 50 mph!

Marscot Plastics, Inc. 1480 East Rodney French Blvd., New Bedford, Massachusetts. Part of the small southeastern Massachusetts enclave of early glass boat makers, and one of several spearheaded by Palmer Scott, Marscot was active by 1954 with an emphasis on do-it-yourselfers seeking seagoing craft. "The great advantages of a one-piece, leakproof fiberglass hull can be yours with the economy of a kit boat," its ads touted. Marscot also marketed the ready-to-run 15½-foot Coastal runabout. "Generous freeboard and level-riding characteristics [keep her] dry in rough water [while] making 27 mph with 25 hp," brochures noted. There was also a 15' 6" Hunter 19, "a new design [for 1960] with tunnel in keel. Tunnel fills with water when boat is at rest, making it stable. Underwater ballast flows from tunnel as speed increases. Boat has three longitudinal skis along underbody for speed." Around 1958, George O'Day Associates bought Marscot in order to distribute its outboard craft.

From its generous wood-framed windshield to ample gunwale coaming, the 15' 6" Marscot Coastal Fisherman was fabricated for salt water angling.

Mark Twain Marine Industries. 5th and College, New London, Missouri (1967)

Masco Corp. 7300 North 60th St., Milwaukee, Wisconsin (1968)

The Mathews Co. Port Clinton, Ohio (1963)

McComb Fiberglass Co. Ratio Drive, Navasoto, Texas (1968)

McGowen Mfg. Co., Inc. "McGowen Boats." 829 Newark Ave., Elizabeth, New Jersey (1961)

Merline Boats. 9740 Firestone Blvd., Downey, California (1959)

Mermaid Marine Mfg. Co., Inc. Manitowish, Wisconsin (1961)

Meyers Marine, Inc. 300 Chicago St., Columbia City, Indiana (1956)

Miami Aeromarine, Inc. 920 N.E. 72nd Terrace, Miami, Florida (1949)

Miami Marine Industries. Lake Providence, Louisiana (1959)

Midwest Marine, Inc. "Mariner Boats." 1000 Levee St., Red Wing, Minnesota (1965)

Midwestern Industries Corp. Route 37, Harlan, Indiana. This is the circa 1961 corporate banner for Abner Crosby's boat second notable enterprise, Hydrodyne.

Milo Craft Boat Co. 7737 South Western Ave., Chicago, Illinois (1962)

Minnetonka Fiberglass & Marine. 9425 Sixth Ave. North, Minneapolis, Minnesota (1958)

Mishey Boats & Motors. "Custom Liner Boats." 2872 Grand Ave., Phoenix, Arizona (1961)

Mitchell Boat Co. 1980 Placentia Ave., Costa Mesa, California (1960)

Mitchell Plastics. "Mitchell Boats." 2911 46th Ave., Bradenton, Florida (1965)

Mobilcraft. 613 South Fremount Ave., Alhambra, California. (1953)

Mohawk Boat Co. Grand Rapids, Michigan (1959)

Mohawk Boat Co., Inc. Gardener Lane, Amsterdam, New York. "A fleet of twenty-two runabouts and outboard cruisers built of fiberglass" was noted in the January 1968 *Motor Boating* show issue. A 14-foot outboard utility started the upstate New York outfit's lineup.

Monelle Corp., North Star Marine Div. 600 West 10th Ave., Monmouth, Illinois (1958)

Montgomery-Ward. Chicago, Illinois. Finding out who built a particular Sea King fiberglass hull could be more of a challenge than locating a vintage one in the first place. Like competitor Sears & Roebuck, Ward was on the lookout for the best deal from its contractors. And during some years, several builders might have been hired by the chain store to produce Sea King boats. No matter what the origin, Ward's line was described as "rugged, classy Sea King fiber glass, scientifically constructed [and] all new for 1958." Most "fifty-ish" was the 14-foot Deluxe Sport Boat. "Bottom and sides are sturdy fiber glass laminate. Plywood seats, two-tone upholstering, red hull, white firegold decking," noted the flyer. Big slanted fins gave this one just the right degree of automotive styling. By 1961, Sea King glass looked completely mainstream with lots of upholstery on the likes of the 14- and 15-foot Sea Fire series. Twin rear hatches, built-in ice chest, and a padded dash compartment made this craft a family favorite. The red decking and white hull made a fashion statement when mated to a fat red and white (Gale Products–built) Sea King 60-hp outboard.

Moorhead Plastics, Inc. "Silver-Line Boats." 2300 12th Ave. South, Moorhead, Minnesota (1961)

Morgancraft Boat & Marine Supply Co. 15017 South Figueroa St., Gardena, California (mid-1960s)

Muir Plastiglas Products. "Muir Maid Boats." Bradenton, Florida (early 1960s)

Multi-Plastics Co. "Fiber-Flite." 2411 Weaver St., Fort Worth, Texas. W. T. Ray, owner. (1958)

Munro Boats. 250-266 Springbank Drive, London, Ontario. Also as **Munro Boats & Motors, Ltd.** (1952)

Muskoka Canoe Co., Ltd. 35 Wellington St., Bracebridge, Ontario (1955)

Myco Marine Div., Myco Co., Inc. 705 East Pleasant St., Belvidere, Illinois. D. L. Myers, president. (1958)

Meyers Marine, Inc. "ThunderBay Boats." Columbia City, Indiana. "ThunderBay is the finest in fiber-glas and the fastest growing name in marine history," claimed Meyers in a 1955 debut ad. The firm claimed its tremendous growth and expansion was because "when craftsmen take pride in making something better, the people's demand cannot be satisfied." Apparently, ThunderBay I, a double-cockpit fiberglass runabout (a 14-footer) was that better thing. Actually, it looked a lot like a Winner PlastiCraft or Glastex Speed Queen of similar vintage. This Meyers was not related to the aluminum boat maker with the same name.

National Marine Plastics. 215 North Detroit, Tulsa, Oklahoma (1958)

Nautilus Fiberglass Boat Works Corp. Motor Ave., Liberty Park, Farmingdale, (Long Island) New York (1961)

Nefco Div. of Ozarka, Inc. Washington & Borden, Woodstock, Illinois (1952)

Newman Industries Inc. "Esquire Boats." 201 South Main St., Commerce, Oklahoma, and later Miami, Oklahoma (1960)

Newsome Fiberglass, Inc. "Newsome Boats." 3199 9th St., South Bradenton, Florida. Also listed as Jake Newsome Boats. (1957)

Nipissing Boat Co., Ltd. Premier Road, North Bay, Ontario (1960)

Norris Craft. LaFollette, Tennessee. This line got its start in 1954 when Mac Crumley, Sr., began making a few fiberglass runabouts in a garage. The Norris name was co-opted from the Tennessee Valley Authority's Lake Norris. The output was visually in keeping with Winner PlastiCraft of the era. Though a check of 1950s–60s trade magazines doesn't reveal a Norris Craft listing, it's apparent that the brand flew under industry radar toward a bass boat clientele on which it has since successfully focused.

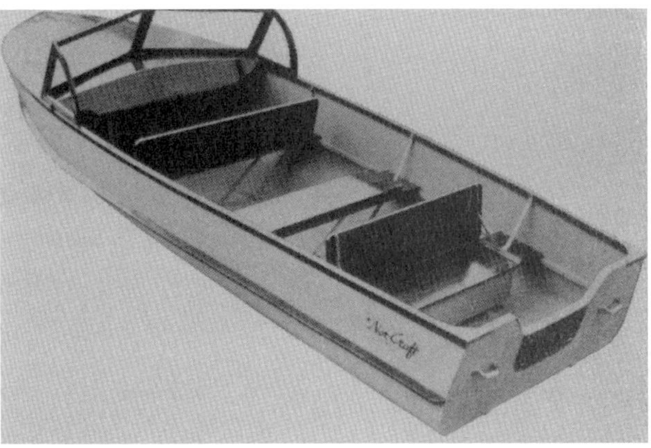

Windshield framing and bench seats with folding backs were among the wooden components of the model "B-2" Nor-Craft 16-foot Utility Runabout. Fair weather anglers attracted to this boat often saved money on a related outboard by selecting a significantly smaller kicker than its 25-hp transom rating.

North American Boat Corp. 3377 S.W. 2nd Ave., Fort Lauderdale, Florida (1967)

North American Marine, Inc., or **North American Mfg. Corp.** "American Boats." Highway 15, North Warsaw, Indiana (1959)

Northern Reinforced Plastics Corp. 206 East Mulberry St., Stillwater, Minnesota (1957)

North Star Marine Mfg. Co. 600 West 10th St., Monmouth, Illinois (1957)

Northwest Mfg. Corp. Iron River, Wisconsin (1959)

Northwest Plastics, Inc. "Nor-Craft." 65 East Plato Ave., St. Paul, Minnesota. Formed in 1951, the marine division of Northwest Plastics offered a 13-model line of fiberglass boats by 1955. The boats ranged from 14 to 23 feet and were fabricated in the company's marine facility in St. Croix, Minnesota. The 14- and 18-foot runabouts appeared to be the firm's biggest sellers. Several, like the model A-2, a 14-foot utility-runabout, could be purchased in "Nor-Craft Fiberglas Kit" form. Also for do-it-yourselfers, Nor-Craft marketed

"Fiberglas recovering kits for wood [and enigmatically] for aluminum boats."

Nylox Corp. 333 North Santa Anita Ave., Arcadia, California (1959) Noted for its snub-nosed ski boat — the Pantom.

O'Connor Lumber Co. 100 Howe Road, Cuyahoga, Ohio. This outfit reportedly offered fiberglass outboard utilities and runabouts in kit form around 1959, though it's not remembered whether or not the line was glass-covered wood.

George D. O'Day Associates, Inc. 9 Newbury St., Boston, Massachusetts. Around 1958, O'Day acquired Marscot Plastics, Inc., a Bay State maker of plastic boats, including outboard craft. The buyout extended O'Day's sailboat line to the then burgeoning market for outboard boats.

Old Town Canoe Co. 58 Middle St., Old Town, Maine (1967)

Orlando Boat Co. "Orlando Clipper Boats." 521 Elwell St., Orlando, Florida (1959)

Ouachita Marine & Industrial Corp. Arkadelphia, Arkansas. The company's 1969 Convincer Deluxe is an interesting example of outboard utility craft in the true sense of the word. The 16-foot Convincer had a center steering station, decking and gunwales suitable for casual seating, generous storage, tri-hull stability, swivel seats, and convenient bow rails.

Outers Laboratories, Inc. Onalaska, Wisconsin, and Tomah, Wisconsin. "Pabst Boats." (1961)

Owens Yacht Co., Inc. Stansbury Road, Baltimore, Maryland. This inboard cabin cruiser firm got in to outboard runabouts for 1958. Owens's 15-foot fiberglass

By 1962, tailfins that had been rather pronounced on most Owens outboard runabouts got moved slightly forward and were muted to the point where they'd barely hold the maker's nameplate. Owens and sister Cutter shared some badge-engineered models during this period when the 15-foot Owens Dover was cataloged. Note that her seats fold down to form a bunk.

runabout is a nice example of its 1960 output, as the boat sports tasteful aft fins and even "fiberglass forward seat foot rests." When purchased by Brunswick, the Owens name was oriented toward larger hulls, and the smaller outboard models morphed Brunswick's Larson and Cutter brands.

P-14 Fiberglass Boat. Pilot Grove, Missouri (1959; see Seaswirl and note possible connection with the "P-14" listed with Fiberform Products.)

Pacific Marine Supply Co. 1223 Western Ave., Seattle, Washington (1961)

Pacific Plastics Co. 2727 7th Ave. South, Seattle, Washington (1953)

Pallu Products. 430 South Schuyler Ave., Bradley, Illinois. Russell Kaufman, owner. (1957)

Parsons Corp., Lake'n Sea Div. Traverse City, Michigan. The story starts in Boca Raton, Florida, where the tiny Lake'n Sea Boat Corp. began making some 15-foot fiberglass runabouts. For some reason, big Chris-Craft was attracted to Lake'n Sea and quickly

Before it became discouraged and quietly sold its Lake'n Sea fiberglass outboard boat "experiment" to Parsons, Chris-Craft had high hopes for the good looking 15-foot Lake'n Sea Sea Pleasure runabout offering. Debut 1957 color options on the $755 plastic boat included: "Boca White deck and seats with Sunrise Pink, Seafoam green, or Yellow Chartreuse hull."

acquired the company in order to get into the glass game, which appeared to be leaving traditionalists behind. The boats, however, essentially plywood framing encased in fiberglass, proved to be a headache for Lake'n Sea owners and consequently for Chris-Craft executives. In numerous cases, the glass unstuck from the wood and caused the little runabouts to take on enough water to be nicknamed "Leak and Sink."

As fast as it had acquired the marque, Chris-Craft sold the Lake'n Sea fiberglass outboard runabout business to Parsons, which facilitated the latter's 1958 re-entry. The Traverse City, Michigan, manufacturer had more experience in glass than did Chris-Craft, and added a few more models to the line (some with special "extension hull drain plugs") before selling it to a Holland, Michigan, firm in 1960. With more delaminating and leaks reported by concerned customers, the brand was silent by 1964. No matter the problems, any incarnation of the seemingly jinxed runabouts (especially a Chris-Craft version) would be a fortunate find for the classic boat enthusiast.

A postscript related to the Lake'n Sea story is Coast Manufacturing & Supply Co., a Livermore, California, firm, which advertised in 1958 that, since 1948, its Trevarno-brand fiberglass sheeting had been "the largest selling Glass Boat Fabric in the country. When Chris-Craft engineers designed [the] fibre glass 15-foot Lake'n Sea pleasure runabout," Coast's ad noted, "they specified Trevarno Glass Boat Fabric for maximum strength and toughness. The seamless, molded hull is stress free. It won't shrink, swell, rot, or dry out," Coast promised. The promotion appears to have dissipated after some Lake'n Sea owners experienced leakage-related problems with their new craft.

Pearson Corp. 1 Constitution St., Bristol, Rhode Island. Also, Pearson Plastic Corp., Seekonk, Massachusetts. The 1958 15-foot Marauder with its tail fins would make a nice find for glass runabout buffs who love automotive accents. Pearson got into the outboard market in 1957 with the more subdued Maiden 15. A few years later, Grumman Aircraft executives, looking to add a glass line to Grumman's aluminum boat catalog, acquired Pearson around 1961. The resulting "Grumman Boats, Division of Pearson Corporation, Subsidiary of Grumman Aircraft Engineering Corp.," offered Grumman-branded aluminum hulls and glass sailboats, inboards, and outboards with the Pearson "finest name in fiberglass" tag line. An example of the latter for 1961 is the 14' 7" Pearson Mate fiberglass runabout. Soon, however, Pearson focused on what would be its core market, the cruising sailboats for which the firm is best remembered.

Peninsular Fiberglass Products, Inc. "Vanguard Boats." 1067 East 30th St., and later 950 West 20th St., Hialeah, Florida (1957)

Penn Yan Boats, Inc. Foot of Waddel Ave., Penn Yan, New York. The famed canvas-covered wooden-boat maker showed up in 1951 with a "plastic" listing which related to the resin coating on the canvas rather than full-fledged fiberglass production. *The Boating Industry*'s 1961 "Stock Boat Builders" directory shows Penn Yan beginning to make the transition from wood and "composite" categories to pure fiberglass reinforced plastic.

Pere Marquette Fiberglass Boat Co., Inc. First St., SW, Scottville, Michigan (1955)

Performer Boat Corp., Div of U.S. Fiberglass Products. 17923 Santa Fe, Compton, California, and 14720 Lakewood Blvd., Paramount, California. From the latter address, Performer debuted its 1960 line by promising "Laminac resins made by American Cyanamid Company [are used to fabricate] each of its ten models." (1960)

Peterborough Canoe Co., Ltd. Peterborough, Ontario (1959)

Pilot Grove Boat Co. Pilot Grove, Missouri. (1961)

Pipestone Sales Co. "Pipestone Fiberglass" and "Silver Arrow Boats." Pipestone, Minnesota. Known for its arrow design on the bow of the fiberglass boats molded from an Aluma Craft, Pipestone cracked the glass game in 1958 when it contracted to fabricate plastic boats for Aluma Craft. The agreement only ran for a year, but Pipestone had the wherewithal to continue making fiberglass hulls for its own sale through a network of regional dealers. The company had enjoyed a decade of firm footing when it was sold in the late 1960s and eventually ended up with Bayliner as a production facility.

Planet Products, Space Liner Boats. Pompano Beach, Florida (1962)

Plas-Steel Products, Inc. "Safe Line Boats." 309 Tennessee Ave., Walkerton, Indiana (1959)

Plastic Boats, Inc. Auburn, New York (1947)

Plastic Industries, Inc. "Playcraft." 1108 East 33rd St., Kansas City, Missouri, and 11900 Old 40 Highway, Route 5, Independence, Missouri. One of a bevy of early 1950s 14-foot "plastic" outboard utilities, Playcraft didn't mention fiberglass in its 1953 ads. Instead, "Resilite — a reinforced plastic glass of astonishing characteristics" — was highlighted. Whatever the stuff was, such resin was reportedly "found only in Playcraft."

Plastic Fabrications, Inc. "Thunderbird Boats." 940 SW 69th Ave., Miami, Florida, and later 605 West 25th St., Hialeah, Florida (1955)

Plastics, Inc. Plant Hi-Way 75, Sherman,

Texas (1959)

Plastyle Co, Inc. "The 400-Line." 2809 South 11th Street Road, Niles, Michigan (1959)

Pleasure Craft Boat Co. 827 North Van Buren St., Auburn, Indiana (1960)

Pleasure, Inc. Fort Worth, Texas (1965)

Polymer Engineering Corp. "Victor Boats." 1100 Houston Club Bldg, Houston, and later RFD 1, Hitchcock, Texas (1957)

Pontoon Boat Co, Inc. 3434 Colfax Ave. South, Minneapolis, Minnesota. Though its name evokes quiet craft for calm waters, Pontoon's 1955 listing even includes outboard runabouts and stock racing boats.

Power Cat Boat Corp. 13512 Lakewood Blvd., Paramount, California, and by 1967 at Foster Field, Victoria, Texas (1959).

Power Craft Boat Co, and Powercraft, Inc. Middlebury, Indiana (1961)

Prestige Boat Mfg., Inc. "Champ Boats." 410 NE 1st Ave., Hallandale, Florida (mid-1960s)

Princecraft Div. of Aluminum Boats & Canoes, Inc. Princeville, Quebec (1969)

Progressive Plastic Products, Inc. "Javelin Boats." 4533 South Flores, San Antonio, Texas (1959)

Proma Mfg., Inc. 800 North Cummings Road, Covina, California (1968)

Provo Boat & Sport Shop. Provo, Utah. H. F. DeWeese, owner. (1957)

Quality Plastics, Inc. "Quality Glass Boats." 109 Main St., Reeseville, Wisconsin (1959)

Razorback Fiberglass Corp. Route 1, Malvern, Arkansas (1957)

Ratio Mfg. Co. Navasoto, Texas (1962)

Rayson Craft Boat Co., Rayson Industries, Inc. 115 East Gardena Blvd., Gardena, California (1967)

Red Fish Boat Co., Inc. Clarksville, Texas. Begun in 1955 as a wooden hull maker in an erstwhile farm building, Red Fish moved to glass for '57. The following year, a notorious, but clever "splash" of a Glastron design spawned the marque's signature 15-footer, the Shark Capri. For a hot automotive effect, it wore a trio of big aluminum hood scoops, and was later considered unique enough to be featured in the goofy movie, Ernest Saves Christmas. Iola Molded Products handled overflow production after Red Fish devoted much of the Texas factory space to build Scott/McCulloch boats. When the Scott deal expired, the two brothers who owned Red Fish soon left the marine business, though Iola kept the line alive. For the Canadian market, Muskoka Lake Craft, Ltd. of Brace Bridge, Ontario, built Red Fish craft under contract.

Regalite Industries, Inc. 500 Amsterdam Ave., NE, Atlanta, Georgia (1960)

Reinell Boats. Marysville, Washington. Ed Reinell, owner. (late 1950s)

Remco Marine Co. Railroad, Walker & Smith Sts., Emporia, Virginia (1961)

Renken Boat Manufacturing Co. 808 Folly Road, Charleston, South Carolina (1960)

Revline Boats, Inc. Arnold, Maryland. Tri-hulled outboard utilities of 15-, 16-, and 18-foot lengths formed this line's late-1960s fleet.

Richland Mfg. Co. "Sea Fury Fiberglass Boats." Richland, Missouri. This aluminum fabricator introduced a line of Sea Fury fiberglass boats in 1960. Any of the four models would represent a lucky find today. Most desirable might be the 14' 3" Sea Fury Clipper 15, a two-toned (from "atom red," "sunset yellow," "Florida tangerine," "surf green," or "sea blue") stylized beauty with healthy tail fins. The 19-foot Seminole Queen, 14' 1" Sea Fury Rocket, and 15' 11" Sea Queen 17 had nice lines, but were more subdued than Clipper. It may seem odd to dub a boat that's under 16 feet, a "17," but a Richland copywriter explains, "True to its name, this sparkling number is saucy and sharp as a 17-year-old youth…as pert, pretty and alluring as his senior prom date!" Though a perky effort, the company only danced with fiberglass for a few years. By 1965, catalogs were promoting an all-aluminum line.

Rickborn Industries, Inc. 93 U.S. Highway 46, Caldwell, New Jersey (1961)

Ritz-Craft, Inc., Marine Div. Sarasota, Florida (1964)

H.S. Roberts Co. "Skagit Boats." This trade name was also used by Skagit Plastics, Inc., a small firm similarly listed as being based in La Conner, Washington. A connection probably existed. (1962)

Rocket Marine, Inc. 1547 Tyler Ave., El Monte, California (1959)

Rose Fiberglass Boat Co. Pleasant Ridge Industrial Distributors. 2308 Sycamore Drive, Knoxville, Tennessee (1960)

Sabre Craft Boat Co., Inc. 329 West Ewing, Seattle, Washington, was home to this company at its 1959 debut. Within a decade, Sabre Craft became a division of American Marine Industries, Inc., 311 East Alexander, Tacoma, Washington. The 1969 outboard runabout group came in 14-, 16-, and 17-foot versions. Sabre Craft purchased the old Bell Boy line around 1963.

St. Croix Marine Corp. "St. Croix Boats." Park Falls, Wisconsin (1960)

St. Louis Boat & Canoe Co. 220 Benton St., Valley Park, Missouri (1952)

Salerno Shipyard, Inc. "Goldcoast Fiberglass Boats." Salerno, Florida. By the mid-1950s, this outfit offered "custom-built fiberglass boats" in 15' 6", 18-foot, and 22-foot sizes. The smaller two could be ordered as outboards.

Schenkel Brothers Mfg. Co. "White Water Boats." Brookville, Indiana (1959)

Scott (Boat) Div., McCulloch Corp. 6101 West Century Blvd., Los Angeles, California, and McCulloch of Canada, Ltd., 25 McCulloch St., Rexdale P.O., Toronto, Ontario. When Robert P. McCulloch's company (best known for superchargers and chainsaws) bought the Scott-Atwater outboard business in the late 1950s, it did so with an eye for aggressive product line expansion. Coincidentally, the go-kart industry was taking off and McCulloch quickly developed karts to package with its new series of (saw-based) high-revving kart engines.

By 1961, the Scott Division got into boat, motor, and trailer packaging, leading the way for a trend that has long since become the norm in the marine industry. "Thanks to McCulloch," a 1963 brochure notes, "boat buying no longer has to be done in bits and pieces. Scott boats are as complete as your car. Boat, motor and trailer are made for each other, factory matched to each other like parts of a fine car."

While McCulloch's fiberglass hulls ranged from open fishing craft to sporty runabouts, the sexiest of the marque was "a 14½-foot 3-point hydro, matched to the high speed Scott 75 [hp] boasting [a] 17:19 gear ratio, and hydraulic engine lift [for] prop-riding or pulling skiers." It had individual windshields for driver and passenger, as well as a spoiler in front of the outboard. The 1962 Flying Scott (17' 3") family runabout is also noteworthy, because of its "sound-deadening engine hood (covering the front half of the matched 75.2-hp Flying Scott outboard), generous hardware ensemble (including a stylized rear flagpole/stern light/ski rope pylon), flip back windshield (that accessed the walk-through sun deck), bow ladder, and car-like dashboard. A 43.7-horse Royal Scott motor could be mated to the 15-foot Royal Scott boat and matching trailer. It was a smaller version of the Flying Scott. Even though it marketed a beautiful product that is coveted by many classic boaters today, the Scott Division, renamed McCulloch in the mid-1960s, had departed the boating picture by decade's end. Designed by naval architect, David Beach, Scott boats were produced at the Red Fish plant in Texas, with a few hulls reportedly crafted at Red Fish's contract-builder, Iola Molded Products.

Palmer Scott & Co., Inc. New Bedford, Massachusetts. Pioneer fiberglass boatbuilder, Palmer Scott appeared in *Motor Boating*'s January 1953 listing as offering outboard runabouts (over 14 feet) in glass. By 1955, his Palmer Scott & Co., Inc., had been replaced with an entry for Marscot Plastics, another fiberglass-related firm that Scott had founded.

Scottie-Craft Boat Mfg., Inc. 1300 Beecher St., Indianapolis, Indiana. This line began as a brand of International Shipbuilding, 1815 N. 144th St., North Miami, Florida. The firm introduced fiberglass boats for 1958, and changed its name to Scottie-Craft Boat Manufacturer, Inc., (some sources say "Manufacturing") later that year, and relocated to Indiana during 1959.

SeaBird Industries, Inc. 1775 West Okeechobee Road, Hialeah, Florida (1967)

Sea Built Boat Mfgrs., Inc. 986-998 SE 8th St., Hialeah, Florida (1957)

Seabreeze Boat Co., Div. of Lyn-Craft Boat Co. Tampa, Florida. Appearing in 1964, Seabreeze Boat Co. changed its name to Seabreeze Marine Corp. by 1967, although it retained a Tampa address.

Sea Craft. Miami, Florida (1967)

Seaform Molded Products Co. 470 Allard Road, Gross Pointe, Michigan (1951)

Seafury, Inc. "Seafury Boats." 5595 NW 9th Ave., Fort Lauderdale, Florida (1960)

Sea Hunter Boats. 18924 South Western Ave., Gardena, California (1964)

Sealander, Inc. 2228 East McElderry St., Baltimore, Maryland (1962)

Sea King. (see Montgomery-Ward)

Sea Lark Boat Co. Rt. 1, Islamorada, Florida. For 1968, the 19-foot Sea Lark sported "a deep-vee forefoot that leads into a flat afterplane in which a tunnel has been built along the centerline." The patented design enabled the boat "to lift higher than conventional hulls and to run in very shallow water." The boat had a center-console configuration.

Sea Lion Boat Works. Sierra Madre, California.

Though not appearing in the consumer trade listings, Sea Lion was fabricating fiberglass outboard craft as early as 1947. The boats were built using the then novel female molding process., Much of the output was reportedly bought by Sears & Roebuck, a retailer pleased enough with the product to continue the contract even after Sea Lion sold its entire operation to what had recently become Glasspar.

Sea Otter Boats. 3134 North Clark St., Chicago, Illinois. J. L. Prather, owner. (1956)

Sea Ski Corp. (early 1960s)

1962 Sea Ski sports runabout measured 14' 3" and mimicked Glasspar's G-3. Wavy aft lines are due to curvature in close-up camera lens.

Sears & Roebuck. Chicago, Illinois. By 1950, the then world's largest retailer was selling its Elgin fiberglass runabout built by California-based Sea Lion. Elgin glass hulls of the 1951–54 period were reportedly manufactured by Glasspar, which had acquired the Sea Lion operation. From that point until Sears dropped boats and motors from its catalog in the late 1990s, Elgin/Sears fiberglass craft production followed a maze of contract builders that could fill an entire chapter of our study. Determining lineage is often an interesting investigative exercise in comparing the store's boats with those of known hull manufacturers. Sears' 1957 boating catalog made such sleuthing easy, though, as it is an exact copy –except for substituting the Elgin name- of an earlier Lone Star brochure. Ostensibly, Sears offered two-year old Lone Star designs (aluminum and

This late 1950s Elgin runabout is a 15-footer made by some "phantom boat builder" under Sears' contract to deliver low to moderately-priced craft suitable for the giant retailer's family-oriented, bargain-hunter market. Glasspar, Whitehouse, Lone Star, and Arkansas Traveler were a few of these masked makers.

glass) that were either new/old stock overruns or newly fabricated re-badged, circa 1955 Lone Stars.

Sea Sled Industries, Inc. 3800 Dempster St., Skokie, Illinois (1959)

Seamaid Mfg. Co., Inc. "Seamaid Boats." West Mitchell St., Kendallville, Indiana (1959)

Seamaster Boats. South Duxbury, Massachusetts (1968)

Seaswirl. Canby, and Culver, Oregon. Also known as Hi-Way Products, Inc. This line appears to be connected to several small companies that each traced their lineage to the 1955 fiberglass P-14, a plastic version of a 14-foot naval speedboat reportedly used in the World War II Pacific theater to transport officers from ship to shore. The 1950s edition sported an elaborately cast aluminum bow handle embossed with "P-14." *Trailer Boats* (July 1991) mentions the unusual craft as having been Seaswirl's "no-nonsense, bare-bones stock-in-trade" from 1955 to 1971, although Seaswirl is said to have built a few basic utilities in 1954. Parentage of the boat also appears to be claimed by the P-14 Fiberglass Boat

Company of Pilot Grove, Missouri, as well as Wilmar Boat Co., Inc., a Richmond, Indiana, maker noted in *Motor Boating* (January 1960) as makers of P-14 and Swordline boats. *Trailer Boats* called Seaswirl "a regional boatbuilder with limited distribution throughout only the eleven Western states." This could signal the fact that Seaswirl had licensed other firms to build the P-14. In any event, Seaswirl management began expanding its line, while staying focused on affordable outboard runabouts, during the 1960s and attracted a buyout by Outboard Marine Corp. in the late 1980s.

Sebago Boat Co. Sebago Lake, Maine. Charles A. Kalil's boatbuilding operation got into glass around 1955 with solid performers like the Sportsman twin-cockpit, 16-foot runabout.

Shawnee Plastic Co., Inc. Servant & Long St., Chester, Illinois (1959)

Shell Lake Boat Co. "Shellglas." Shell Lake, Wisconsin. Following a half century of wooden boat production, Shell Lake dove into fiberglass for 1955. The early "Shellglas" runabouts used wooden decks, as was common in the era. The company's best-loved model, however, was was the all-fiberglass Rocket. This colorful, tastefully tail-finned runabout could be had in 14- and 16-foot versions and became one of the firm's best sellers. Even so, things got fiscally bumpy in 1960. The 15-foot Vixen and the 15-foot Raider replaced the Rocket for 1961, shortly after some local entrepreneurs had bought Shell Lake from a bankruptcy court. Most attractive of the 1961 line was the 16-foot Corsair, with its gently sloping aft decking and slight tumblehome. Eventually the Lund boat folks picked up Shell Lake. They retired the Shell Lake name around 1972.

Signal Craft Boats Div. of Security Signals, Inc. Cordova, Tennessee (1959)

Unused newspaper ad mat for 14-foot Shell Lake Vixen is arguably almost as rare a find as the runabout it depicts.

Silver Star Fiberglass Products, Inc. Corner of 1st & Race Sts., Wolcottville, Indiana (1957)

Skagit Plastics, Inc. (Also H. S. Roberts) La Conner, Washington (1958)

Ski-Craft Co. 3227 Kilbourn Road, Lafayette, California (1964)

Slick Craft Boat Co. 791 Washington Ave., Holland, Michigan. Leon R. Slikkers, owner (1958)

Sooner Boat Co. "Sooner Craft." Eldorado, Oklahoma (1958)

South Bend Laminated Products Co. 215 Garst St., South Bend, Indiana (1955)

South Seas. Lake Helen, Florida. The highly stylized Samoan catamaran served as this rare marque's top-of-the-line, late-1950s runabout.

South Shore Boats, Inc. 2506 Merrick Road, Bellmore, Long Island, New York (1964)

Southern Mfg. 647 North St., Daytona Beach, Florida (1958)

Southern Wire & Iron, Inc. "Swico Boats." 3707 East Ponce de Leon Ave., Scottdale, Georgia (1960)

Span America Boat Co. "Span America–V.I.P. Boats." Fort Dodge, Iowa. The boating company with the funny name was actually a nod to its trio of locales spanning the US. By 1959, it had facilities in Iowa; Santa, Ana, California; and Crescent City, Florida. The latter pair served as factories. The 1960 line included the 14' 2" Pirate runabout. It was dwarfed by the 18' 3" Span Shore, which was suitable for twin outboards of high horsepower. The company also marketed marine accessories.

Sport-Craft. Perry, Florida. Outboard runabouts in this maker's 1968 fleet were the 14-foot Ski Liner, the 15-foot Ski King, and the16-foot Adventurer, as well as the Safari in 17- and 19-foot models.

Sportster Mfg. Co. Paramount, California. "Sportline." (1962)

Squall King Mfg. Corp. Miami, Florida. Royal-sounding model identities such as Emperor, Prince, Empress, Duchess, and Duke were craft names in Squall King's court. The 16' 2" Duke for 1962 was a hardy offshore utility with center console steering and transom space for a pair of 40-horse outboards.

Stamas Boats, Inc. 300 Pampas Ave., Tarpon Springs, Florida (1960). This now well-known fiberglass utility maker began boatbuilding in wood but added fiberglass models to its line by late 1959.

Stamm Boat Co. "Stamm Fiber-Jet Boats." 1764 Milwaukee St., Delafield, Wisconsin (1956)

Stan-Craft Corp. Somers, Montana (1956)

Stanray Corp., Traveler Boat Div. 1901 East Voorhees, Danville, Illinois. This is the late-1960s producer of the former Arkansas Traveler line. By this period, many big companies sought to grow by shedding a regional bias. Perhaps Stanray figured that Arkansas wouldn't play particularly well in what are now commonly called the "blue states."

Standard Glass Products, Inc. 3184 South Austin Station, Austin, Texas. By November 1957, early Glastron listings appeared in publications like *The Boating Industry.*

Starfire Boat Corp. 809 Kennedy Bldg., Tulsa, Oklahoma (1962)

Starline Products. 660 West 17th St., Costa Mesa, California. One Gerald F. Stahr founded this small fiberglass boat operation in Glasspar's hometown circa 1957.

Starliner. (see Boat Distribution, Inc.)

Steury Boat Co. 924 East Lincoln Ave., Goshen, Indiana (1958)

Stevens Boat Mfg. "SK Boats." 1501 West El Segundo Blvd., Gardena, California. Worth seeking is the 10'

4" three-point Mini-Hydro Skier from Stevens's 1968 catalog. Either of its two upholstered bucket seats would provide a thrilling ride when the boat was fitted with a maximum 35-hp motor. Above the waterline, this one looked a bit like a fancy high heel shoe.

Surf Liner Corp. (1960)

Su-Mark, Inc. 34 Rear Pleasant St., Watertown, Massachusetts, and Stone St., Walpole, Massachusetts (1957)

Supercraft Boat Mfg. Co. 14915 Nebraska Ave., Tampa, Florida (1967)

Superglas Corp. "Superglas Boats." 6401 Centennial Blvd., Nashville, Tennessee (1961)

Swiftwater Industries, Inc. 872 East Washington St., Chagrin Falls, Ohio (1960)

Switzer Craft, Inc. 7109 Pingree Road, Crystal Lake, Illinois. A cutting edge maker of sporty and full-race hulls, Switzer got into the glass game rather late (around 1965), but did so with models like the Switzer Wing, a competition craft with an aileron between its double hulls. During a test run, Bob Switzer pulled the aileron lever and suddenly everything went quiet and speed increased, signaling the fact that the boat was no longer touching the water! By 1967, the glass Switzer line included a dozen models from the 13' 3" Shooting Star 140 to an 18' 3" four-point bottomed Hydro-Kat. As was the case in the marque's production years, any Switzer is worth the consideration of classic boating buffs.

An all-out competition version of the Switzer Wing ready to perform for spectators at the 1000 Islands (NY) based Antique Boat Museum in 2004.

Tarpley Boats, Mfg. 13400 Allyn Drive & Highway 395, Riverside (Edgemont), California (1960)

The 13 Co. 190 North West St., Hillsdale, Michigan. Also known as **Marlin Marine Division of the 13 Co.,** this is the interesting maker of the ultra-streamlined Glass Slipper runabout. After being dreamed up by talented 1950s runabout designer Ervin Kiersey, production got under way in 1958 and ended by 1960. About 20 boats were made, but the impressive sounding company — actually consisting of just a few folks — got its name in *The Boating Industry* roster, a list requiring the annual construction of at least 25 craft. Like Lone Star's far-out Meteor, the Glass Slipper had lots of cast aluminum hardware accents, like jet exhausts. Over four decades after the Glass Slipper factory closed, molds for an updated 1959 version (with quadruple headlights and longer fins) were rescued from some midwestern woods.

The Tequesta Corp. Jupiter, Florida (1967)

Terry Plastic Co. 3733 East Belknap, Fort Worth, Texas (1965)

Tempar, Inc. "Jayhawk Boats." Parsons, Kansas (1961)

Texan Boat Mfg Co., Inc. "Texan Boats." San Angelo, Texas (1961)

Texas Boat Mfg Co., Inc. "Texas Maid Fleet." 1120

Texas, Lewisville, Texas. Begun in the late 1950s as a dual (aluminum and fiberglass) full-line boat maker, Texas Boat Mfg. Co., Inc., quickly looked a bit like it was trying to keep up with its wealthy neighbor, Lone Star. A check of the Texas Maid Fleet's 1962 catalog shows four respectable outboard runabouts starting with the 14-foot Astro and running to the Medalist at 16' 2." As were most of Lone Star's products from this period, Texas Maid output wore solid, middle-of-the-road styling that appealed to a wide variety of boat buyers.

Texas Glass Fiber Corp. Grandview, Texas (1958)

Thompson Boat Co. Peshtigo, Wisconsin, and Industrial Park, Cortland, New York. One of this traditional wooden-boat maker's early glass offerings was the 14-foot Starfire for 1956. The two-tone runabout's one-piece topside and molded seats and motor well was gently contoured. By 1965, Thompson's annual industry listing shows it as a subcontractor for Chris-Craft production, typically fabricating the Chris-Craft Corsair.

Thunderbird Products Corp. "Thunderbird Boats." 2901 South Bayshore Drive, Miami, Florida (1961)

Trailorboat Engineering Co. 923 Francisco Blvd., San Rafael, California. Having achieved a good reputation for its aluminum outboard craft throughout the 1950s, this West Coast manufacturer entered the fiberglass fray for the 1959 model year. One of its best glass offerings was the 14-foot Spider runabout with a seven-foot beam! Nicely upholstered, this 1964 sports hydroplane could handle the era's biggest motors and reportedly hit 60 mph.

Triangle Boat Co., Inc. 1455 West 16th St., Long Beach, California. Though short-lived and not now well remembered, Triangle was truly one of the cornerstone plastic boat makers. It was producing runabouts for at least a year before *The Boating Industry* first listed the marque in 1949.

Tri-Star Division. Detroit, Michigan. It's not certain of what Tri-Star was a division. The listing simply appeared without further explanation in a late 1959 *Boating Industry* magazine.

Tri-Vee Boats, Inc. 8315 West 20th Ave., Hialeah, Florida (mid-1960s)

Tropicraft Mfg Co., Inc. 7700 NW 37th Ave., Miami, Florida (1958)

Tomahawk Boat Mfg. Corp. Tomahawk, Wisconsin. "Ask no favors in any competition," Tomahawk brochures sometimes headlined. By 1956, the wooden-boat builder jumped into the competitive glass fray. The 14' 3" Ski Mate for 1959 serves as an example. "Slick, sleek lines high-lighted by raised canted fins make the Ski Mate a top 'looker' as well as a top performer [and] sports car of the waterways." With relatively modest freeboard, the 14' 4" Ranger added a neat mid-level model to the Tomahawk runabout lineup. Its tail fins were not as pronounced as Ski Mate's but did have similar grommet portholes through which steering

Ten feet and a couple inches of fun! The '58 Tomahawk Play-mate is a 100-pounder meant for no more than a 10-hp (by 1962 down graded to 7.5) fishing motor and a couple of lightweight boaters looking to enjoy a spin around some sheltered waterway.

The Tomahawk Ski-Mate had fins tall enough to require grommet detailed holes through which steering and motor control cables can be run. The 14' 3" hull for 1958 was "designed with the water skier in mind [so] has a wider, flatter planning area aft for good load carrying and pulling capacity."

cables ran. Entry-level boaters could take advantage of one of the era's most interesting hull and accessory marketing plans. The 14' 5" Trailer Mate Convertible could be purchased as rowboat, but later "converted" into a decked runabout with seats and seat backs

The 1958 Ranger was 13' 3" long, had nicely covered gunwales — usually found in a more expensive boat — and served as Tomahawk's (1958) runabout "priced for the family budget." Though rated for a 40-horse motor, Ranger buyers typically watched their pennies, so powered her with something in the 10- to 25-hp range.

"simply by adding a few Tomahawk stock accessories (like the deck) as you can." This transformation process could be a do-it-yourself affair or by dealer installation as one's pocketbook allowed. In the late 1950s "big and comfy department," Tomahawk offered the 16' 4" Spirit (with generous aft wings and fins) and the 18½-foot Sea Mate.

Townley Co., Inc. "Hydro Swift." (1960)

United Boat Builders, Inc. "Uniflite." 14 Squalicum Fill, Bellingham, Washington. The 1959 Uniflite/ United Boat Builder's umbrella represented a new name and corporate structure for the old Bellingham Shipyard's Bell Boy line.

U.S. Fiber Glass Products, Inc. "Performer Boats." 1711 Anaheim Ave., Costa Mesa, California. Initially

A lack of light on the cockpit of US Fiberglass Product's Esquire Performer resulted in obscuring the 17' 3" runabout's most interesting feature — bar stool-type swivel seating.

noted in 1955 as a Costa Mesa company, U.S. Fiber Glass Products Inc. had moved to 14720 Lakewood Blvd., Bellflower, California by 1960.

U.S. Outboard, Inc. 159 Morgan St., Rockford, Illinois (1955)

U.S. Plastics of Florida, Inc. Pompano Beach, Florida (1958)

Vali IV. Coldwater, Michigan. Suitable for a starring role in some 1950s space invasion sci-fi flick, runabouts from Vali IV are considered by many vintage fiberglass boat buffs as one of the genre's icons. Ervin Kiersey, designer of the almost-as-unusual Glass Slipper, put this one on the drawing board, too. It is believed that the craft hailed from 1957 when an estimated 75 were fabricated.

C.S. Van Gorden & Son. "Chippewa Boats." Eau Claire, Wisconsin (1961)

Viking Marine, Inc. "Viking Boats." 741 North Coney Ave., Azusa, California. By 1967, a firm with the identical name was headquartered at 5225 Touhy Ave., Skokie, Illinois (1961)

Vio Holda Mfg. Co. 844 North Madison St., Topeka, Kansas (1958)

Volksboat. Chicago. (about 1960)

Wabash Industries. 324 Bush Lane, Terre Haute, Indiana (1958)

Wacanda Marine. "Wacanda Boats." Colville, Washington. "Pioneer manufacturers of fiberglass boats," headlined some of this firm's brochures, though it's unclear when in the 1950s production began. Built in the Wacanda Native American territory near Spokane, these boats included runabouts like 14' 4" Vandal 15, the 16' 2" Husky 16, and 16' 6" Grizzly 17 for 1967.

Wagemaker Co. 566 Market SW, Grand Rapids, Michigan. Long a molded-plywood (and aluminum) boat maker, Wagemaker (after its merger with Cadillac) focused its attentions on fiberglass around 1959 in an effort to breathe new life into its operation.

Water Wonderland Fiberglass Boat Co., Inc. "Aero-Glas Boats." 2041 Bristol Ave., NW, Grand Rapids, Michigan. Interestingly, Aero-Glas is the same trade name used on Aero-Craft's early glass line, but it's unclear whether there was a connection, perhaps relating to subcontracting for Aero-Craft, which was also in Michigan. An undated brochure from about 1955 contains no mention of Aero-Glas, but promotes the Water Wonder Laminated Fiber Glass, "a wonder on the water," in 12- and 14-foot lengths. Central to its runabouts, named Hurricane, Lightning, Tornado, Cyclone, and Thunder, was a "Wonderful Honeycomb structure" apparently foamed into the space between hull and floor. "Store it outdoors!" was just one of the wonderful suggestions Water Wonderland employed as a sales pitch.

Webell Marine. South Kilson Drive, Santa Ana, California. For 1968, Webell cataloged its 16-foot Rebel, "high performance runabout with a double fiberglass bottom filled with foam flotation and reinforced with extra laminate."

Wellcraft Mfg, Inc. 8151 Old Bradenton Road, Sarasota, Florida (1967)

WesCraft. Bazine, Kansas (1961)

West American Industries, Inc. Fort Worth, Texas (1964)

Western Plastics. 243 Marion St., Norwood, Manitoba. Gerald Prefontaine, owner (1956)

Western Plastics, Inc., Chemold Div. Glendale, California. After securing a 1943 military contract to build rescue dinghies for the Army Air Corps, Chemold used its experience with cotton-fabric-reinforced resin to fabricate outboard pleasure craft after the war. Chemold is the first such maker to appear in a June 1945 *Motor Boating.* The line included seven boats by January 1946. Surviving examples would be among the rarest of "plastic" boats, but are probably not true fiberglass reinforced hulls. It is believed that sometime in mid-1946, the Chemold Division and its boat-fabricating information was sold to Wizard Boats.

"Westerner" Boat Div., Western Rubber Products Co. 5001 East Firestone Blvd., South Gate, California. Begun around 1955, the firm was still actively listed as a fiberglass boat maker in the late 1960s.

White Canoe Co., Inc. 156 South Water St., Old Town, Maine. (1964)

White Hawk Cruisers. Charlotte, North Carolina (1962)

Whitehouse Boat Co. Route 3, Fort Worth, Texas. After entering glass in 1958, Whitehouse kept working on innovative designs. Among them was the 16-foot Dolphin, sporting stubby stylized tail fins (with side accents) and raised deck accentuation. "Fashionable and functional" was the 13½-foot Apache, with tail fins, contoured hull design, and decent upholstery, which made the $545 model a good buy in 1958 and one to seek for a restoration project today. The 1960 lineup included Eureka, a "three-point in reverse" outboard

One of many Texas-based glass boat makers, Whitehouse Reinforced Plastic Company was for awhile an industry leader thanks to reasonably priced models like the 1958 Apache.

runabout with a snub-nosed deck. "With two high-horsepower motors," promised the maker, "it can attain 50 mph."

Willis Boat Works. 3319 Grand, Dallas, Texas (1959)

Wilmar Boat Co., Inc. "P-14" and "Swordline Boats." Round Barn Road North, Richmond, Indiana (1959) (see P-14, Seaswirl)

Winner Boats of Tennessee. Dickson, Tennessee. This firm was reportedly started by erstwhile Winner/Wizard employees who set up an independent shop in the 1970s and continued building Winner-designed craft for local sale.

WisCraft Boat Co. 7804 2nd Ave., Kenosha, Wisconsin (1962)

Wizard Boats of Tennessee, Inc. 1st & Pickering, Dickson, Tennessee. This was the division name for the Wizard (and subsequent Winner) southeastern manufacturing facility.

Yellow Jacket Boat Co., Inc (and Yellow Jacket Sales) Denison, Texas. This respected maker of molded plywood outboard boats tried fiberglass around 1958. The company — or a subsequent incarnation — operated from 111 Cypress Lane, Delhi, Louisiana, by mid-1962 and disappeared from national boating rosters several years later.

The Zimmerman Co. 213 South Harrison St., Garrett, Indiana. F. D. Zimmerman, pres. (1958)

Chapter 7

The Colorful World of Classic Runabouts

This chapter presents a sampling of the wide variety of manufacturers and the runabout models that they once offered. The chapter is organized alphabetically by manufacturer. The illustrations, whether photographs of restored boats or reproduced pages from company literature, should help owners of similar boats who seek to create an authentic restoration.

Few boats sum up better the Nifty '50s runabout ideal than this 1956 Lone Star Meteor with its Cadillac-inspired tailfins, two-tone paint, and abundant chrome trim. This Meteor, which was being used as a utility trailer to haul garbage, was in fair to poor condition when found by owner Kevin Mueller who completely restored it. He replaced all the structural wood reinforcements and had aluminum castings made for needed hardware. The trailer is a highly collectible Tee Nee. (Kevin Mueller photo)

Clamp a 25- to 35-hp mill on a Flying D, and even a relatively trim dad can join in on family water ski fun. Walk-through center deck on this 14-footer made the proverbial, "Mom, tell Jimmy to sit back here so I come up front with you and dad!" seat shifting a breeze.

Color, comfortable seating, and capacity for 60-hp worth of outboard are three popular late 1950s aluminum boat features that Aluma Craft incorporated into its 15-foot Super "CS."

Model "R" runabout from Aluma Craft represented an opportunity for rowboat shoppers to upgrade to a utility runabout without sacrificing ease of trailering, storage, and light weight.

Merrie Lady 17 actually measured 16' 6" LOA, but nonetheless went a long way towards nicely debuting Aluma Craft's 1958 fiberglass line — Aluma Glass. Note the Aluma Craft aluminum water skis in foreground.

Aluma Craft's 1960 Torino was among the firm's fiberglass models. It was billed as the "finest all-around 14-footer on the water." Color choices included Deep Scarlet, Peacock Blue, and the Tawny Brown seen here.

Aluma Craft Cruisabout 19 might have looked like plain-wrapper aluminum, but its undeniable ruggedness and ability to host twin Mercury Mark 75 (60-hp apiece) motors made it popular with the big lake crowd.

Aluminum tubular-framed/slatted wood seatbacks on this 11' 7" Model "R" Aluma Craft made cruising to those islands in the background a little more comfortable.

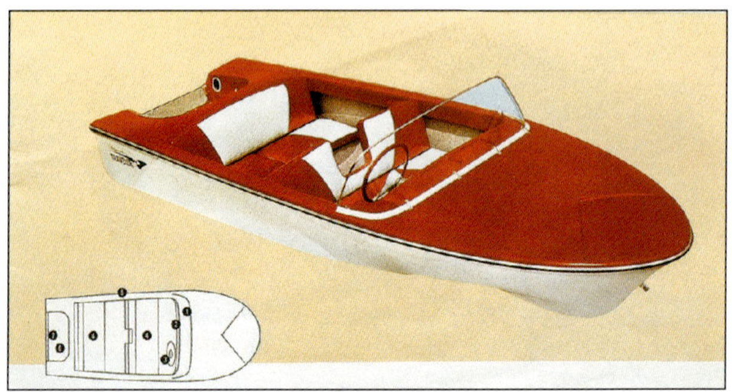

More than a few boat makers utilized "rocket" as a model name. "Like a jet on water," boasted its publicity, here's Rocket Runabout from Arkansas Traveler's glass menagerie. Compared to some of the maker's earlier aluminum speedsters, though, this 14-footer appears to be more comfy than compellingly quick.

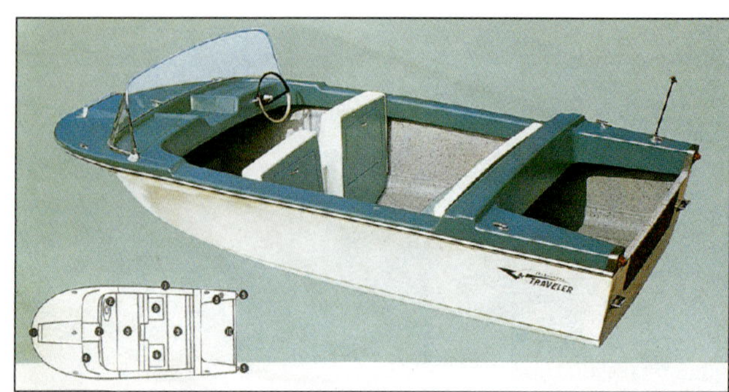

Look closely and you'll see lots of nifty compartments on Arkansas Traveler's 16-foot Custom Sports Runabout. Stuff could be stowed behind the seats, in the motor well, or perhaps on the dashboard shelf.

Dig that crazy steering wheel on the otherwise conservative 15-foot Custom Runabout in lapstrake glass by Arkansas Traveler.

"Tall Merc, Tall Fins, Tall Mountains," might make a descriptive title for this 1959 Bell Boy publicity still. Height was an ideal American subtext during the pioneer years of the space race and public rocket launches. (Courtesy Kevin Mueller)

A green and gold Scott-Atwater 33-hp motor contrasts beautifully with this Blue Star's black, yellow, and natural aluminum hues. The tinted windshield and hydraulic steering are unusual accents on this otherwise simple, rear bench seat-equipped 14-foot Surfrider from 1957.

The tailfins of this 1958 Cadillac Constellation highlight its otherwise conservative lines. The boat was restored by Patrick Wren using some New Old Stock hardware supplied by a fellow collector. (Patrick Wren photo)

This circa 1959 model carAqua might look right at home in a Star Wars movie. Much of this runabout's hardware came from 1955 – '57 Chevy/GMC trucks. This boat, powered by Kennedy-era Scott/McCulloch outboards was restored by owner Del Van Emerik who took the picture.

The entry-level Chrysler Cadet has predecessor Lone Star lines, but the 13' 7" junior runabout for two is mated to a dome-top electric start unit unique to that 20-horse Chrysler outboard.

It's a good bet that the girls modeling in Viking Convertible 14's stern seat noticed the neat plaid top more than anything else on this Crestliner. Of course, smart boat manufacturers looked for such details that'd get "mom" eyeing their products at dealer showrooms or boat shows.

One of several fiberglass craft styled by an internationally known industrial designer, this 1959 Dorsett cruiser was created by Raymond Loewy, also credited with designing the late-1930s Waterwitch outboard motor. (Kevin Mueller photo)

Larson Watercraft's 1954 cover theme included two words which pulled a lot of folks into the aluminum hull genre –"carefree boating."

A more down-to-earth incarnation of its sister metal Rocket Boat, Eshelman's simple fiberglass version of the fun craft looked a lot like a big plastic toy.

Sport 14 was Evinrude's foray into what it predicted would be a growing, upscale hobby angler market focused on middle-aged, mid-1960s executive (golf) types who had disposable income and liked things — such as their fishing boat, motor, and trailer — matched. This model was only cataloged in 1965, however, making it the rarest of Evinrude's fiberglass hulls.

Some call this Evinrude Lark concept craft/motor combo the boating boom's most photogenic runabout/outboard. The April 1956 Popular Science *said that sports car designer Brooks Stevens's $11,000 creation was "the most expensive outboard runabout ever built." (Others recall that figure being Evinrude's budget for two such boats.)*

"Deluxe sport runabout styling with long sweeping foredeck and tumble home aft decking" were design features touted by Feather Craft copywriters describing the 15-foot Vagabond. While the Vagabond I had a solid center deck, the Vagabond II seen here (a 1959 model) featured a walk-through center deck with step-aboard pads. (Boyatt Photography photo)

By the late 1950s, some boat makers stopped dating their catalogs in order to avoid being caught up in model/year frenzy, which demanded quicker change than small- to medium-sized companies could handle. Believed to be from 1959 output, The Siesta was Feather Craft's fiberglass flagship that year. The 15-footer was joined by 13' 6" glass sisters, Amigo I and Amigo II, the latter with rear seating.

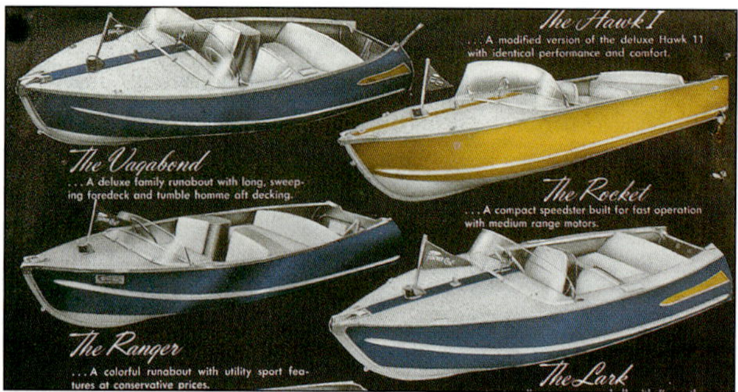

What classic aluminum boat collector wouldn't like to ride a time machine back to when this 1958 Feather Craft catalog page was current, and say, "I'll take one of each!"

Fiberglass' nearly unlimited compound curving "moldability" is certainly evident in this late '50s runabout, presumably a Fleetform.

Glasspar's attractive 1963 catalog cover with G-3 ski boat keeping up with a seaplane. To the 30-something suburban executive set the image courted, this graphic suggested sophisticated fun.

Citation by Glasspar is a roomy 16-footer for 1960. Note the four flip-down rear seats, important for families with several baby-boomers aboard.

The Glasspar Marathon hails from 1963, and was advertised as a "go ahead [14-foot] boat for go-ahead people who like to fish, cruise, water-ski, and enjoy life on the water. [its] sleek new deck [was] designed for smart appearance and safe footing."

The 14-foot Lido by Glasspar for 1960 offered quality a glass runabout at a budget-friendly price.

This 1960 Glasspar Citation was restored by its owner, James Arbella. The work included replacing the floor, transom, seat bases and rubrail, and re-gelcoating the hull. (Neda Atash photo)

Automotive styling is unmistakable in the 1958 Glastron hardtop runabout. (Courtesy of Kevin Mueller)

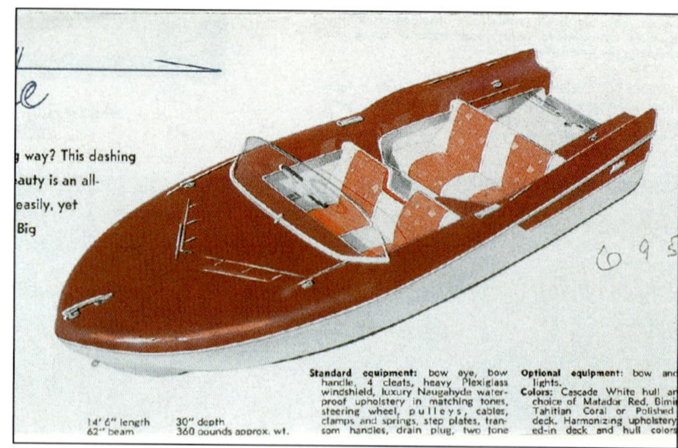

Designed for a big two-cylinder 35- to 40-horse Evinrude or Johnson with three-blade power prop, the 1958 Glastron SKIflite employed forward-pointing rear seats, a position later ski-oriented runabouts would reverse to facilitate more comfortable skier observation.

"Chrome MYLAR side panels, durabrite aluminum trim, chrome nameplates, plus two glove trays in the rear seats," gave Glastron's '58 FIREflite an automotive accent. A glass hooded Scott-Atwater 40-hp provided a stunning color match for this 15-footer's publicity still.

SKIflite for 1965 offered mid-sized runabout buyers a quality boat steeped in Glastron's great reputation for comfort, style, and performance at affordable prices.

Even a modest "fishin' motor" in the 7 ½- to 10-hp range would allow Grumman's Junior Runabout to go right along. Convince Pop to swing for a sexy, late model Mercury Mark 25, and — with just the driver aboard- this little craft could whip the pants off most of the bigger, expensive boats that'd dare to an informal race.

By 1958 color television and colorful cars represented an American status symbol of progress. Grumman joined several other aluminum boat makers in marketing runabouts capitalizing on attractive hues and tailfin style.

A 150-hp motor on this 15' 1" G-W Invader could conquer just about anything – including I/O-powered show-offs — on the market during the early 1970s.

Ready for the classic boat show! The late '50s Herter's Flying Fish and period Merc outboard combo looks like a candidate for a prize. A stickler judge, might want the flag removed from the fin unless the owner can demonstrate it's as "factory" or "period-appropriate" as the cast aluminum accents on those generous tailfins. (Courtesy of Kevin Mueller)

A Johnson-branded offering in OMC's valiant foray into boat/motor packaging.

This meticulously restored Larson Falls Flyer is ready to spark some vintage boat talk at a Canadian sportsman show. (Patrick Wren photo)

What's the fastest way to identify a Larson runabout? Look for the telltale "spear" or "mermaid kiss" running along the hull. The uncommon circa 1963 Homelite 4-stroker was capable of generating 55 hp, but sometimes presented a challenge when needing spare parts. This 1959 Larson All-American is owned by Bob and Peggy Van Diem. (Neda Atash photo)

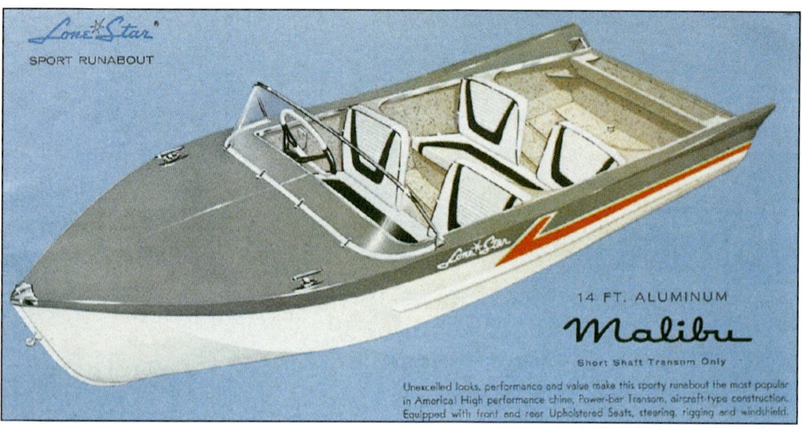

Lone Star was one of several boat manufacturers to spray the inside of many of its late 1950s/early 1960s hulls with Zolatone, a speckled anti-skid coating also meant to jazz-up an otherwise stark interior. In 1966, the author's family bought a used 1960 Malibu (like this one), a 30-horse 1957 Johnson Javelin, and Sea King trailer for $450 and, after enjoying it for years, sold it to another family for $500. They later conveyed it for a bit more to some folks who still use the hardy craft.

Cushy, tufted upholstery provided a major pathway towards making Lone Star's solidly constructed, sturdy Admiral shout "nice comfort" louder than "highly functional."

The 15-foot aluminum Saratoga was Lone Star's 1960 "family-size 'cruisette' for any kind of boating fun."

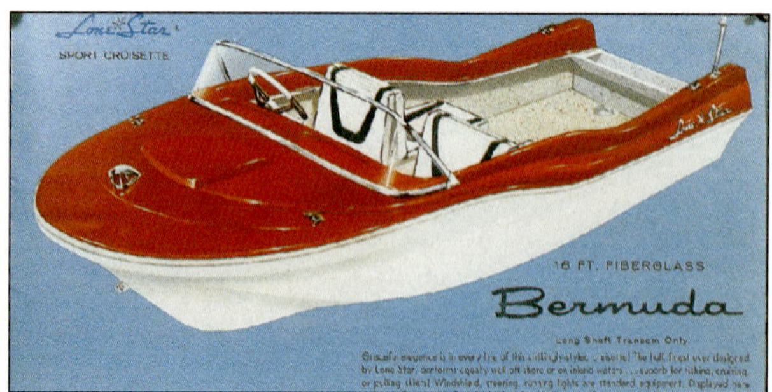

Lone Star's 16-foot fiberglass Bermuda to her aluminum sister 1960 fleet mate Malibu, and it's evident that glass produces smoother contours.

Rear bench running fore and aft, as well as gunwale railings and small driver-side windshield make the 1964 Lone Star Mystic unusually appointed, though nicely equipped as a sports runabout/ski boat.

Perhaps because Mirro Aluminum was respected by millions of North Americans who already owned Mirro pots, pans, and small kitchen appliances, the company gained a quick reputation among freshwater boaters for basic, quality runabouts like this.

Flooring and deluxe seating/upholstery transformed a 16-foot Mirro Craft hull into a Super Sport of a runabout.

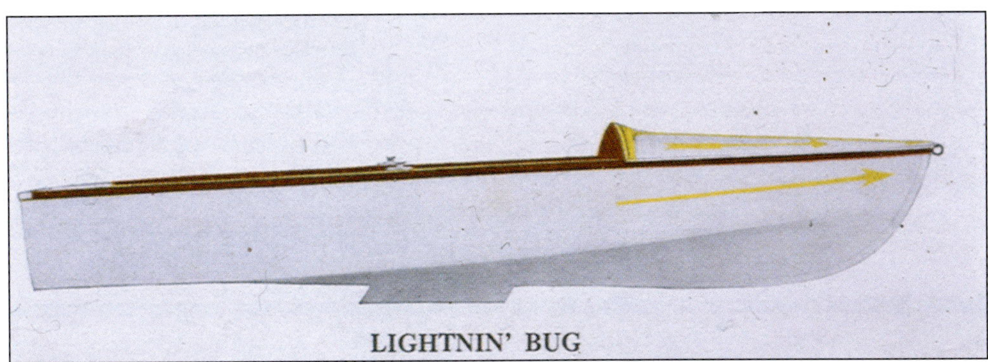

Arguably the grandfather of every fast aluminum runabout is the 1928 Mullins aluminum Lightnin' Bug with mahogany trim, a 12' 9" racer weighing 135-pounds. Note underside stabilizer fin needed for control when boat just kisses the water at plane.

Some of the nicest boat pictures could be found within outboard motor catalogs. Mercury featured a couple of its mid-range products on a subdued-styled Crosby (left) and more curvaceous Red Fish.

Reinell built several incarnations of its Jet Flight, including this edition of its most remembered creation, a runabout with the 1959 Chevrolet fins and taillights interpreted in the stern. This 1960 model was bought new with a trailer for $792 in 1962 by Mel and Shirley Rose who passed it on to their son Rich in 1992. The boat is in excellent original condition. It is powered by a 1969 Merc 650. (Neda Atash photo)

In catalog store parlance, low price beats sophistication. Few boat buyers expected Glasspar or Glastron quality at Montgomery-Ward prices, and consequently were reluctant to buy "bigger" (than a rowboat) craft from mail order establishments. Of course, there's a chance that the likes of this 1962 Sea King Sea Venture II was fabricated for Wards by a big name boat builder.

The 1962 Sea King Sea Knight I represented the kind of entry-level simplicity for which Ward's aluminum marine offerings were noted. Match it with a private-brand/badge-engineered Sea King outboard, and you've got a potential classic boat show crowd pleaser.

That sure doesn't look like Captain Kirk at the center-station controls nor Mr. Spock delivering those groceries, but Starcraft conjured up images of the duo's now legendary voyages by naming this 1969 utility Star Trek V.

Gunwale Length	Center Line Length	Height Forward	Amidship Depth	Transom for Long Shaft Motors	Beam	Stern Depth	Stern Width	Deck Length	Horsepower Rating	Carrying Capacity	Approx. Weight
17'10"	16'	38"	34"		74"	30"	74"	62"	90	1,770 lb	680 lb

Fold down seats, ample dash area, and high hull sides gave the 16-foot Shell Lake fiberglass Corsair a comfy automotive-like interior.

Though the 1966 Starcraft 16-foor Newport V makes for a good picture, the high-sided fiberglass runabout is eclipsed by that marina milieu background. Note the classic Coca-Cola machine offering sodas for a dime. And even at premium "marine prices" the gas is setting back the boater just 36-cents a gallon!

Starcraft's 1958 Ski Champ held a promise of 14-feet of colorful fun for families just getting into boating. Don't forget to budget an extra 20 bucks for a pair of brightly painted water skis!

The 16-foot Jupiter V by Starcraft shows the kind of vinyl upholstery and floor carpeting considered requisite to attract late 1960s aluminum runabout buyers.

Starcraft's 1969 catalog employed photography models in catchy costumes — such as the hooded masks donned by this duo — to add pizzazz to runabouts that looked like… well, runabouts. The traditional vee-hulled 16-foot glass V-160 is shown here.

Built around 1957, these Sputnik-era Vali IV runabouts were stylistically outdated by the time America began Project Mercury manned space missions, and got tired of fanciful fins. What goes around, comes around, however, making even one of the uncommon craft a fantastic find today. (Kevin Mueller photo)

Chapter 8

What to Look For

In a Vintage Aluminum or Fiberglass Runabout

"Boats are an investment in pleasure and health.
For real boating pleasure, seek a boat that is safe and carefree.
Consider a design that gives stability yet is highly maneuverable.
Now choose the model that is best suited to your purpose."

— 1959 Newport fiberglass boat pamphlet

When not at the tiller of a classic outboard motor, one of my luckiest vintage boat friends drives a concrete truck through rural New England. From that vantage point, he sure seems to encounter a lot of old hulls. Because most have been sitting outdoors for at least several years, the wooden ones — these days few and far between — are totally shot, and fiberglass examples (often containing a surprising amount of lumber) typically serve as the nautical equivalent of fool's gold. That's why, unless they're incredibly rare and include salvageable deck hardware, or motor, he stays in his vehicle. Besides, it's classic aluminum he's really seeking.

Whether flipped upside down across some firewood behind a ramshackle garage or full of green water on a rusted trailer with flat tires, almost all of the old aluminum runabouts can be brought out of retirement with little more than some old fashioned elbow grease. In fact, aluminum's relative imperviousness to rain, snow, and sunlight is often reason enough for the owner of an obviously neglected runabout to keep it around — just in case he ever wants to go fishing or something. My compatriot usually returns with cash near the end of the month and makes an offer. He actualizes the old boat hunter's motto: *If you don't ask, it's a "no!"* Mortgages and other bills coming due a dozen times annually have a way of making those "someday" fishing trips suddenly seem farfetched.

Vintage runabouts can turn up just about anywhere. This orange and white Lone Star sold quickly. (Stan Grayson photo)

Curious to many old aluminum runabout buffs is the question: Given the large numbers built between 1946 and the early 1970s, where have all the aluminum runabouts gone? This isn't just a 21st century question, either. Back in 1988, *Trailer Boats*'s Larry Carpenter mused that "a certain percentage must have been dented or smashed to the point where their owners figured repairs weren't worth the trouble, but this still leaves tens of thousands of [aluminum] boats built during the height of the postwar pleasure boating boom that must still exist somewhere."

While logically choosing to believe that these boats were simply not discarded in large numbers, Carpenter was, "left with the [conviction] that they must be salted away in barns, sheds, and garages, out of range of wandering eyes." He concluded that "those still in plain sight don't begin to equal the numbers that must still exist."

To be sure, polite snoops, consistent readers of classifieds, and diligent detectives have discovered hundreds since then. The craft have surfaced in venues as diverse as church fundraisers, front yards, used car lots, and eBay auctions. Each hunt has potential to yield a neat boat or at least a classic story. "Would you consider selling that?" my buddy asked while pointing to a lopsided craft that was full of rain and practically bonded to a derelict trailer frame wearing a crunched 1982 license plate. "Can't," declared the owner who then gestured towards some swayback horses. "We still use it — for a watering trough. And ole Bucky over there likes to scratch his itches on those metal tail fins." Not one to give up, my friend offered to replace the boat with a legitimate farm trough and scratching post. Even so, the owner speculated that he might put it back on the lake next summer.

Some of the best vintage marine finds turn out to be 10- to 14-foot runabouts that were carelessly camouflaged as duck boats by an interim owner wielding a few cans of paint. And, budget-minded anglers wanting a cheap bass boat have hacked their share of center (wheel) decks off more than a few classic runabouts, or removed the decking altogether. Vintage boaters with a good idea of what they're looking for, however, are in the optimum position to recognize such diamonds in the rough, be they metal or glass.

This uncommon Red Fish Shark DeLuxe popped up in the author's riverside neighborhood after having been bought inexpensively by a family scanning the local classifieds for "an old boat that the kids can use." Some buffs would travel a thousand miles to snag such a craft.

First, though, determine what you like. Establish a "specialty." It's probably because I'm mainly an antique (aluminum) outboard motor nut that, over the years, my boating interest has run the gamut, but always returns to oohs and ahs for small aluminum runabouts — the shorter the better. The iconic 10-horse 1947 Mercury Lightning performs best on a featherweight aluminum hull. 10- to 14-foot glass speedsters run a close second when powered by an older motor. Of course, these (typically) two-seaters are much harder to find than an average family runabout primarily because an average 1950s–60s family's mom, dad, and 3.2 kids couldn't fit into such sporty craft, and consequently few were sold. But small, fast boats are what I coveted as a kid at the marina, so they influence my search engine today.

I can also report, however, that having spent a year or so regularly delving into old boating literature while preparing this book, I've developed a new interest in the more traditionally sized 15- to 17-foot garden variety runabouts. Watch out for getting too tolerant, though. No garage or barn offers infinite space. Be comfortable with passing up boats — no matter what the bargain — that are not central to your focus, and then pass along those leads to others. Among honorable collectors, what goes around comes around.

"Does it leak?" certainly seems like a good question

Here's the stuff classic aluminum boat buff's dreams are made of — happening upon a forgotten Feather Craft in back of some old barn! Generally with aluminum, what you see is what you get, making the assessment decision easier than might be the case with an old wooden or glass hull that's been long exposed to the elements.

to ask someone selling an old aluminum boat, but even a definitive "no" doesn't usually come with sufficient guarantees to be meaningful. Consequently, buyers should assume there are a few leaky spots in which existing rivets require some sealant, hammer-snugging, or where drilling out the original and installing new oversize rivets will be needed. Nasty-looking gouges, dents, cracks, bent framing (stringers), corrosion from having been mired in mud, loose metal, or ripped or chopped-up decking should be of the most concern, depending on one's aluminum repair confidence level.

Over one summer, I made several trips to a marina advertising a 1957 Feather Craft Rocket Runabout among its used boat inventory. On top of what was originally anodized green and gold, the boat had been painted a hideous brown, possibly to mask a mass of lumpy dents literally from stem to stern. Even so, I came very close to buying her, and have sometimes

Until vintage non-wooden craft are embraced by the traditional classic boating crowd, models such as this still brightly anodized Feather Craft aluminum runabout can be had for a lot less than their mahogany sisters in line at the local marina or antique boat auction.

regretted finally walking away. My eventual departure can be credited to a painful realization that I had no background in knocking a boat smooth. Wisdom reasons that a hull requiring repairs beyond a boater's abilities — or monetary means to pay someone else to fix it — seldom helps make any dreams come true.

Incidentally, by fall, I began to wistfully reconsider the little aluminum gal, but learned that she'd been sold to someone in the auto body trade who was very excited

When you see a nicely equipped, beautifully preserved — or lovingly restored — classic runabout and proper period motor offered for sale, don't be afraid to ask for a demonstrable proof that all is shipshape. And if the price is fair, neither should you lowball the seller or agonize to the point where someone else swoops in and closes a deal. Instead, calculate what it might cost — fiscally and time wise — to buy, revitalize, and outfit a similar boat into such a condition. Often, it's a package like this shiny Feather Craft and Johnson Sea Horse 25 that is the actual bargain.

Along the way, this 10-foot Feather Craft stock outboard utility racer was unmercifully modified by someone who loved purple stripes, Naugahyde vinyl, shortened decks, and jerry-rigged front steering. A model this rare, though, is worthy of the time and money required for restoration.

to have found her. To him, restoring the Feather Craft was not much of a problem. Where his rubber mallet wouldn't do the trick, aluminum patches could be riveted over cracks, rips, or holes, once this area was well-cleaned with lacquer thinner. Such dents are best repaired with a rubber or neoprene gasket, the exact size of the patch. The patch is coated on both sides with adhesive and riveted over the damaged area. To avoid electro-chemical deterioration, the rivets and patch need be aluminum like the hull. This amateur riveter can attest that consumer-grade hand rivet tools take a lot of squeezing. Neither is it always easy to find an enthusiastic riveting partner who'll patiently press a small sledgehammer (or equivalent backstop) against the factory rivet head so you can properly peen the other end.

Popular Science had its eye on a mystery that occasionally pops up in classic glass boating circles — how to identify the origin of a boat with no brand name. When the magazine's editors made space for "How to Tell a Copycat Boat from a Good One," in their January 1964 issue, they did so because readers had reported getting burned on a purchase. While it's quite plausible to assume that there are examples of no-name, fly-by-night craft on the vintage market, the most egregious ones have probably crumbled away decades ago. Still, *Popular Science*'s advice can be useful to anyone trying to size up a second-hand boat's integrity.

"Check the interior of the boat for the woven pattern of fiberglass cloth under lightly applied paint. You wouldn't normally see the weave in a good boat. Occasional tufts of glass fiber, without the slick feel of polyester resin, suggest resin starvation and a potential weak spot. A slick, smooth bump with a glass feel to it suggests resin over-richness. Thump the sides of a glass boat with your fist. A good boat reverberates like a drum. A cheap boat rattles."

A long-time student of glass outboard craft, Bill Loveland, admits to having lost count of how many vintage plastic boats he's dragged home on decrepit trailers. And just when he decides to curtail his collecting, another inviting classic glass runabout will appear, seemingly out of nowhere, begging for triage in his late-19th century barn turned hull hospital. A knowledgeable generalist, Loveland always queries the seller (or "giver" on more than one occasion) about hull leaks. He understands, however, that a boat that "seemed to be fine" on her most recent voyage, often a decade earlier, has likely since suffered some degradation by just sitting. He is seldom a Pollyanna about the condition of those great quantities of core or support wood in most fiberglass hulls either.

"The plywood in the transom is probably a goner," Loveland says. "Water has a habit of seeping through every small space it finds, including through splits in the floor, gel coat cracks, transom fasteners, and hardware mounting holes. Figure that to do things right," he suggests, "the whole floor and transom has to be cut out so you can get at the rotten support boards. What a

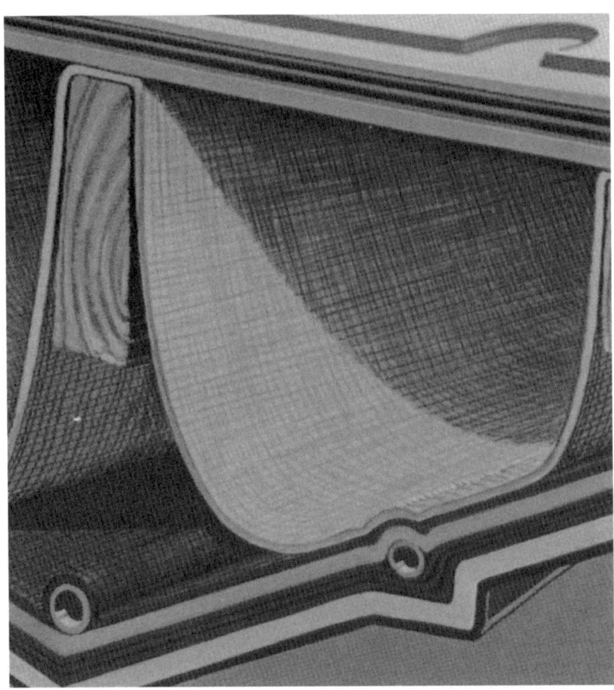

Fiberglass boats don't look like they contain any wood, but most do, as noted in this artist's rendering of flooring and related supports. To restore a classic glass hull that has seen sustained leakage or been left to fill up with several seasons worth of rain and melted snow, one should figure on ripping out and replacing such lumber.

messy job!"

That's probably why classic fiberglass's tail fin–era expert, Kevin Mueller, stresses that it requires just as much work to restore a "common" plastic runabout as it does to revitalize one of the incredibly unusual models, such as a Lone Star Meteor or Bee-Line Sapphire. "When it comes to choosing a project boat, nothing exceeds like excess!" he's fond of preaching to folks trying to decide what kind of craft to seek out and submit to months of surgery. Admittedly though, beauty is in the eye of the beholder. A big, rubbery-looking 1950 Beetle Boat utility, a "girl next door" 1970s Chrysler trihedral, or a generic 16-foot runabout with no trace of an ID (save for a fudged "homemade" registration descriptor) can prove to be just as worthy of a restoration as might some low-production seagoing rocket ship. Again, determining one's intended focus is the best way to get into the hobby.

Mueller has taken that step and reflects, "I've been trying to build a fairly inclusive, outboard boat collection since 1991, and as of 2005 have twenty-five pieces. I began by compiling a list of what should be included, under ideal circumstances, defined as unlimited time for restorations, unlimited funding for restorations, and unlimited storage and shop facilities for restorations. My passion is for the following: brightly colored fiberglass boats with fins! Lots and lots of fins! Fins so big I cannot dock them in even a light crosswind with six experienced deck hands. Did you know that cutting a few inches off the windshield can actually make the fins *look* taller?" Here's the short list Mueller takes whenever sleuthing vintage glass.

1) Begin with a dog-eared catalog and a daydream. "After reviewing the idyllic photographs and dubious claims in the surviving literature, I already have a good idea what classic boats I want. Experience reveals that they all take roughly the same amount of work, so I figure I better hunt for whatever I think will look the most spectacular when it is done. What will be the final appearance? This is probably the foremost guide in my 'Should I get this one?' decision making."

2) Conspicuous conservation. "Another strong consideration is a boat's rarity. I love finding something that may become extinct without my efforts. Take the car collector philosophy, for instance. If a person saves a forlorn '57 Chevy, well, that's great. It's a fine car and parts availability is a breeze. No danger of the car languishing though. If you don't buy it, the next guy will. Heck, the next thousand guys will. Now what about a '53 Packard Sedan? If you don't save it, who will? Obscure and odd classic outboard boats fall into that second 'needy' category. When found, most old wooden boats, like '57 Chevrolets, enjoy a well- represented following and so seem to be in no real danger of extinction. As for the flock of 1970s–1980s tri-hulled bow riders, they're not on the endangered species list yet, either.

3) What am I going to do with the darn thing? "Practicality should be a real consideration. If you are going to have only one vintage boat, like most *normal* people, then it's vital that the craft fits your needs. Small, two-person boats, with exotic, expensive styling, are as rare today as they were in the '50s, due to poor sales. You might want to ask yourself the same question now, as was silently asked in thousands of marine showrooms when the classic boat was new. Can I justify a sporty little Wizard Wasp for my family of six? Do I have a sheltered body of water on which to run it? Most of the early flat-bottom boats were astonishingly poor performers on all but smooth waters. Sure it looks sexy, but can you imagine yourself and five landlubber passengers on a rough lake in that bouncy Wasp? How about a roomier nineteen-foot Lone Star Caribbean or big Balboa hardtop, instead? With a seven-foot beam and ample weight, either will be a lot better boat for demanding conditions, like a serious wake from a carelessly passing cabin cruiser at half-throttle."

4) Realism 101. "Honestly, what is the boat's probable condition? Actually, I always said this doesn't really matter because they all contain a foot of topsoil and need transom replacement by the time we find them. True, there are some rare exceptions out there worth considering, boats that have led sheltered lives, well away from deciduous trees and gobs of wet, decomposing leaves. I wouldn't pass on a truly rare boat, regardless of its condition, but if conducting a painfully difficult restoration isn't your idea of fun, you don't need to have a giant tail light–festooned Cadillac Sea Lark 'eternal project boat.' Instead, you would be happier cruising around in a teensy-tiny little tail fin-equipped plain-Jane Span America brand runabout. So make one of those your personal top priority. You may never discover a 'mint' Meteor, but you can probably expect to find a nice Glastron."

5) Location, Location … Vacation. "Don't be afraid to travel to find your dream boat. Make a memorable family excursion out of it and enjoy the trip. Be sure the trailer is in good shape, or obtain one that's State Police–roadworthy at your destination. I often bring my own trailer and load the boat there. If the craft is on a junk trailer, just have the seller take it to the dump, or advertise it for gas money later in your local swap sheet paper. Keep in mind that some trailers were equally as stylish as the 1950s boats and could be worthy of restoration. Backing the good trailer up to the hopeless one, removing the old winch stand, and dragging the boat forward onto the new trailer has worked extremely well for me. Trailering often comes with the territory, as the most unique boats are rare enough to make them unlikely to be found in someone's storage shed just ten minutes from home. I have located a few close by, but most precipitated cross-country trips as follow-ups on Internet leads for a real neat boat. Before you leave your driveway, always recite the boat hauler's creed: If you pack a spare trailer tire, you will never need it. If you don't, you most certainly will!"

6) Even after a long boat-hunting trip, think in terms of puzzle pieces. "Completeness of what's there on the hull should be the key consideration. Are there any hard-to-replace components absent? That's why it's good to have done homework studying period catalogs and talking to other owners of that model so you can test the boat for original equipment. Some collectors are willing to loan other enthusiasts particular parts for duplication. I have had literally dozens of missing pieces fabricated for these boats in the same way that they were made to begin with — sand castings and Fiberglas molds. Often, when collectors need to have a part made, we network with others who need the same thing, and share any tooling costs involved. Ideally, though, it's best to get a boat that's already got what it needs.

7) Get a prescription for *"Leaverite."* "All in all, buying a classic glass or aluminum outboard boat is a matter of personal taste and tolerance for the work that lies ahead. If the boat *isn't* what you had in mind when you get there, then it is not a bargain at any price. *"Leaverite"* there and just keep on looking. Enjoy the hunt!"

When inspecting a boat, interview the seller with questions that tell him or her that you are a polite, knowledgeable person but not a pushover. Inquire about the craft's history, as that might get the owner reminiscing. Very few average boat owners, however, are infallible about dates and details relating to how long the thing has been in the side yard or — if it's mated to a mill — whether the outboard's innards have issues. Ask to see the registration for boat and trailer. These documents have a way of defining many issues. You want to know things like when the craft was last used and what make, model, and year it is, as well as who owns it. I once sadly passed on a rather robust little Rich Line utility because it turned out that the seller didn't actually own it and had no documentation except for an illegible note on a flattened McDonald's bag that allegedly transferred the boat over to the seller, who then told me he could only sell it for cash and had to do so that night.

"I can write you a bill of sale alright," the fellow offered, "but I can't sign it." In many states, a boat with a questionable or no title or registration won't prove any more beneficial that the proverbial screen door on a submarine. Another time, I bought a bargain 1962 Arkansas Traveler Little Fisherman pram for which the seller produced the current registration from his wallet. It looked fine and had worked for him. Fortunately, the lady at the Department of Motor Vehicles was a friend of the family and accepted paperwork that listed the LF-1 model designation as the serial number and was blank in the "model" space. "A cranky agent could have sent you and your cute boat back to square one," she smiled. In the good old days, folks were able to register almost anything that floated by indicating it was a homemade boat. Few jurisdictions still have such loopholes.

Don't get hemmed in by the asking price. Beware of being pressured to act immediately and without having the opportunity to ask the owner to consider your offer, a figure within a range you should have established prior to seeing the boat. Also beforehand, on a piece of paper you can hold and study, realistically estimate what it will cost to get the craft to the level of revitalization that suits your purposes. Ignore the seller's predictions (especially if bidding in an online auction) about how easy such a fixup will be. If restoring the boat really is so simple, ask the person why he or she doesn't make the improvements. Be careful about rationalizing the purchase price based on how much you might subsequently get for the trailer, motor, water skis, or plaid picnic cooler that is being thrown in with the deal. My experience has been that mentally subtracting $250 for the trailer, $500 for the

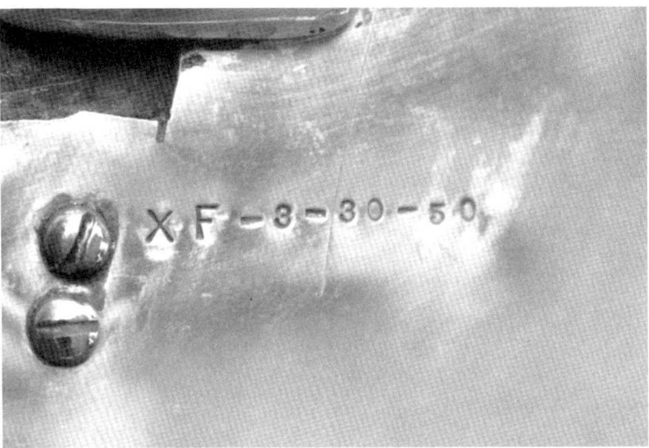

Many vintage boats do wear identification. Because few manufacturers were consistent in their ID techniques, the trick is knowing where to look — under the deck, on the transom, on the seat frame, on the gunwale, etc., etc. Here's a rare serial number stamped into the stern of an experimental (X) Feather Craft Flyer model (F) built on March 30, 1950. Too bad such genealogy isn't always that obvious!

outboard, and $100 for the other valuable equipment, in order to convince yourself that the $1,000 Larson All American is really only going to cost 150 bucks, seldom ends up being fiscally prudent.

What are old boats worth, anyway? As the author of *The Old Outboard Book*'s vintage motor price guide, and having researched pricing trends on pleasure craft–related items for several decades, I must admit that I don't exactly know. Nobody does. Sometimes things go surprisingly high and on other occasions incredible bargains can be had. Get on the web and go to hobby sites like *www.fiberglassics.com*. There you can conduct vital research and email other collectors who will have a feel for approximate current boat values on the model you're considering. Though Internet sites tend to come and go, FiberGlassics (thanks to founder Kelly Wood and the legion of helpful hobbyists congregating there) has demonstrated its staying power.

Thinking of great deals reminds me of a family that rented a camp down the beach from ours around 1970. The dad heard I liked old boats and wanted to show me a late 1950s Sears Elgin salmon-colored fiberglass runabout, matching West Bend-built Elgin 30-hp outboard and trailer with pert, teardrop fenders — all in nice shape. "Got the package from a couple relocating to California," he smiled, "The moving van was in the driveway and so was the boat." He admired it and admitted to having only $100 in mad money. 'OK,' they said, 'cuz we're sure not pulling it to L.A." Remember always that one key buying or selling reality remains constant — "you just never know." Whether or not you close the deal, consider leaving contact information. More than once, either the seller later phoned me to accept a month-old offer, or somebody who the seller knew called to ask if I was the guy who buys old boats and motors.

After saying, "yes" to such a query, chances are you'll be buying more than just the boat and outboard. As Kevin Mueller noted, there are time and monetary expenses related to any restoration, even if they're just a Saturday afternoon, and some soap and water. Once the craft is at its new home and gets a thorough cleaning, it's almost certain that trouble spots not previously noticed will show up. A quality polish and wax — ask for advice at the auto parts store or from a FiberGlassics person — helps show a fiberglass hull's good and bad external areas. Glass repair is trickier than aluminum revitalization and often necessitates taking out the seats, and cutting out the floor and transom in order to replace the stern and support network. In 1960, Owens-Corning published a 16-page booklet (O-C pub. No. 5-BO-584A) called *Repair Guide For Fiberglas Reinforced Molded Boats.* For those really committed to studying period literature on the topic, a copy shouldn't be too tough to find.

Wherever originally hidden, Styrofoam or air chamber flotation needs to be evaluated against legitimate safety standards. Even buffs who get some satisfaction from slowly slicing through FRP and scraping away the mushy remains of the boat's balsawood core, admit it can be a tedious, dusty, sweaty and itchy endeavor that spouses often don't appreciate. One's better half might be more willing to help with re-upholstery. Many early, entry-level runabouts had some kind of Naugahyde or vinyl (available from fabric and craft stores) stapled to a wooden seat or seat back with foam rubber in between. Others used snap-in or even loose marine "flotation" cushions, most of which are no longer legal flotation devices. A set of modern cushions should be figured into the budget.

Deluxe upholstery may be a greater challenge, but the robust auto restoration hobby makes it possible to access just about any style, texture, and color of material, padding, and fasteners for the job. If your budget isn't tight, know that car restoration shops are usually very willing to re-upholster boat interiors. Even the best ones, though, would find certain proprietary marine patterns, such as Lone Star's asterisk seat-back design, challenging to reproduce. There might be details that the boat will just have to live without. The same goes for missing or blatantly incorrect hardware. Getting in touch with collectors of boats similar to yours will provide you with a palpable sense of the pieces' availability — from "off the shelf" to "off the charts!" One can also network with folks who are planning to fabricate reproductions of the stuff your boat needs to look good.

Throughout your boat's revitalization process, you'll be making decisions about just how far to go on the road from "as found" to transforming the craft into a 100-point Antique and Classic Boat Society show winner. Don't feel bad if you're satisfied with a good, middle-of-the-road, clean, serviceable hull that looks used but loved. As in the vintage auto and old outboard motor hobbies, such a "runner" often generates more enjoyment than a museum-quality example. Most antique outboarders do suggest, however, that one's motor or boat neither be "over restored" nor be irrevocably modified from the original.

Finding a vintage craft with its plastic steering wheel hub insert — or other cosmetic features — intact makes any "restorable" runabout a bit easier to complete.

Matching just the right period motor to your boat can be a fun endeavor not unlike the shopping trip that the original owner savored when visiting his local dealership years ago. While horsepower and engine brand preferences were part of the mosaic, it was color

Cast aluminum identification emblems — like this tag from a rare Vali IV runabout — is a must when restoring with classic boat show trophies in mind. Enthusiasts are often willing to loan such small cosmetic pieces to fellow collectors for duplication at a foundry.

that helped make the sale fun. No matter what your craft's hue — even if bare aluminum — there's an outboard that will look tailor- made for its transom. In fact, there are scores of appropriate kickers in "Happy Days" colors from royal blue and salmon to sunset orange and copper, as well as black and white.

From 1951–55, Evinrude and Johnson's most powerful model rated 25 hp. This increased to 30 for 1956, went to 35 in 1957, 50 for 1958, and 75 by the 1960s. Gale Products' Buccaneer and Sea King brands topped out around 1960 with 60 hp. Mercury's four-cylinder 25-horse model debuted in 1949 and essentially continued through 1953. A 40-hp Merc arrived in mid-1954. Six-cylinder Mercury models appeared for 1957 with 60 hp. That rating climbed to 70 and then 80, before hitting the 100 mark in 1962. Scott-Atwater

Deck hardware can take on a personality all its own. "Warp speed! Engage!" hints this collection of cleats.

Modern gauges and a radio nicely installed in a circa 1960 Reinell runabout. Admittedly, locating original instrumentation is akin to netting the proverbial needle in a haystack, but some buffs and most classic boat show judges say all accessories must be "period" pieces in order to appear shipshape.

(and subsequently just "Scott," and finally McCulloch) offered 30 and then 33 hp during the 1954–56 period. Later 1950s' increases yielded 40 and 60 hp, and 75 by the early 1960s. West Bend motors were rated initially at 30 and 35 hp. The company's biggest motor arrived in the early 1960s as a four-cylinder 80-horse mill. Also a province of the early 1960s, Homelite's 55-hp four-stroke outboard took a small, colorful slice of the runabout-power pie. To access the Antique Outboard Motor Club website, complete with great insight, helpful membership, and a free classified section, type in *www.aomci.org*.

As a closing effort to get you thinking about honing your wish list of vintage aluminum and fiberglass runabouts, I am offering mine. It's likely that yours will include lots of boats not on these rosters. While busily considering and scribbling away, there's always the interesting problem of how realistic one should be. For example, my Number One target was long a Blue Star stock racing runabout and/or hydroplane. However, friends have convinced me that these low production/ high-performance products are so rare that I could no longer endure wasting one of my top-10 wants on what has proven to be a wild goose chase.

Consequently, the Blue got bumped for an Arkansas Traveler, which associates are now telling me is also a hopeless long shot. And what about our hobby's "future gold"? It's probably prudent for some collector to resolve finding a decent 1970s Glastron tri-hull or early Bayliner while these boats are still plentiful, quite usable, and often unbelievably inexpensive. Suffice it to say, pleasure craft wish lists are most lively when allowed to be works in progress. Please excuse the fact that I've had no choice but to double up some hoped-for hulls on one number!

Top Ten Aluminum Runabouts To Look For

1. Arkansas Traveler long fore-decked 12-foot two-seater, Playboy stock outboard racer, or Sportsman series.
2. Feather Craft Rocket Runabout, Firefly, Flash (or any model that comes your way and looks serviceable).
3. Aero-Craft model AD, and models K or L racing versions.
4. Crestliner Commander "12."
5. Arkansas DUT-14 with Fiberglass Deck.
6. Duratech 92R Class "JU" utility racing pram.
7. Aluma Craft model R wheel deck runabout.
8. Trailorboat mini-runabout.
9. Crestliner Jet Streak 12.
10. Starcraft Jet Star.

Top Ten Fiberglass Runabouts To Look For

1. Herter's Eldorado Rocket or any fiberglass craft from this underrated boat maker.
2. Lone Star Meteor or late version Larson Falls Flyer.
3. Beetle BB Skimmer.
4. Starcraft Royal Star.
5. Triangle runabout.
6. Garform outboard runabout.
7. Crosby Sweptfin.
8. MFG (in good shape from the mid-1950s).
9. 13' 3" Boston Whaler.
10. Chris-Craft Lake'n Sea 15'.

Chapter 9

All Decked Out

Equipping a Vintage Runabout

"One of the remarkable things about the boating boom is that it is growing almost as fast in the hinterlands — far from lakes, rivers, and bays — as it is by the water. The automobile and the boat trailer have made it possible for anybody to join the small boat navy."
— *Newsweek*, April 15, 1957

Trailer home an old aluminum or fiberglass boat and you've suddenly got the opportunity to become the head curator of a floating museum. Don't worry about not immediately knowing the craft's history and how to best allow the boat to brag of its past. Researching and gathering little details generates a large portion of our unique hobby's fun. But be advised, even the most confirmed landlubber will ask about your boat's background and may be sparked into his or her own reminiscences regarding somebody they knew with a boat like yours back in the good old days.

So follow the lead of the vintage automobile buffs and spend a bit of time each year making your classic craft as representative of the date it left the dealer's showroom. Actually, a few years on either side is acceptable. But make sure everything on the boat gives it the chance to serve as a relatively accurate time machine for all to enjoy — whether as passenger or passerby. Start by hunting up some original brochures and boating magazines at nautical flea markets or online (or maybe borrow some for photocopying) that can provide a good glimpse of what the craft looked liked when new.

At the same time, and just as important, search for information on what accessories were then available to deck out such a hull. During the boating boom, dozens of companies like Attwood Brass Works (started in 1893 on $300 by Charles Attwood with an eye toward making car parts, and now called Attwood Corporation) got into producing marine hardware that became a profitable line for it and its thousands of boat and motor dealers when the boating boom erupted in the 1950s. No self-respecting proprietor would want to sell a just boat, when a boat, motor, trailer, and accessories "package" could be offered.

Consequently a lot of boats in our interest area were fitted with a bevy of neat gizmos — like a combination glove compartment and beverage rack. Common sense should prevail, so that while tracking down a steering station for your 1953 Duratech utility, stay clear of the 1960 Lone Star "side steering assembly" some flea market vendor tries convincing you "oughta work okay if you just pry out the little Lone Star logo." Aftermarket products (parts and doo-dads sold after their intended subject has been purchased) are the best bets because aftermarket companies like Attwood-made accessories intended for a wide range of boats and tastes.

Basic to the outfitting experience is playing engine and hull matchmaker so your boat can marry just the right motor "mate." Start by determining the craft's original power plant. Proprietary remote controls, solenoid electric starting boxes, and clamp marks on the transom serve as clues. And, those original catalogs and ads will show which outboards the company used to make their boats look nice. Johnson is one motor maker that came out with an annual "Dealer Photo Catalog," which pictured Johnsons on the different craft its various dealers also carried. Don't overpower your hull. Remember that some of the 1950s' manufacturers' horsepower capacity ratings were hyperbolic in a world that topped out at 25–40 hp, anyway. Not that it's everyone's cup of tea, but I've run into many classic outboarders who are perfectly happy with the portability (motor weight-wise), fuel economy and moderate cruising speeds that a 15- or 18-horse Evinrude (as opposed to a 40-hp mill), provides for their 14-foot runabout and three passengers. If you're stuck for ideas, hit the Antique Outboard Motor Club's website, *www.aomci.org,* and request suggestions. Like sports nuts who spend hours considering "dream teams," many an AOMCI folk have cogitated regarding ideal motor and boat combos.

If you might like to show your boat at any one of the growing numbers of antique maritime events, consult the particular organization for hints. A major show each early August takes place on the grounds and docks of the Antique Boat Museum in Clayton, New York. This fine organization subscribes to Antique and Classic Boat Society protocols gladly offered to any interested exhibitor. As a long-time judge at this event, I'm always pleased to award available points to a family who displays their vintage outboard runabout with a period trailer, motor, a few accessories, picnic basket, and something that brought many baby boomers to pleasure boating in the first place — a pair of colorful water skis!

Formatted like the "Latest Boating Accessories" photo essay features in those wonderful 1950s and 1960s *Outboard Boating Handbook* magazines, here's a look at some of the goodies that can get you cruising in style and transform your old aluminum or fiberglass boat into a real museum piece.

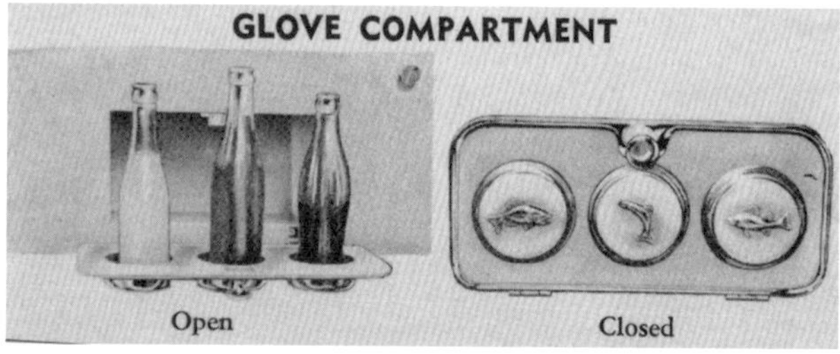

Easily affixed, after-market accessories with a decidedly nautical or fishy theme make for dandy runabout accessories. Here's a Herter's glove compartment/soda bottle holder.

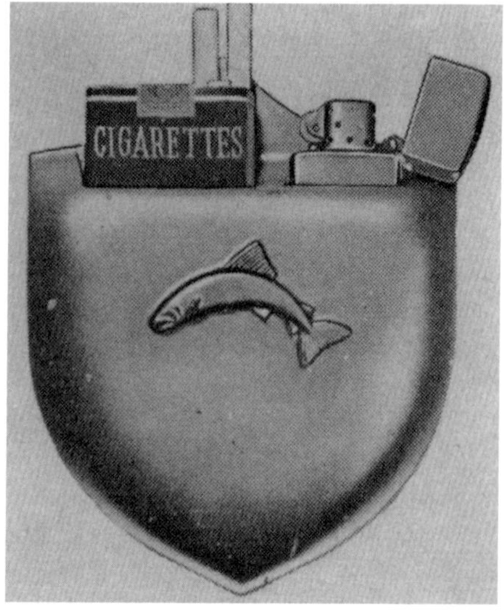

Even the runabouter who is staunchly anti-smoking shouldn't pass up this stylized cigarette/lighter caddy, as it'll just as nicely cradle a deck of cards and a box of breath mints.

Every vintage fiberglass boat should have her own 1960 fiberglass battery box — perhaps for storing ice and beverages. Chances are you'll earn points with the classic boat show judges, even if you don't offer them a cold one.

What'll they think of next? An outboard speedometer for outboard boats! Clamped to any transom, this Airguide novelty is set to produce quick results — or at least serve as a vintage conversation piece.

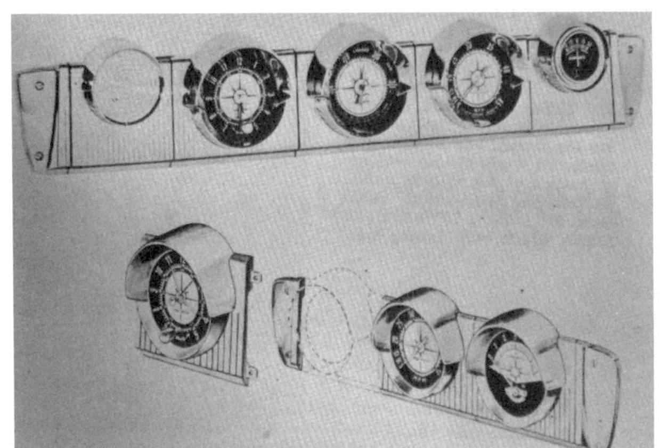

Aqua Meter offered a full range of marine instrumentation in single or panel format. Either format can add a little something to a vintage runabout's dashboard.

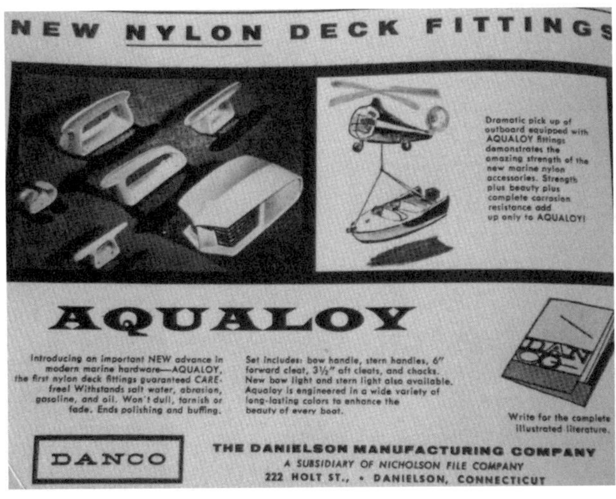

Look for ordinary "old" accessories made of then unorthodox materials. Nylon deck fittings are an example.

Dealer signs and clocks make excellent additions to an antique boater's collection, and score points when displayed on a stern seat during show judging. Repro versions — often sold on-line — are typically much more affordable than originals.

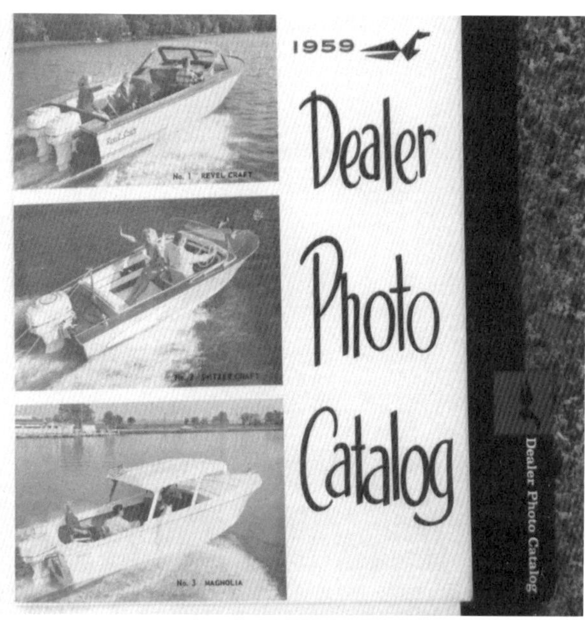

Collecting vintage boating literature has become a hobby in itself and usually starts when a classic boater finds a period brochure picturing his or her now classic craft.

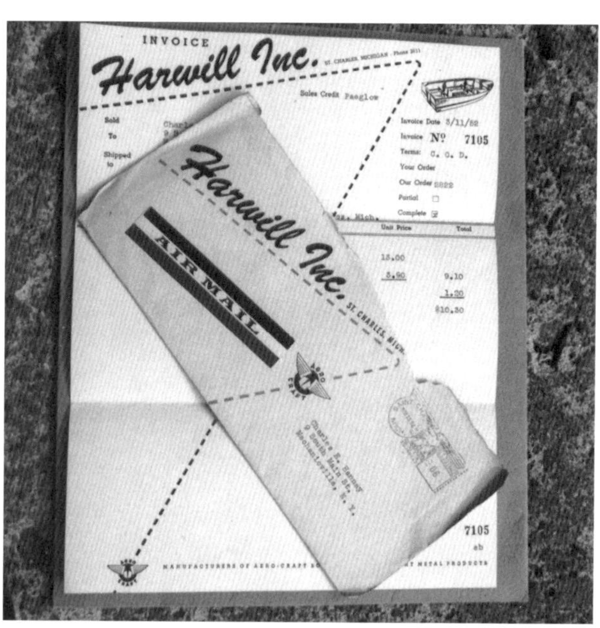

Talk about paper capable of making boat show judges swoon, an invoice or other documentation showing original details is a veritable time machine. When buying an old craft — even if from a seemingly unfriendly seller — pointedly ask if they might have any paperwork related to the boat. That goes double for inquiring about the boat's registration!

Among the many neglected old trailers rusting away are undoubtedly at least a few 1960 Gator models reportedly the recipients of a $100,000 styling budget. Maker, Peterson Brothers, Inc., of Jacksonville, Florida, advertised that Gator trailers' then big budget research and development "blends and compliments the flowing lines of your car, boat, and motor to complete a streamlined symphony of beauty and convenience."

Tee-Nee trailers are favorites of many classic outboarders because of those little teardrop fenders and mustard yellow paint job.

An old boat's top might well be shot after numerous decades of being scrunched-up in the rafters of some dank garage, but take it anyway and use the remains for patterns facilitating a replacement.

An accessory as basic as a spare propeller is both useful and worthy of show display with your vintage craft.

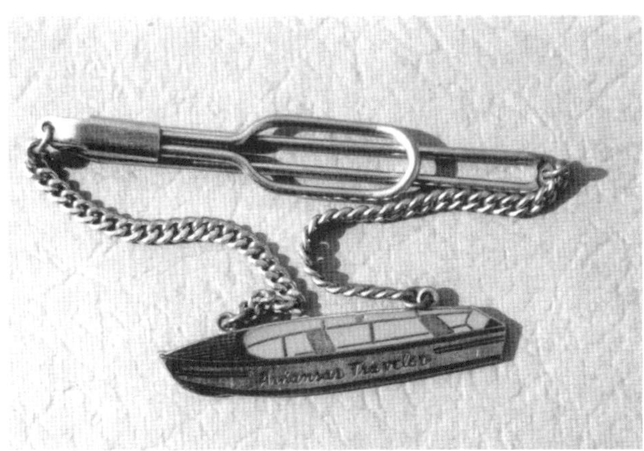

Maybe one would need to be a full-fledged aluminum boat fanatic to wear an antique Arkansas Traveler dealer's tie clip, but donning such an accessory might result in a lead for other vintage craft , or impress the heck out of a show judge.

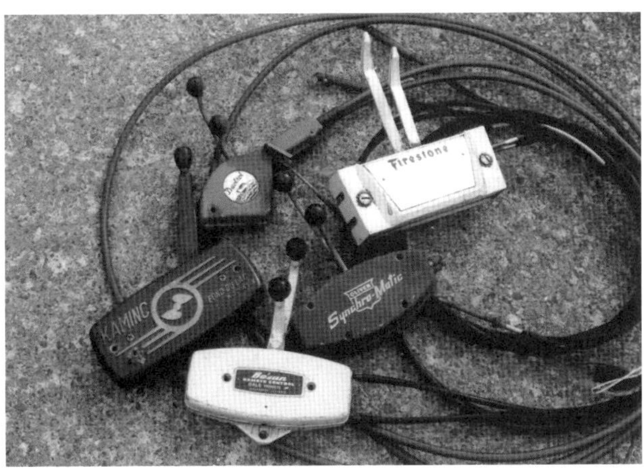

Because of the robust 1950s boating market, there were even more companies making outboard motor remote controls than there were outboard manufacturers. Some brands, like Oliver and Mercury's short-lived KAMINC, are not as easy to scare up as are Johnson/Evinrude boxes. The rule of thumb is — try matching the controls to your motor's brand, and if you can't, go for some interesting after-market set such as Duotrol or Smith. Whatever you find, beware of painting it to match the boat's color, as that's heresy to outboard purists!

Ever since outboarding began, two-cycle motor oilcans have found sanctuary aboard boats. That's why period examples often get co-opted for display in classic runabouts. When building a small collection, don't pass by any decent examples for less than $5. One of those 1950 Allstate cans surprised an incidental boating accessories collector when a more ardent buff gladly handed him a hundred bucks for the quart container!

Wow! What great shape this Feather Craft pennant is in! Well, that's because it, and flags for other classic aluminum and fiberglass brands, are now being reproduced. Check an on-line search engine for the latest details.

Johnson dealer's paperweight and after-market Merc transom pad are the fascinating stuff of nautical flea market shopping. Both instantly add to a classic boat's ambiance.